By the Same Author

Casino

Wiseguy

Blye, Private Eye

Nicholas Pileggi

CASINO

LOVE AND HONOR IN LAS VEGAS

◆

Simon & Schuster

New York   London   Toronto   Sydney   Tokyo   Singapore

SIMON & SCHUSTER
Rockefeller Center
1230 Avenue of the Americas
New York, NY 10020

SIMON & SCHUSTER and colophon are registered trademarks
of Simon & Schuster Inc.

Designed by Meryl Levavi/Levavi & Levavi

Manufactured in the United States of America

10 9 8 7 6 5 4 3 2 1

Library of Congress Cataloging-in-Publication Data

ISBN 0-684-80832-3

For Nora

Acknowledgments

I would like to acknowledge my appreciation and gratitude for the hundreds of people who helped me with this book, but I also wish to extend a special thanks to Gene Strohlein, Mert Wilbur, Dennis Arnoldy, Jack Tobin, Joseph Gersky, Murray Ehrenberg, Wally Gordon, Oscar Goodman, Emmett Michaels, Mike Simon, William Ouseley, Bud Hall, Bo Dietl, Beecher Avants, Jeffrey Silver, Marty Jacobs, Mike Reynolds, Jeff German, Ed Becker, A. D. Hopkins, Jim Neff, Phil Hannifin, Shannon Bybee, Lem Banker, Dick Odessky, Allen Glick, Matt Marcus, Richard Crane, Loren Steven, Russ Childers, Jack Roberts, Brian and Myra Greenspun, Angela Rich, Manny Cortez, Douglas Owens, Frank Cullotta, Ray LeNobel, Melissa Prophet, Lowell Bergman, Tommy Scalfaro, Tim Heider, Scott Malone, Ellen Lewis, Kristina Rebelo, Joey Boston, George Hartman, Bobby Kay, Bill Bastone, Kenny Brown, Bob Vanucci, Claudette Miller, Victor Gregor, Arlyne Brickman, John Manca, Buddy Clark, Joe Coffey, Don Furey, Joe Spinelli, Phil Taylor, Rosalie DiBlasio, Howard Schwartz, Bob Stoldal, Lee Rich, Shirley Strohlein, and, of course, Frank Rosenthal.

Introduction

"Why is my car on fire?"

"**I** had just had dinner and gotten in my car," said Frank Rosenthal. "I don't remember whether or not I turned on the ignition, but the next thing I saw were these little flames. They were only about two or three inches high. They were coming out of the defroster vents. I never heard any noise. I just saw the flames reflected against the windshield. I remember, I asked myself, 'Why is my car on fire?' And then the flames started getting bigger.

"There must have been a strong enough jolt to throw me against the steering wheel, because it hurt my ribs, but I don't remember any of that. All I thought was that my car was having some kind of mechanical problem.

"I didn't panic. I knew I had to get out of the car. I had to get away from the flames. Call the garage. I reached for the door handle. I almost torched my arm. There were flames shooting up between the seat and the door. Now I knew I had to get out of the car or I'd never see my kids again. This time I used my right hand to grab the door handle, and I threw my shoulder against the door at the same time. It worked.

"I fell out onto the ground. There were flames all around me. Some of my clothes were on fire. I was burning. I rolled around on the ground until the flames were out.

"Two men helped me to my feet and got me about twenty or thirty feet from the car. They told me to get down, but I didn't want to. I kept saying that I was all right. They insisted I get down, and when I did, it was as though the atom bomb had gone off. I saw my car jump about two feet into the air, and then flames shot up through the roof about two stories high.

"That's when I realized for the first time it hadn't been an accident. That's when I knew somebody put a bomb in my car."

◆ ◆ ◆

Before his car was blown up outside Marie Callender's Restaurant on East Sahara Avenue on October 4, 1982, Frank "Lefty" Rosenthal had been one of the most powerful and controversial men in Las Vegas. He was in charge of the largest casino operation in Nevada. He was famous for being the man who had brought sports book–betting to Vegas—an achievement that made him a true visionary in the annals of local history. He was a gambler's gambler, the man who set the odds, a perfectionist who had once astonished the kitchen help in the Stardust Hotel by insisting that every blueberry muffin had to have at least ten blueberries in it.

But Frank Rosenthal had been dodging trouble most of his life. He started as a clerk and bookie for Chicago gamblers and mobsters before he was old enough to vote. In fact, before going to work inside the casinos in 1971, Lefty had held only one legitimate job—as a military policeman in Korea between 1956 and 1958. In 1961, when he appeared at the age of thirty-one before a congressional committee in Washington investigating the influence of organized crime on gambling, he took the Fifth Amendment thirty-seven times. He wouldn't even tell them whether he was left-handed—which fact, by the way, had earned him his nickname. A few years later he pleaded nolo contendere to bribing a college basketball player in North Carolina—though he never admitted his guilt. In Florida, he was banned from horse and dog tracks for allegedly bribing the Miami Beach police. And in 1969, along with a dozen of the nation's biggest bookmakers, he was indicted by the Justice Department in an interstate gambling and racketeering conspiracy case that dragged on for several years—until Lefty's lawyer got the indictment thrown out because John Mitchell, the attorney general at the time, had failed to personally sign the case's wiretap orders, as required by law. Mitchell had been out on a golf course the day the court orders were to have been signed and had instructed an aide to forge his name.

Frank Rosenthal came to Las Vegas in 1968 for the same reason so many other Americans have—to get away from his past. Las Vegas was a city with no memory. It was the place you went for a second chance. It was the American city where people went after the divorce, after the bankruptcy, even after a short stint in the county jail. It was the final destination for those willing to drive halfway across America in search of the nation's only morality car wash.

It was also the city where you could strike it rich—a kind of money-happy Lourdes where pilgrims got to hang up their psychic crutches and start life anew. It was the end of the rainbow—American city as pot of gold—the only place in the country where the average guy had a shot at a miracle. Long odds? Sure, but for many of those who went to live in Las Vegas and for many who went to visit, the longest odds in Las Vegas were better than the odds they had been dealt in their lives back home.

It was a magical place, the neon capital of the world. By the 1970s, the stigma of its mobster history was on the wane, and there seemed almost no limit to its potential for growth. Bugsy Siegel, after all, had died way back in 1947. And he wasn't even killed in Las Vegas. He was shot dead in what is now the 90210 zip code—Beverly Hills.

By the 1970s, Las Vegas was poised for such unprecedented growth that the city was much too big to be dominated, or even influenced, by a bunch of men with funny accents and pinky rings. Public corporations like Sheraton, Hilton, and MGM, along with Wall Street investment bankers and Michael Milken's Drexel Burnham Lambert, were becoming increasingly interested; tentative investments had already begun to turn what was essentially an inhospitable, crop-defying, windblown, alkaline-salted town on the eastern end of the Mojave Desert into the fastest-growing city in the United States. From 1970 to 1980, Las Vegas would double the number of its visitors, to 11,041,524, and the amount of cash left behind by those visitors would increase 273.6 percent, to $4.7 billion. The heart of all this growth was, of course, the casino business—and by 1993 visitors had dropped $15.1 billion in town.

A casino is a mathematics palace set up to separate players from their money. Every bet made in a casino has been calibrated within a fraction of its life to maximize profit while still giving players the illusion that they have a chance.

Casinos mean cash. From the nickel slots to the $500 progressive superslots, cash is the blood that enlivens everything and everyone in a casino. The buildings are nothing but a cacophony of money. From the noisy geysers of a winner's silver change tumbling into the purposely hollow metal trays to the bells and buzzers and lights announcing minute-by-minute wins, cash dominates the room. Normal business techniques of fiduciary responsibility and cash accountability crumble under the mountains of paper money and silver coins that pour into casinos every day.

There is probably no type of business in the world where as much paper money is handled on a daily basis by more people under more security than in a casino. Dealers have to clap their hands under the Eye before leaving the table to make sure they're not carrying any chips away with them. The small aprons they wear are to cover their pockets—and keep them from filling them. Every $100 bill changed for chips at the table must be called out by the dealer so the pit boss can watch it being slid into the narrow drop box slit with a metal paddle.

No matter how busy a craps or roulette table might be, the chips must be evenly stacked by color to facilitate the almost continuous counting by supervisors, and blackjack dealers have to learn to cup the hole card against side readers to make sure players in cahoots aren't swapping paints (face cards) to beat the house. An experienced stickman at a craps table is trained never to take his eyes off the dice, especially when the noisy drunk at the end of the table spills his drink on the felt, drops his chips on the floor, and takes a swing at his wife. It is at precisely these distracting Kodak moments when the shavers, or baloney dice, are slipped into the game. Trying to beat the casino—through a miraculous win or, alternatively, through the more reliable methods of being a crook—is what brings everyone to town. In Las Vegas, beating the casino by hook or crook has been raised to an art form.

But, of course, the greatest amount of casino theft has

nothing to do with cheating players or crooked dealers. Most of the major theft in a casino doesn't even happen on the casino floor. The largest amount of larceny takes place behind closed doors in the casino's sanctum sanctorum, the casino's most sensitive and security-conscious area, the place where all of the cash churning its way through the hundreds of games and slot machines ultimately heads, the casino's sacred count rooms.

Usually a windowless, double-locked, bare-bones workroom with straight-back secretarial chairs, clear plastic tables, and reinforced-steel shelves and floors to bear the tons of coins and stacks of cash that must be counted daily, the count room is the place where the hundreds of double-locked metal boxes under every table game are emptied, their contents of $10, $20, and $100 bills sorted into inch-thick $10,000 bricks and, on busy days, stacked against the walls chest high.

There are no strangers stealing this money in the count room. This money is taken in spite of the fact that cameras are often in use, that guards check everyone walking in and out, that only a very limited number of people can even enter (state law bars even casino owners), and that every dollar counted out of every single drop box on every shift must be signed and initialed by at least two or three independent clerks and supervisors.

Count room workers go about their tasks with the deadened glaze of people who must steel themselves against the dazzling daily experience of being immersed in the sight, smell, and touch of money. Tons of it. Stacks of it. Bundles of cash and boxes of coins so heavy that hydraulic lifts must be used to move the tonnage of loot around in the count room.

There is such a daily fortune of stacked paper bills pouring into the count room that rather than being counted, the cash is assembled into various denominations and weighed.

A million dollars in $100 bills weighs 20½ pounds; a million in $20s, 102 pounds; and a million in $5 bills, 408 pounds.

The coins are poured into specially made Toledo electronic coin-weighing scales manufactured by the Reliance Electric Company—model 8130 being the scale of preference when Lefty ran the Stardust—that sort and count the coins. A million dollars in quarter slot machine winnings weighs twenty-one tons.

The dream for many of those who find themselves owning casinos, or even working in them, is to figure out exactly how to separate the count room from its loot. Over the years, the methods employed have run from owners getting their hands on drop box keys to employees grabbing fists full of cash before the boxes are even counted. There are complicated methods of misdirected fill slips and maladjusted scales that weigh only one-third of the loot coming through the count room doors. The systems for skimming casinos are as varied as the genius of the men doing the skimming.

◆ ◆ ◆

In 1974, only six years after arriving in Las Vegas, Frank Rosenthal had managed to get from Las Vegas exactly what he'd hoped—a new life. He was running four Las Vegas casinos. He had married a gorgeous former showgirl named Geri McGee, and they lived with their two children in a $1 million house facing the fourteenth tee on the Las Vegas Country Club golf course. He had a swimming pool and a housekeeper. His bedroom closet had over two hundred pairs of custom-made silk, cotton, and linen slacks—most of them in pastel shades—which he had specially fitted by tailors flown in from Beverly Hills and Chicago. He was the man to see at the Stardust, and his reputation as an innovative and successful casino manager was soon to be recognized throughout Nevada. He saw himself as part of an elite group of casino impresarios, union pension fund officials, investment bankers, and Nevada politicians who were about to transform Las Vegas from its cowboy and gangster roots into the family-oriented $30-billion-a-year adult theme park it would eventually become.

It should have been perfect.

But ten years later, Frank Rosenthal was under investigation as the mob's casino man in town and the suspected mastermind behind a multimillion-dollar skimming operation. He had been denied a gambling license and was hosting an inadvertently hilarious ninety-minute talk show—which he had modestly named *The Frank Rosenthal Show*. He was suspected of working in cahoots with his boyhood friend Anthony "Tony the Ant" Spilotro, who the FBI said was the Chicago mob's main muscle in town, a hit man suspected of at least a dozen homicides. At the time of Lefty's explosion, Spilotro was under indictment along with eight members of his gang for running an extortion, loan-sharking, and burglary ring out of a jewelry shop he owned just off the Strip. He was also the prime suspect in Lefty's attempted murder, and he was a man with a motive: he was having a love affair with Lefty Rosenthal's wife. Well, maybe not a love affair— very little that happened in Las Vegas had to do with love— but an affair nonetheless, one that had been documented by the FBI agents who were assigned to follow Spilotro and that had eventually become public knowledge.

How it could have come to this in just a few years was a question that would haunt not just Lefty but the mob bosses who had put him in to run the casinos in the first place. Instead of calm, Lefty gave them chaos. Instead of a quiet path into the new Las Vegas, Lefty and his pal Spilotro had created so much turmoil and caused such law enforcement scrutiny that rather than retiring with their tidy nest eggs of skimmed millions as planned, the septuagenarian mob bosses of Chicago, Kansas City, and Milwaukee were facing the rest of their lives in prison.

It should not have ended this way. It should have been so sweet. Everything was in place. It was better than an even-money bet. It was a wager you couldn't lose. And yet, eight years later, the whole thing blew up in the parking lot on East Sahara Avenue.

Part One

BETTING THE PASS LINE

◆

1.♦

"My pals thought I was the messiah."

Lefty Rosenthal did not believe in luck. He believed in the odds. In the numbers. In probability. In the math. In the fractions of data he had accumulated copying team statistics onto index cards. He believed that games were fixed and that referees and zebras could be bought. He knew some basketball players who practiced the art of missing basketball rim shots for hours every day, and he knew players who bet the middles between the odds spread and got a return of 10 percent on their money. He believed that some athletes played lazy and some of them played hurt. He believed in winning and losing streaks; he believed in point spreads and no-limit bets and card mechanics so good they could deal out cards without breaking the cellophane on the deck. In other words, where gambling was concerned, Lefty believed in everything but luck. Luck was the potential enemy. Luck was the temptress, the seductive whisperer taking you away from the data. Lefty learned early that if he was ever to master the skill and become a professional player, he had to take even the remotest possibility of chance out of the process.

♦ ♦ ♦

Frank "Lefty" Rosenthal was born on June 12, 1929, just a few months before the stock market crash. He was raised on Chicago's West Side, an old-world, syndicate neighbor-hood, where bookie shops, crooked cops, corrupt aldermen, and closed mouths were a way of life.

"My dad was a produce wholesaler," Rosenthal said. "An administrative type. Good with numbers. Smart. Success-ful. My mother was a housewife. I grew up reading the rac-ing form. I used to tear it apart. I knew everything there was to know about the form. I used to read it in class. I was a tall, skinny, shy kid. I was six foot one when I was a teenager and I was kind of withdrawn. I was sort of a loner, and horse racing was my challenge.

"My dad owned some horses, so I was at the track with him all the time. I lived at the track. I was a groom. A hot walker. I hung around the backstretch. I mucked out. I'd get there at four thirty in the morning. I became a part of the barn. I started hanging out there when I was thirteen and fourteen, and I was an owner's son. Everybody left me alone.

"I got some resistance at home when I started getting into sports betting. My mother knew I was gambling and she didn't like it, but I was very strong headed. I wouldn't listen to anyone. I loved going over the charts, the past perfor-mances, jockeys, post positions. I used to copy all that ma-terial onto my own eight-by-ten-inch file cards in my room late into the night.

"I cut school one day to go to the track. I went with two pals. Smart guys. We stayed for eight races and I punched out seven winners. My pals thought I was the messiah. My dad turned away when he spotted me there. He wouldn't talk to me. He was pissed that I had cut school. I didn't say anything to him when I got home. It wasn't discussed. I didn't say anything about winning, either. The next day I cut school again and went back to the track and lost it all.

"But I really learned gambling in the bleachers of Wrigley Field and Comiskey Park. There were about two hundred guys up there every game and they bet on everything. Every pitch. Every swing. Everything had a price. There were guys shouting numbers at you. It was great. It was an open-air casino. Constant action.

"If you were talented, and you had some ego, and you knew your game, you'd be tempted to take them on. You've got money in your pocket and you feel like you can take on the world. There was a guy named Stacy; he was in his fifties and he had a pocket full of cash. He'd fade anybody. 'Hey kid, they gonna score this inning or not?' Instead of passing, your pride gets in there and you make a bet and you pay the price. Stacy always got you to make a price.

"Say Chicago is winning six to two in the eighth and you want to bet they score again, or that they'll lose in the ninth. Or that they'd hit into a double play to end the inning. Or hit a home run to win the game. Or a double or a triple or a flyout. Whatever. Stacy would take the action and he'd lay the odds. He'd make a homer twenty-five to one. Bam! Just like that. A fly ball was twenty to one. An 'out' was eight to five. If you wanted the action, you made the bet and he gave you his odds.

"I didn't know it at first, but every one of those bets Stacy faded had odds backing them up. A strikeout at the end of a game was, say—I don't remember the real odds now, but say it was a hundred and sixty-six to one, not thirty to one, which was what Stacy was laying.

"A home run on a game's first pitch could be three thousand to one, not seventy-five to one. And so forth. If you were betting Stacy, you had to know those odds, or you'd be picked clean.

"After I caught on, I'd just sit and listen to him make his odds and I'd write them all down and keep a record. After a while, I started making proposition bets out there on my own. Over the years, Stacy made a little fortune in the bleachers. He cleaned up. He was terrific at getting everybody all around him to start betting. He was a great showman.

"Back then, you didn't have sports channels and magazines and newspapers and radio shows that specialized in betting sports. If you were in the Midwest you couldn't easily find out what was happening to the East and West Coast teams behind the scenes. You'd get the final score and that was about that.

"But if you're betting seriously, you've got to know a lot more than that. So I started reading everything. My father got me a shortwave radio, and I remember spending hours listening to the play-by-play of out-of-town teams I was thinking of betting. I began subscribing to different papers from all around the country. I'd go to this newsstand where they had all the out-of-town papers. That's where I met Hymie the Ace. He was a legendary professional. I don't call people legends unless they are. Hymie the Ace was a legend. He would be there at the same newsstand buying dozens of papers, just like me. He'd get into his car and start reading. I'd be there, too, except I didn't have a car. I had a bike. After a while we got to know each other. He knew what I was doing.

"Hymie was about ten or twelve years older than I was. I made it a habit to always say hello to him and to the other pros, and I was lucky that they'd all talk to me. I was still a kid, but they saw that I was serious and I had an aptitude, and they were willing to help me. They were very kind. They allowed me into their circle. I felt great.

"But I'm also getting chesty. I'm doing pretty well. I'm feeling good. There was a Northwestern-Michigan basketball game that was coming up. I had people at both schools feeding me information and I felt really strong. I liked Northwestern.

"Now I don't mean I *liked* Northwestern. That I was a fan. That I had their pennant in my room. I mean I liked them as a bet. That's all teams were to me. Bets. I'd been waiting for this game. I'd been watching it. So I bet Northwestern to beat Michigan State. It was a sellout crowd. I walked in and I saw Hymie the Ace. Hymie knows more about basketball than any man alive. We say hello. It's ten minutes to tip-off.

"I told him I played Northwestern and asked what he was doing. I was so certain about my information that I had made what I used to call a triple play—I'd bet two thousand dollars. It was as far as I could go with my bankroll. A single play for me at the time was like two hundred, a double play was five hundred, and a triple was two thousand. I'm just a kid. It's my limit. We're talking about a time when my whole bankroll was eight thousand.

"'What?' Hymie says, surprised. 'Why are you playing Northwestern? Don't you know about Johnny Green?'

"'Who?' I asked him.

"'Johnny Green. What's wrong with you?'

"Now Johnny Green was a black player who had been ineligible for the whole season. It turned out he had suddenly become eligible a couple of days before the game. I'd missed it.

"'Green's going to take every rebound in the game,' Ace said, and my heart sank.

"I ran to the phones, but there were just two booths and there were twenty-five people waiting at each booth. I'm looking to lay off some of my bets. Get rid of them. Balance some of the action. I'm still standing in line waiting for the phone when I hear the announcer and I know I'm dead. I can't get off.

"I go back and sit down. I watch Green. Just like Ace said, he controlled both backboards. At halftime I had seen enough. Michigan annihilated Northwestern. Ace had done his homework and I hadn't.

"Ace not only knew that Green was eligible, he knew what kind of a player he was, knew that he was a great rebounder, knew that that was the element that could beat Northwestern. Green went on to be an All-American and top pro player.

"I learned a hell of a lesson. I found out I wasn't as smart as I thought I was. I had depended upon people for too much. I had given them the power to make up my mind for me. I realized that if I wanted to spend my life gambling, pitting myself against the best bookmakers, there was no such thing as listening to people. If I was going to make a living doing this, I was going to have to figure it out for myself and do it all myself.

"So I started out with college basketball and football. In college games I subscribed to all the school newspapers and went through the sports pages every day. I'd call the reporters at the different schools and make up all kinds of stories to find out extra bits of information that didn't get into the papers.

"At first, I didn't tell them why I wanted the information, but pretty soon they caught on, and I picked up some sharp kids out there and I brought them along. When I won, I threw them a few bucks, and after a while I had a whole network of people who kept me informed about college games.

"As I got older I'd go to games with a tape recorder. I had spotters working for me. I'd tell some guys to just watch specific things. I'd have them watching two or three players only. I didn't care what else was happening; they had to watch who I told them to watch. I'd take their notes. Then I'd fly to the next town where the team played and I'd watch them again. I'd match lineups. The final score's never the main thing to look at if you want to make money instead of losing it. I knew if a player had hurt his ankle and was playing slower. I knew when a quarterback was sick. I knew if his girlfriend got knocked up or left him for somebody else. I knew if he was smoking dope, snorting coke. I knew about injuries that didn't get in the papers. About injuries that players kept from their coaches.

"Now, with this kind of information, it wasn't hard for me to see when the bookmakers had made an error in their odds. I didn't blame them. They were covering lots of sports and lots of games. I was concentrating on a few. I knew everything there was to know about a certain limited number of games, and I learned a very important thing—I learned that you can't bet on every game. Sometimes you can only bet one or two games out of forty or fifty. Sometimes, I learned, there wasn't a good bet on the whole weekend. If that was true, I wouldn't bet or take a serious position.

"I used to hang around a cigar store on Kinzie. George and Sam ran the place. Out front they had cigars and stuff. But in the back there was a Western Union wire, telephones, and a tote board. In those days, they had the most up-to-date information. During the baseball season, the latest list of starting pitchers would come over the wire just before game time.

"George and Sam were really big bookmakers. They had come to Chicago from Tarrytown, New York. And they had an okay from the powers that be to operate the book. It was wide open. They even had the okay from the local police captain to run poker games, which were very illegal.

"They had a bar and they'd serve drinks and food for free. The wire was always banging away. It was like a stock market ticker. The Western Union machines were hard for a bookie to get. They were meant to be sold to newspapers, but if you filed certain papers with the company and knew how to go about it, you might be able to get one. At that time I was so dumb I tried to get one for my house, and I was turned down.

"George and Sam were independent operators, but they still had to pay protection. All the card rooms and bookie rooms paid off in those days. Bookmakers took care of the cops and they took care of the outfit. And sometimes the outfit took care of the cops. In the end, everybody could wind up taking care of everybody, just as long as everybody made money.

"When I was nineteen," Rosenthal continued, "I got a job as a clerk at Bill Kaplan's sports service, Angel-Kaplan. It was great. We would be on the phones all day giving out our line to bookmakers and players. Everyone from all over the country was hooked into each other. We had special phone lines set up by retired telephone company workers. We all knew each other's voices and code names, but after a while, you get to know everybody's real name.

"I'm just a kid and still in Chicago, but now I'm hooked into the biggest office in the United States at the time—Gil Beckley's in Newport, Kentucky. Gil had the whole town of Newport locked up. The coppers. The politicians. The whole fucking town.

"Gil was Newport's main industry. He had thirty clerks working. He ran the biggest layoff operation in the country. It was where every bookmaking office in the country called to lay off bets if the action on one side was getting too heavy.

"For instance, if you're a bookmaker in Dallas, you are naturally going to get more Dallas bets than you want, because you won't have enough people betting on the other side to offset any win. So a Dallas bookmaker would call Gil Beckley's layoff operation, and Beckley's clerks would pick up enough of the Dallas bookmaker's bets to balance his book. Since Beckley is national, he can offset the Dallas bets against their opponents that week, and everything becomes even again.

"Wherever he went, Gil was the boss. In the winter he'd be in Miami. He'd invite twenty or thirty guys out to dinner. 'Let's go to Joe's Stone Crab!' 'Let's go here!' 'Let's go there!' He always had an entourage with him, and he always picked up the check.

"Naturally, I got to meet Gil Beckley only by phone. For a couple of years we're talking and he recognized that I was an up-and-coming kid. A whatever-you-want-to-call-it kid. A handicapper and a player. And my little reputation was building. But the more I talked to Beckley, the more I realized the most unbelievable thing. If you asked Gil Beckley how many men were on a baseball team, he'd have to ask someone. Literally.

"He could not tell you. That wasn't one of his things. I'm being honest. Mickey Mantle? Who? Beckley just didn't know. He didn't have a fucking clue. But then, he didn't have to know. He was a bookmaker and layoff man. He didn't bet. He just ran the biggest accounting office in the country. I was stunned.

"But I found out pretty soon it didn't matter. All a layoff man's gotta do is make sure he keeps the bets balanced and take his ten percent. You don't have to be an expert on teams or even know about the games. I was amazed, but it turned out to be true of lots of layoff men and bookies. Some of the biggest guys didn't bet. In Chicago we had Benny the Book. Benny was the biggest bookmaker in town. Benny made millions and millions as a bookmaker, and just like Gil Beckley, Benny couldn't tell you who Joe DiMaggio played for. I'm serious.

"I was betting and getting good information at the time my friend Sidney was Benny's top clerk, and he asked me, as a favor, if I would call his office if I learned something about a game, something that might affect the outcome, like that there was a fix or one of the players was injured.

"So, one day I came up with an injury that hadn't been reported, and I called my friend Sidney, but he wasn't there. Instead, I got Benny. The big boss himself. So I told Benny about the player. I remember the player. Bobby Avila. Second base for the Cleveland Indians. I said 'Avila's out.'

"I wanted to alert him so he could adjust his line and not get smashed by all the pros, who, I can assure you, would have already gotten the same information I had.

"Benny takes the information like he knows what I'm talking about, but when I finish he asks me, 'Don't they have another second baseman?' I think, 'Another Bobby Avila? Is he serious?' I couldn't believe it.

"That night I met Sidney and I asked him if he was working for a crazy person. He said Benny didn't follow the games, just the price. Benny was the biggest bookie in Chicago, not because he knew about the players and sports but because he paid on Monday. No matter what he owed you after the weekend, Benny paid on Monday. His clerk would be down there with an envelope and brand-new bills. And if you owed him, he'd always give you more time. So, whether he knew Bobby Avila or not, he had a tremendous clientele and laughed all the way to the bank."

2 ♦

"One of these days I'm gonna be the boss of the whole syndicate."

Tony "the Ant" Spilotro grew up in a two-story wooden gray bungalow in an Italian neighborhood just a few blocks from Lefty's home. Tony and his five brothers—Vincent, Victor, Patrick, Johnny, and Michael—slept in one room in three sets of bunk beds.

Tony's father, Patsy, owned Patsy's Restaurant at the corner of Grand and Ogden Avenues. It was small place famous for homemade meatballs that attracted customers from all over town, including outfit guys like Tony Accardo, Paul "the Waiter" Ricca, Sam Giancana, Gussie Alex, and Jackie Cerone. Patsy's parking lot was often used for mob meetings.

"Tony and I met when we were kids," said Frank Cullotta, who became part of Spilotro's crew. "We didn't like each other. We both had shine boxes, and I would shine shoes on one side of Grand Avenue and Tony would shine shoes on the other side of the street. We had a big argument. He told me I had to stay on my side of the street. I told him he had to stay on his. We started shoving. Nothing really came of it, and he went on his way and I went on mine."

Like Tony Spilotro, Frank Cullotta was born on the South Side of Chicago. Cullotta was a thief. He had been one as far back as he could remember. He started boosting stores and apartments when he was twelve, the year his father was killed driving a getaway car in an armed robbery; the circumstances of his father's death were a badge of honor in the neighborhood.

"Tony and I were both little short guys, you know," Cullotta said, "and he was a little shorter than me, so he didn't scare me at all. But Tony always had a lot of guys hanging around him. He used to have about fifteen guys that used to follow him around. I had about six guys that hung with me.

"Then one day he was talking to his brother about me and his father heard my last name. He told Tony to find out if I was Joe Cullotta's kid.

"My father was an independent bad guy, and a long time ago, Spilotro's father was getting shaken down by some old greaseball black handers. He went to my father, and my father straightened it out. So when it turned out that I was Joe Cullotta's son, Tony father's said that was the end of our feud.

"The next day, Tony walked up to me and said, 'I want to talk to you.' I said I wasn't running away, and he said, 'My father and your father were friends, and we're going to be friends forever.'

"My father was a wheelman for a gang of crooks. He was considered the best driver in the city; there wasn't anybody else who could outdrive him. From the stories I heard, he could go in reverse faster than most people could go in forward gear. Anyway, my father died behind the wheel during a car chase. He wasn't shot or anything. There was a police car chase and he got killed.

"From the moment we became friends, Tony and I ran the streets. I was in his house as much as my own. Even though Tony's mother, Antoinette, was a witch, I went to the house anyway. She used to give me dirty looks. I'd come in the house she'd snarl at me, 'Go sit over there!' and not even offer me a drink of water. Tony was the toughest kid I knew. He was so tough that his brother Victor used to offer guys five dollars to see if they could beat him up. Usually, Victor got a taker and the guy would try to kick Tony's ass, but if it looked like Tony was gonna lose, we'd all jump on the kid and break his head.

"Tony and I stole together. We rode around in hot cars. We hated school. We wound up in a trade school filled with black kids.

"Nearby there was a Jewish neighborhood with lots of stores, and every day Tony and I and a couple of other kids used to go and rob them and either jump on the streetcar or have a hot car parked nearby. We'd take the stuff to our own neighborhood and sell it.

"We used to fight with the black kids a lot, and one time, when I wasn't there, they jumped him. But Tony had a knife and he stabbed one of the black kids. Everybody knew Tony did it, but the kid didn't press charges.

"A week later I got into a fight and I got six months in a reform school. My mother visited me in there every time she could. Faithfully.

"When I got out, Tony was hanging around with a blond kid named Joe Hansen, and I started hanging with Paulie Schiro and Crazy Bob Sporadic, doing armed robberies. One day, Tony saw us getting chased by a police car after we shot three guys in a tavern. He came looking for me. We didn't kill anybody, just wounded them, but Tony explained that we had to dismantle the guns and throw them into the Des Plaines River.

"He said, 'You guys can't do this; you're gonna get killed. You're better off robbing banks.' And he starts to tell us about how he's been robbing bank messengers. He'd have one guy outside the bank and one guy inside. The guy inside would stand on line and he would spot the people who were taking out lots of cash and bringing it back to their businesses to cash checks for customers or whatever. There was usually between three thousand and twelve thousand in a bag.

"The man outside would watch everyone who left the bank and he'd remember which way they went. Then we'd follow them until we got their route down, because you knew they were gonna do it over and over again. The next time, we're waiting for them. We're seventeen, eighteen years old and we're making twenty-five thousand a month apiece. We were doing really good. We were doing so good we decided to go out and buy new cars. I remember when I pulled up and parked a brand-new Cadillac in front of the Mark Seven Tavern where we all hung out.

"Tony walks out. He looks at the car parked there. He says, 'I bet you money I know whose car this is.' Nobody says anything. He asks if it's mine and I said, 'Yeah, it sure is.'

" 'Well,' he says, 'you can't own these cars. They're gonna get mad at us.' Now I know he's talking about the outfit guys.

"I showed Tony my bankroll. 'Look at this money, Tony,' I say. 'We're stealing and we can't enjoy it and buy what the fuck we want to with it?'

"He said, 'Yeah, but they don't understand. They want us to keep on driving Fords and Chevys.'

"That didn't make any sense to me. If you're stealing and taking the risks, you might as well enjoy it, but Tony didn't just want to be a thief like all of us anymore. He wanted to be a racketeer.

"Within a couple of years, Tony starts hanging with a guy by the name Vinnie 'the Saint' Inserro, who was even shorter than Tony. He was about five one, but he was the guy who introduced Tony to all the outfit guys like Turk [Jimmy Torello], Chuckie [Charles Nicoletti], Milwaukee Phil [Philip Alderisio], Potatoes [William Daddano], Sammy Pigs, Joe the Clown [Joseph Lombardo], and Joe Doves [Joseph Aiuppa], who later became the outfit's top boss.

"As these guys got bigger, Tony stayed close. He did whatever they wanted. 'Brahma,' he said to me one day—he used to call me Brahma because I was built like a bull—'Brahma,' he said, 'one of these days I'm gonna be the boss of the whole syndicate.'

"I never cared that much. I was more interested in money. Enjoying myself. But Tony was waiting for an opportunity to make his bones, and that came right around here. There were two sharp stickup men we knew named Billy Mc-Carthy and Jimmy Miraglia. I did some work with them. They had been hanging around an outfit lounge on Mann-heim Road, getting loaded and getting into arguments with Philly and Ronnie Scalvo.

"Anyway, one night Billy McCarthy went drinking there again and wound up getting into another beef with the Scalvos, and a week later Jimmy Miraglia goes into the place and gets into a worse beef with the Scalvos in front of his wife.

"The next time I see McCarthy and Miraglia they tell me they're going to kill the Scalvos. I said they were nuts. If the outfit ever heard they killed the Scalvos without an okay, they'd be dead.

"The next morning, it was on my way home, about seven

thirty in the morning. I'm listening to the radio when a newscast came on and said two men and a lady were gunned down in Elmwood Park, gangland style, early in the morning. And it gave their names.

"I knew this was a disaster. First, McCarthy and Miraglia didn't have an okay for the hit. Second, it's definitely out of the question to kill anyone in Elmwood Park. So far, they're two for two. I started to get worried about myself, because everybody knew I had been doing business with the two guys.

"That day Spilotro calls and says he wanted to meet with me. I met him in the bowling alley. He was all business. I could tell he was on an assignment from the boys. I knew this was where he was gonna prove himself, and I didn't want to be his proof.

"I had two guns with me just to be sure. Two thirty-eight snubs. I was scared and ready for trouble. When Tony came in he told me that I had no problems, but I had to call McCarthy at home and tell him to meet me that night. I was supposed to tell McCarthy that I had a great score lined up.

"I didn't want to make the call, because I knew McCarthy was in trouble, but Tony assured me there was no trouble. He wanted information on the situation with the Scalvos. That's all. He just wanted to talk to McCarthy for about a half hour.

"I didn't tell him what McCarthy and Miraglia had threatened to do, and since he didn't ask to talk to Miraglia, I hoped maybe the outfit guys weren't sure who did it as yet.

"I called and Billy's wife answered. She said, 'Hi, Frankie,' and she got Billy. I told him to meet me at the Chicken House, which was located in Melrose Park, another outfit suburb. I told him I wanted to show him a very good score I found.

"He said okay, and all the while I was on the phone, Tony stood right alongside of me. I wondered whether Tony was staying that close because he wanted to see if I'd tip Mc-Carthy off that he would be waiting.

"Tony never let me out of his sight. About eight thirty, we started to drive over to the Chicken House in my car, but we stopped at another restaurant on the way. We didn't go into the place; Tony just had me pull around in the back of the parking lot, and there was a guy sitting in a dark blue Ford waiting for us.

"The guy in the car waiting for us was Vinnie Inserro. The Saint himself. We pulled up to his car and Tony walked over. They talked a minute and then Tony came back and told me to wait in the car with the Saint.

"Then Tony jumped into my car and drove away. I sat with the Saint for about forty minutes. All the while I sat in the car with him I kept one hand on my gun. The car we're sitting in was definitely a work car, and the Saint and I said absolutely nothing to each other the whole time.

"Tony rolled up about forty minutes later in my car. He walked over to where we were sitting and told the Saint he had to drive him back to the Chicken House to pick up Billy McCarthy's car. Tony also told Saint everything went fine. When they drove off I got in my car and drove home.

"The next day my phone rang. It was Billy's wife. She asked me if I had seen Billy last night. I told her no and asked why. She said it wasn't usual for Billy to stay out all night without calling her, but Billy had used her father's car last night and he never pulled a shot like that on her father.

"I told her I'd check around to see if I could find him. I really started to worry. I figured for sure I was next. I made sure I always carried a gun. Three nights after Billy disappeared I ran into Jimmy Miraglia at the Colony House restaurant. He was with his wife.

"I pulled him on the side to talk. I asked him if he had seen Billy in the last three days. He said no, and I said if I were him I would leave town in a hurry. He laughed and said, 'Why? I have nothing to hide from or run from.'

"Two days later, Jimmy Miraglia disappeared. Eleven days later both of their bodies showed up in Jimmy's car trunk.

"About a week after the bodies popped up, Tony called. He was excited. He wanted to talk.

"He told me how he grabbed Billy McCarthy at the Chicken House the night I was waiting in the car with Saint. He had parked my car in front of the place so when Billy got there he thought I'd be inside. Instead, he sees Tony.

"Billy asked Tony where I was, and Tony said he was waiting for me, too, and that he had seen my car parked outside. So they just bullshitted a little bit and when they got tired of waiting for me, they both walked out the door.

"Right as they walked out the door, Billy spotted Chuckie Nicoletti and Milwaukee Phil Alderisio right next to him. Tony grabbed Billy and they all threw him into the car. Billy had to know right then that it was up. Chuckie and Phil were known guys. They were fifteen, twenty years older than Tony. When they grab you you're gone.

"They knew Billy had a gun on him, and they took it off him right away. Then they held him down on the car floor as they took off.

"That's when Tony came back with my car and we swapped. He jumped in the car with Saint and drove off and I got in my car and took off.

"Tony said that the Saint first dropped him at a workshop where they had shanghaied Billy. Then Saint dumped Billy's car.

"Tony said they didn't kill Billy right away because they didn't know who was with him when the Scalvos were murdered. He said they had to torture Billy for a long time before he would give up who was with him. They had to beat him. Kick him. Even put an ice pick through his balls, but Billy never gave them nothing. Tony said he never saw anybody as tough as Billy McCarthy.

"Finally, Tony said he dragged Billy over to a workbench and put his head in a vise, and he started screwing it tighter and tighter.

"He said while Phil and Chuckie watched, he kept tightening the vise until Billy's head began to squish together and one of his eyes popped out. Tony said that's when Billy gave up Jimmy Miraglia's name.

"Tony really sounded like he was very proud of what he accomplished that night. It seems as though it was the first time he had ever killed anyone. It was like he made his bones. That's the way it appeared to me at the time. Like he was recognized now that he participated in a mob hit. I remember he was really impressed with Chuckie Nicoletti.

"'Boy, this is a heartless guy,' Tony said about Chuckie. 'This guy was eating pasta when Billy's eye popped out.'"

3.

"Practically a papal request."

Lefty had nothing to do with the violent end of the outfit's business. He grew up knowing most of the same bosses as Spilotro; he just provided them with a different service. He provided them with the very likely possibility of winning bets.

According to the Feds, Fiore "Fifi" Buccieri, the outfit's boss of the West Side, was one of the men who profited the most from Lefty's early handicapping talents. He was a scholarly-looking man with a stocky build, eyeglasses, and a partial upper dental plate. He started his criminal career as a juvenile delinquent, and at the age of nineteen he was already a top enforcer for Al Capone. His arrests dated back to 1925, and he had been charged with extortion, bribery, larceny, and murder. His only conviction came on a burglary charge that was reduced to petty larceny.

Lefty had known the solemn-looking street boss most of his life. Lawmen suspect that Lefty's family knew Buccieri since the mob boss and Lefty's father were in the same close-knit fruit and vegetable supply business. By 1950, when Lefty was twenty, he was already spotted traveling around the city with Buccieri. At the end of a day at the track, Buccieri would often invite Lefty to drive around with him for a few hours, according to the Feds. "Lefty knew who Buccieri was," retired FBI agent Bill Roemer said, "and that kind of an invitation was practically a papal request."

Usually, young bookmakers and handicappers were kept far away from the men who controlled the outfit, but according to the FBI, the Chicago police, and the Chicago Crime Commission, Rosenthal occupied a unique place with the outfit's bosses.

"Lefty would be seen moving all around town with some of the top guys," Roemer recalled. "He'd go for coffee with them. He'd go places outfit guys didn't usually take outsiders. We had information that he went to many of their homes and their farms in Wisconsin and on Lake Geneva. He knew everybody, but he was especially close to two guys who later became bosses—Turk Torello and Joey Aiuppa. And Fifi Buccieri probably would have become a top boss, too, except he died of cancer first."

As a result of his friendship with up and coming outfit bosses, Rosenthal always had unusual access to the outfit's top echelon. Since he was Jewish and could never be a member of the organization, he did not have to abide by many of the traditional rules of protocol that restricted aspiring members like his pal Tony Spilotro or even made men. Lefty did not have to get permission to talk to Buccieri, or Turk, or anyone else in the outfit's top echelon. According to the Feds, Lefty acquired this unique position because he made them money. First, he was a great handicapper, and second, he was able to provide the kind of inside betting information denied even mob bosses.

"Lefty was in a position to hear about doped horses, fixed

fights, crooked referees, and just about every gambling scam you could dream up, and he always knew just the people to share that information with," Roemer said. "Later, the bosses began using him whenever they found that their own bookmaking or numbers operations were not making as much as they had been making in the past. We had very good information that the outfit's top guys would often call Lefty in whenever there was a question about their gambling operations. He was like the bosses' troubleshooter. He could question people, even made men.

"Running an illegal gambling franchise is not as easy as you might think. The people who work for the bosses are constantly trying to rip them off. We are dealing with very greedy and very crooked people. The mob guys are always trying to steal from each other. Even when they know somebody's going to wind up in the trunk of a car if they get caught, they still try and steal a few bucks here and there.

"Hanging around outfit guys was the way Lefty grew up. He didn't really know anything else. To him it was all very normal." Lefty may not have been a part of the outfit's violence machine, but it was never very far away.

"While Rosenthal likes to pretend all he did was make bets and maybe take a little book, you can't be as close to these outfit guys without getting bloody," Roemer said.

One night, according to Roemer, Lefty was in the Blackamoor Lounge. The place was owned at the time by a legitimate businessman, even though it was a place where outfit bookmakers and gamblers, like Lefty, hung out.

"This night it was really crowded," Roemer said, "when in walks one of the outfit's made guys. He was by himself. The man knew Lefty fairly well, and they said hello. Our undercovers were taking it all down.

"About a half an hour goes by. This must have been about

midnight, and all of a sudden four other outfit guys walk in the front door. They were rough guys. They nod to Lefty, and one of them walks over to the owner and says, 'You're closed for the night. Everybody out!'

"The owner usually closed down around three or four in the morning, but when these guys said, 'Turn out the lights!' everybody, including Lefty and the owner, went outside.

"When the outfit guy who had come in alone tried to walk out, the goon squad stopped him.

" 'You fucking stay,' they said. 'Sit on your stool.'

"Our agents no sooner got outside with everyone else when the goons started beating that poor guy to death. One of our men got to a phone and called the police. Lefty hung around outside listening to the bloody murder just like everyone else. When the goons walked out, they had left the guy for dead. In fact, one of them said to Lefty and a few of the other guys standing around, 'Okay, get him some help, if he's still alive.'

"The guy was in the hospital for two or three months. He barely lived. His kidneys were gone. He's been in a wheelchair for the rest of his life. I think he's still alive, because we once asked about him.

"We later found out that the guy received that beating because he got into a dumb argument with another made man's wife and made the mistake of saying, 'Fuck you. Fuck your husband, and anybody around him.' With that, the wife told her husband and the husband went and told the boss that he and the wife wanted satisfaction. That's the world Lefty grew up in. That's how easy it was for even a made guy, one of the outfit's own people, to wind up in a wheelchair for the rest of his life. That's why guys like Lefty grow up being very, very careful. They know that no matter how much money they make for these guys, they cannot make any mistakes."

Still, according to Frank Cullotta, Lefty did once speak up to Buccieri and probably helped save Spilotro's life.

"There was this one time when Buccieri had everybody in Chicago terrified. I heard about the story at the time, but later Tony told me what happened. As crazy as it might seem, some psycho had actually gone to Fiore Buccieri's house with a gun and robbed Fiore's wife. When Buccieri got home he was insane. He wanted to know everything. The wife told him that the guy was a dapper-looking fella with a New York accent. She said he came to the door, showed her a gun, and made her open the safe. The guy took about $400,000 in cash and almost all of the wife's jewelry. Since the guy hadn't even bothered to wear a mask, he was probably not local, but Fiore had the cops bring him a dozen mug shot books, and he made his wife go through thousands of pages looking for the guy's face.

"Two weeks later, Buccieri still doesn't know who robbed him, and he's going wild. And everybody's terrified. If he even suspects you know what happened, you're dead, but the truth was nobody knew anything. Then, one guy looking to make a few points with Buccieri says the only guy he knew who might be crazy enough to maybe know somebody who could do such a thing was Tony Spilotro.

"Years later, when Tony found out who that rat bastard was, he wanted to kill the bum, but the guy was already dead.

"But at the time, Buccieri sends the word he wants Tony to show up at his house. Tony knows that Lefty is close with Buccieri, and he said he asked Lefty if he knew what the old man wanted. Lefty said he didn't know, and they go over to see Buccieri together. Lefty used to be at Buccieri's house all the time.

"When they got there, Tony said, Buccieri had two guys the size of refrigerators in the doorway. When he walked inside, Fiore's wife glares at him like he was the devil. He said she didn't even acknowledge him. He said now he was not very happy. He and Lefty were led down into the basement where Buccieri tells Tony to sit down in a chair. Tony said Buccieri didn't pay any attention to Lefty, who was just standing there in the dark. Then Buccieri looks at Tony and asks him, 'Do you know what happened to me?'

" 'Yeah,' Tony says, 'and I'm sorry.'

" 'I didn't ask you that,' Buccieri says, 'just answer my question.'

" 'Yes,' Tony says, 'I heard about it.'

" 'Do you have any idea who fits that MO?" Buccieri says.

" 'No,' Tony says, like he's getting a little annoyed at all this bullshit. It's like he's answering a cop.

" 'Are you sure?' Fiore asks.

"Now Tony gets pissed and he says, maybe a little sarcastically, 'I already answered that question.'

"Before his mouth was closed, Tony said, Buccieri had him by the throat, and he started strangling Tony right there. Tony thought he was going to die. Tony said he began to lose his breath. He started to gag and feel weak.

"And then he realized that Lefty was standing right next to him and that Lefty was begging Buccieri to stop. He could hear Lefty say that if Tony knew who did it he would already have given the guy up. Lefty said that Tony had a stupid mouth, but he didn't mean to be disrespectful. Tony said he could see that Lefty was talking right in Buccieri's ear until finally, Buccieri let go. He stepped back. Tony was gagging and coughing. He was dizzy.

"Buccieri looked at him and said, 'I don't want to see you in Cicero ever again, and, if I find out you know what took place in my home and didn't tell me, I'll wipe out your whole family.'

"Tony said even though Lefty saved his life, he and Lefty got out of there before the old man changed his mind."

4.

"I'd give half of what I own if I was as clean as you. Stay that way."

Lefty was probably the youngest employee to have ever worked for Donald Angelini, the Wizard of Odds. Angelini and Bill Kaplan had the best-known and best-connected book in Chicago. They had outfit bosses as their partners and the city police as their protectors. Their clients either owned the city or ran it. To work for Angel-Kaplan meant you were a seasoned veteran of the bookmaking wars. The office was full of old guys chomping on yesterday's cigars, *Guys and Dolls* rejects, gamblers who had spent years matching wits against every variety of scamster. Lefty was in heaven.

"I'd been working at Angel-Kaplan a couple of years when Gil Beckley rented a couple of big suites at the Drake Hotel and invited me," Lefty says. "There was some major fight in town. I don't remember exactly who was fighting, but I was feeling on top of the world. I had just been invited to a party by the most prominent bookmaker and layoff man in the United States.

"I knew I was picking up a little reputation at the time, and I felt like it was Gil's way of making me a part of the fraternity.

"There were no clients at this party. No high rollers. Nothing like that. Everyone there was a professional. The top pros in the business. Bookmakers. Handicappers. Lay-off men. And a couple of professional players who made their livings by betting sports. There were no suckers. No politicians.

"I had never even seen Gil Beckley before. I'd been talking to him over the phone for a couple of years. Talking to him six, seven times a day, and we're very friendly.

"Now when I meet him in person, he's really nice. He was surprised I was only in my early twenties. There were about fifteen guys at the party, and every one of them had me by twenty or thirty or forty years.

"So Beckley takes me around and introduces me to everybody in the room. It's spectacular. There was food and broads all over the place. He took care of the broads.

"And after the party's going for a while, he says to me—he called me Lefty; he didn't call me Frank—he said, 'Lefty, I want to tell you something. You're a young fellow. You've got a very, very bright future. I'm going to tell you something that you need to keep precious to you for the rest of your life.'

"He said, 'I'd give half of what I own'—and this is a wealthy man at the time—'if I was as clean as you. Stay that way.

" 'You've got the brains. You've got the know-how,' he's telling me. 'Keep clean!'

"I never forgot that, but at the time, I didn't really know what he meant. I didn't respond. But he was telling me to play it smooth. Don't get pinched. Watch your reputation. Don't get labeled.

"I didn't listen to him. I didn't know how important those words were. I was too fucking young. I had too much energy. There was too much ego. There was too much of the challenge. I wanted to become the best there was. Who's worried about getting arrested? Bookmaking? A fifty-dollar fine. Ten days suspended sentence. Fuck the coppers.

"But Gil Beckley knew that. He knew everything that I knew, plus. He knew the price you had to pay when you got to be well known. He was warning me to play it safe. Keep a low profile. Stay away from the limelight. He didn't say this, but I could sense he meant for me to stay away from being too closely associated with outfit guys.

"I just listened to Beckley and nodded. But I'm full of young blood. I'm ready to challenge the world. I know what I'm doing. I can handle it.

"About a week after the party I saw Hymie the Ace. I know he had been invited, but he never showed. I told him he had missed a great party. I told him I finally got to meet Gil Beckley and that he was a great guy.

"Ace looked at me like I was diseased. He didn't want to hear about the party. He didn't care who was there. Gil Beckley or anybody. But then, Ace never wanted to know about anything. He had no interest in street gossip, or in outfit guys, or in anything except his basketball. Ace never went to parties. Never went to outfit restaurants or hang-outs. And as a result, the Ace never took a pinch in his life."

♦ ♦ ♦

On May 26, 1966, when Gil Beckley was fifty-three, he was arrested along with seventeen others, including Gerald Kilgore, the publisher of *J. K. Sports Journal* of Los Angeles, and Sam Green, who headed the Multiple Sports Service of

Miami, in a raid of his layoff operations, which were said by the FBI to exist in New York, Maryland, Georgia, Tennessee, North Carolina, Florida, Texas, California, and New Jersey. He was tried, convicted of interstate gambling violations, and given ten years. In 1970, before the appeal of his sentence could be heard, he disappeared. The FBI believes he was murdered because mob bosses feared he might talk if faced with such long prison time.

♦ ♦ ♦

By the early 1960s, Tony Spilotro was living the outfit life. He was making money and putting it in the street. He was getting $100 a week for every $1000 borrowed. He had teams of burglars—like Frank Cullotta's—working all over town, and they kicked in between 10 and 20 percent of their takes to him. Tony was basically in the mob's main business: franchising crime. And of course, Tony had to kick in a percentage of everything he got to the street capos and lieutenants above him, to guys like Joe "the Clown" Lombardo and Milwaukee Phil.

Tony was also a master thief. He knew the best pick men, alarm guys, and fences. He could put together a team and pick a place clean. Mostly he worked with jewelry. He knew everything there was to know about stones. He could have been a jeweler. In fact, later on he opened up a jewelry store.

In the summer of 1964, Tony and his wife, Nancy—a former hatcheck girl from Milwaukee—joined their friends John and Marianne Cook on a European vacation. John Cook owned a water-skiing business in Miami, but the FBI had him listed as an international jewel thief. The Spilotros and the Cooks flew to Amsterdam, rented a Mercedes-Benz, and drove to Antwerp, Belgium, the diamond capital of

Europe. Interpol and local police were watching them every step of the way.

The Belgian police watched them check into the hotel. They watched Spilotro and Cook casing dozens of jewelry stores and wholesale shops. They spotted the two checking alarm systems, window displays, and security. Then they visited the shop of Solomon Goldenstein, a local jeweler, who became suspicious when Cook used a fake name and gave a wrong hotel address when he tried to make a credit card purchase. The jeweler activated a silent alarm, and when Spilotro and Cook left the store they were arrested. Police found that Cook was carrying a high-powered slingshot and ball bearings, a small crowbar, and passkeys for Yale locks.

When he was questioned he told police that he had the passkeys because he was afraid of being locked out of his car and that the slingshot and ball bearings were for his son.

When the police took Spilotro and Cook back to the hotel, they found the two wives waiting with the luggage packed. When the police searched the luggage they found more ball bearings.

Belgian authorities ordered the Spilotros and Cooks out of the country.

The two couples left Belgium and continued their holiday, driving through the Swiss Alps and into Monaco for a couple of days in Monte Carlo, and then back to Paris before returning home.

Spilotro and Cook did not know that they had been tracked since Belgium. When they got to Paris, the gendarmes swooped down again. This time the French police found a couple of dozen lock picks.

When the Spilotros returned to Chicago, they were searched by customs agents, who found packets of diamonds, including two that had been sewn into Spilotro's wallet. The customs agents confiscated the loot, which also included more lock picks and burglary tools.

"I went to pick Tony up at the airport," said Frank Cullotta, who was now Spilotro's right-hand man. "The cops were going through everything they had. Tony was really surprised, but Nancy was fuming. I don't think he knew they had had a line on him from Paris. I don't think he knew that he was now hot and getting hotter.

"When we got home I remember they gave Vincent, the kid, something to eat, and then Tony got a white towel and put it on the kitchen table. Then Nancy bent over the table, and one by one she began dropping diamonds out of her hair. They kept coming out one after another. He had made her hide them there. The customs people might have confiscated some of the diamonds, but I think the prize stones got through in Nancy's beehive."

Two months later, the French police found out that Spilotro and Cook had burglarized an apartment in the Hôtel de Paris in Monte Carlo on the night of August 7 and made off with $525,220 in jewels and $4,000 in traveler's checks. The apartment had been occupied by a wealthy married American woman who had been staying there with a young man and was therefore reluctant to get herself involved in an investigation. By the time she did, Spilotro and Cook were back in the United States.

Spilotro and Cook were convicted in absentia by the criminal court in Monaco and sentenced to three years, if and when they ever cared to return.

♦ ♦ ♦

"I was with Tony's crew for five years before I ever met Lefty Rosenthal," said Cullotta. "I was with his burglars and goons. Lefty was part of his gambling stuff. Mad Sam was with his loan-sharking and leg breaking. Tony liked to keep everybody separate.

"For instance, if he wanted you to drive somewhere, he wouldn't tell you who would be there or anything. You just went there, and then, maybe, he'd tell you the next step. Meantime, when you get there, the guy who's there doesn't have any idea that he's gonna meet up with you.

"So on this afternoon I get a call from Tony asking me to drop by his apartment. I knew he needed me to do something; he doesn't say what or anything. I don't expect him to. So I go right over.

"Tony and Nancy had a nice little two-bedroom, fourth-floor apartment in Elmwood Park. When I get there I see that Tony is playing gin rummy with a tall thin white-faced guy. It was Lefty.

"Nancy was running around the apartment making coffee or on the phone. I just stood behind Tony as he played a few hands, but I didn't say a word. Sometimes I'd whisper something to Nancy, but I can see Tony is beating this guy bad.

"You've gotta know that Tony played gin rummy very, very well. He'd play two hundred points across and he never lost. The guy could have been a professional gin rummy player. One night he was in Jerry's Lounge, and he's at the bar playing gin with Jerry. Jerry kept getting interrupted by customers, so Tony told me to take over the bar.

"So I took over behind the bar and they played until Tony beat the poor guy for fifteen thousand dollars. Jerry fell off his own bar stool and started crying. 'I can't pay,' he tells Tony. Tony says, 'Okay, I'll take the lounge.'

"I never saw Tony pay. He'd make you play until his luck turned around. Usually, if he beat a guy for, say, fifteen thousand dollars, he'd have me take the guy to the bank, and I'd be there while he cashed a check, and then he'd give me the money and I'd take it back to Tony.

"On a fifteen-thousand-dollar score, Tony would give me three thousand dollars just for making sure the guy doesn't skip and for bringing him back the money. Tony was a very generous guy. When he was moving around town he always picked up checks. It didn't matter. Twenty, thirty people, Tony always got the check. And he'd get really pissed off if you tried to take care of the tip. That was his, too. Nobody paid for his food.

"Finally, Lefty stands up. He says he's had enough. 'That's it,' he says. I know that these guys go back a long time. Lefty just dropped about eight grand and he says he doesn't have the cash on him, and that he'll get it and give it to Tony later.

"I knew they were close, because Tony didn't ask me to go with Lefty to get the money. He just asked me to drive Lefty to a cabstand at Grand and Harlem Avenues, on the borderline between Elmwood Park and Chicago.

"That's the only reason why Tony had me come to his house in the first place. He didn't want Lefty calling a cab from his house. He didn't want any record of cab pickups from his address. This way, when I dropped Lefty at the cabstand, nobody knew where he came from. That's why Lefty didn't take his own car to Tony's. He didn't want anybody picking up his plates outside Tony's. Back then, Tony was very careful about things like that. He was very, very cautious.

"During the ride Lefty hardly said a thing. He just sat there real glum. I guess Lefty wasn't used to losing.

"Lefty was weird. You couldn't read him. Tony loved to hang around him, because even then Lefty was one of the best handicappers in the country, bar none. We'd be hanging around on a Friday night before putting down our bets. Tony would ask Lefty, 'What about Kansas?' And Lefty would just say, 'I have no opinion.' Then Tony would ask him, 'What about Rutgers–Holy Cross?' And Lefty would say, 'No opinion.'

"Now Tony's got this list of college games printed with the odds as long as a supermarket tape, and he's going down it game by game, and he's throwing every one of them at Lefty, and Lefty's standing there, leaning against the bar, drinking his Mountain Valley water, watching some fight rerun on the TV, and he's just no-opinioning Tony to death.

"Finally, Tony blows up. He grabs the list and shoves it in Lefty's hands. 'Here, you pick 'em. Pick 'em yourself.'

"Without hardly taking his eyes off the fight, Lefty takes Tony's list, makes two quick little pencil marks on it, and hands it right back to Tony.

"Tony looks at the list. Lefty keeps looking at the TV. 'Hey!' Tony says. 'What is this? I've got a hundred plays here. Every college basketball team in the country is playing this weekend, and you give me two picks?'

"Now everybody in the joint is very quiet. You don't want to get in between these two. Lefty turns to Tony like Tony is some kid and says, 'There are only two good picks.'

"'Yeah, yeah,' Tony answers him. 'I know all that, but what about Oklahoma–Oklahoma State? What about Indiana–Washington State? Jeezus, look at that spread.'

"'Tony, I gave you the two good picks on the sheet. Forget the rest.'

"Now Tony gets hot and he starts waving the sheet in Lefty's face. 'Two picks out of a hundred? This is the way you bet?'

"Lefty looks down at Tony like he's a bug. 'I assumed you wanted to win,' he says.

"'Of course I want to win, but I want to have some fun, too. Why don't you loosen up for once, for Chrissake?'

"'How much are you betting?' Lefty asked.

"'Couple of grand, whatever . . . What are you betting?'

"'I'm wagering more than that,' Lefty says. Lefty almost never said he 'bet'; he was always 'wagering,' 'having an opinion,' or 'taking a position.'

"'More than what?' Tony jumps on him. 'You're only playing two fucking games. What the hell did you bet?'

"'You don't want to know,' says Lefty.

"'I do wanna know.'

"'You going to make it good if I lose?'

"'C'mon, tell me. I just wanna know. I told you, didn't I?'

"Lefty gets close to Tony and he says very quietly under his breath, and I'm right there between them watching his lips as he says the words, 'We were down for fifty each.'

"There would be the day when Tony bet fifty and sixty thousand dollars on a football or basketball game, but not back then. We were still in our early twenties. Lefty was about thirty. He was betting for himself and some pretty big people, outfit people, and we all knew who they were.

"'Oh, excuse me,' Tony says, grabbing the list and going down it game by game again. 'I forgot who I'm talking to. I shouldn't even be alive. I'm betting nickels and dimes over here.'

"And just as Lefty turns back to the TV, Tony asks him, 'What about West Virginia? They got that seven-foot kid from Africa. How the hell can they lose?'

"'I have no opinion on that,' Lefty says, without even turning around.

"Now Tony blows it. He rolls up the betting sheet and starts bopping Lefty over the head with it. 'If I lose, you prick,' Tony yells, 'you're gonna buy us all dinner.'

"We're all on the floor laughing, including Lefty, and Tony turns to us and says, 'The prick's got me thinking negative.'"

5.

"I respectfully decline to answer the question, as I honestly believe my answer might tend to incriminate me."

By the late 1950s, before the horror of drugs had invaded the country, illegal gamblers were considered public enemy number one. The FBI had started nationwide roundups of known gamblers. Federal laws were passed that made it an offense to transmit sports scores or race results over interstate lines. The Kefauver Crime Committee hearings—one of the first television inquisitions—also made it hot for the local sheriffs and county commissioners who had allowed bookies, layoff men, and illegal casinos to operate in their territories for a price. Even Chicago, the home of Capone, a community where the police had had difficulty closing down even one of Al's forty thousand speakeasies, was beginning to apply pressure on the city's bookmakers. In 1960, Lefty Rosenthal had his first pinch as a bookmaker. His name suddenly appeared on various lists of KGs—known gamblers—churned out for the press by the Chicago Crime Commission.

In 1961, at the age of thirty, Lefty Rosenthal moved on.

"I decided to go out on my own," he says. "Stop making money for other people. I felt it was time to start playing for myself. I moved to Miami. My father had gone down with some of his horses, and it seemed like it was the right thing to do.

"I was going to play small. I had five thousand of my own to invest and two guys took a piece of me at five thousand dollars each. I had a fifteen-thousand-dollar bankroll. I said we'll start with two-hundred-dollar plays, then double plays at four hundred dollars, and all out at a thousand dollars.

"By the end of the college basketball season, with two weeks to go, we had moved our fifteen-thousand-dollar bankroll up to seven hundred and fifty thousand dollars.

"I had friends in different parts of the country. We used to back each other up. I'd help them and they'd help me.

"One day I got this call from a pal in Kansas City. He said that he didn't think Wilt Chamberlain, who played for Kansas City at the time, was going to play that night.

"Chamberlain was the team. If he didn't play, they didn't win. I asked why. He said he didn't know, but somebody, maybe a nurse, said that Chamberlain's balls had somehow swollen up so big that he could hardly walk.

"My pal said he was sure of his information, but I checked around and found out that Chamberlain's doctors agreed about his condition.

"I took the lead early. I had nothing to lose, because I could always switch my bet later in the week. I went as far as I could go against Kansas, prior to the announcement that Chamberlain would not play.

"I gave my pal who called me with the tip a free five-thousand-dollar bet on the game. Chamberlain never missed a game except this one.

"Also, when I made the bet, I told the bookmakers what I

heard. That's the professional courtesy. You keep your bookmaker informed. You know these men. You talk with them all the time. Of course, first you make your bet and then you tell him what you've heard. It's the right thing to do in the profession. Sometimes they listen and sometimes they don't. In my case, they started to listen. It gave them an opportunity to lay off some of the Kansas money.

"On a bet like that we—my partners and myself—were all trying to get down as much as possible. We were calling bookmakers all over the country. We had special phones installed in my apartment.

"Retired telephone company guys would fix our phones so we had speed dialing before there was speed dialing. When we pounced on a game and made our bets, it would take only three or four minutes for that information to go across the country. No exaggeration. That's all it took.

"I'd punch the phone and get Washington, New Orleans, Alabama, Kansas City, just about everywhere except places like North Dakota, South Dakota, and Wyoming. I could place my bets all over the country. The bookmakers knew my code name. They knew, if I lost, I paid.

"You have a settlement number with a bookmaker and they had their own credit rating system. They didn't need D and B. They'd size you up.

"Say they decide I'm good for twenty-five thousand dollars. That meant I could be into them for twenty-five. We'd bet back and forth, and when we came up with the twenty-five thousand dollars, we'd pay off. Either you send a courier to me or I'd send one to you.

"My partners and I had it set up like a business. We had beards who would make bets for us so as not to alert the line. We had couriers. Gofers. We all had different jobs in the operation. You'd tell the courier, 'Here, take this to

Tuscaloosa.' Couriers usually wanted to be part of the organization. They were hang-around people. They'd get a piece of the pie. It was a trade-off. I was the guy who studied. I was the handicapper.

"I was betting twenty thousand dollars and thirty thousand dollars a game. Then, in the final two weeks of the season, with all this machinery working so smooth, we lost a hundred and fifty thousand dollars. I took a real couple of hits. Still, we closed the year with four hundred thousand dollars in wins on the fifteen-thousand-dollar investment and called it quits for the season.

"But in the end, the odds are built against you. You have got to walk and balance a delicate line. When I was a kid in Chicago I always heard them say, 'In the winter, the bookies go to Florida and the players eat snowballs.'

"Still, things were okay. My father and I had bought a few yearlings together. In fact, I started spending more of my time at the track. We had thirteen horses down there. We had to pay attention. It cost us about seven thousand dollars a month just to feed them. I was practically living at the track. I just loved being there."

About this time, Lefty says, he had a visit from a man known as Eli the Juice Man. Eli the Juice Man had a store in Miami, where he shipped oranges and grapefruits all around the country. He was really the middleman for the Beach, the guy who collected money to provide immunity along Miami Beach. He suggested to Rosenthal that it would be in his interest to pay him $500 a month.

Rosenthal says he told Eli he wasn't doing anything illegal—he was handicapping and working with racehorses. "I told him if I was booking I'd be happy to accommodate him, but I wasn't booking. I was strictly a player now," Lefty said. "A week or so later, Eli the Juice Man came back and asked if I had changed my mind. This time I wasn't very cordial. So, one word led to another, and I told him to go fuck himself. I made the mistake of telling him to take his best shot. He did. On New Year's Day the cops broke down my door and arrested me."

◆　◆　◆

The arrests were made by the North Bay Village Department's Chief Martin Dardis and Sergeant Edward Clode from the Dade County Division of Public Safety. Lefty was sitting on his bed in blue pajamas watching a game that afternoon when he was interrupted by the two-man raiding party. He turned what should have been a routine arrest into a disaster.

The police were no sooner in the door than Lefty started yelling that they were only there because he had refused to pay off Eli the Juice Man. "What's the matter," he said. "You didn't get your piece? Is that why you're here?"

His accusation of Chief Dardis was an unpardonable breach in the Kabuki ritual attached to cop-and-crook etiquette.

"After that," Lefty now admits, "I was fair game."

Chief Dardis later testified: "When I went into the bedroom, Mr. Rosenthal was seated on the bed. He had a telephone in one hand and a small black book in the other. The search warrant was read to him by a deputy sheriff, at which time I took the telephone from him and I asked the person on the other end who was talking. I said I was Lefty.

"He said, 'This is Cincinnati.' He said, 'You have ten and ten on Windy Fleet, and I will take four and four of it.' We later learned that Windy Fleet was a horse running at Tropical Park that afternoon. It came in second."

♦ ♦ ♦

A couple of weeks after his arrest, Lefty said, he got into a traffic dispute with two men who turned out to be federal agents. He said he and the agents were on a side street near Biscayne Boulevard. Lefty had been on his way to a popular restaurant nearby. He knew they were agents because he had just been ticketed for failing to signal a right turn by the local cops. The agents had been tagging along right behind the police and started cursing him while he was being given the ticket. Lefty said the cops giving him the ticket acknowledged they were FBI agents.

"One night I was driving down a very dark road in Miami and a couple of agents were behind me," said Rosenthal. "This actually happened; I swear to you it happened. And it's a real dark road and it's very narrow, and this car's closing in on me. And they pull me over and I stop. And the two agents identify themselves, and they start giving me some shit, and I gave it right back to them. One of them was a real big guy. We were in this wooded area. He got out of the car and pushed me off, physically pushed me off to the side, and he said, 'We finally got you. We are going to take you into the fucking woods and beat you to a pulp.' And he looked like he meant it. As he's talking, who's driving the other way on that street by mere accident? So help me God—Tony Spilotro. He sees my car. He pulls over. He gets out of the car. He challenges both of the fucking agents. He went nose to nose—and he's only five two or five three. He says, 'You two gutless sonofabitches, you ain't gonna do nothing to him.' So help me God.

"Now Tony and I grew up together. I used to say I knew him from the time he was conceived. We frequented the same places in Chicago. But the relationship really grew more from North Miami. Tony would come down there about three times a year, and the first person he'd get hold of is me. Tony's first love, really, was gambling. Tony felt, in those days, he could not make a play without me. That to make a bet on anything would be disastrous unless he had my opinion. And he would call me all the time. He could hound me to death for an opinion. He was habitual. You're talking about alcoholics when it came to gambling and Tony.

"One night we're having dinner on Biscayne Boulevard in an Italian restaurant with about six or seven people. All guys. There's Tony, all his guys, and me. And there were some rough hombres at that table. And for some reason, one of them had a real hard-on for me. He didn't like Frank Rosenthal, for whatever reasons. And he insulted me at the table. About three or four minutes went by. Tony says he's going to go to the men's room. And he gets this kid off to the side. Before they even get to the men's room, what he fucking told this guy! Holy shit. The language. 'You son of a bitch. I will cut your fucking head off if I ever, ever hear you even look at him like that again. You go back to that fucking table and tell him you're sorry, you son of a bitch.' So the kid comes back to the table and he apologizes. He says, 'You know, I shouldn't be drinking. I'm drinking. I didn't mean it. Would you forgive me?' I said, 'Sure, no problem.'"

◆ ◆ ◆

In 1961, the newly appointed Attorney General, Robert F. Kennedy, started looking into the connections between the mob, illegal gambling, and the Teamsters Union.

The FBI already knew most of the players. They knew

more about what was happening within the mob than many of the mobsters. Frank Rosenthal's connections to the Chicago outfit were well known. In Miami, he had been spotted in the company of Chicago street bosses like Turk Torello, Milwaukee Phil, Jackie Cerone, and Fiore Buccieri. The bureau believed that in addition to betting in Miami, he was also booking bets. His arrest by the local police raised his profile high enough to guarantee a friendly visit from the feds asking him to become an informer in exchange for immunity—he refused—and subsequently a subpoena from the McClellan Subcommittee on Gambling and Organized Crime arrived.

Senator McClellan did not see any charm in the roguish guys and dolls with their buffed nails who paraded before him accompanied by high-priced lawyers who'd provided them with neatly-printed cards containing the Fifth Amendment.

The committee had lined up several cooperating witnesses who would testify to the mob's power in illegal gambling and their influence in the sports world, where it was not uncommon for athletes and coaches to be offered cash to shave points or throw games.

Lefty got a lawyer and flew to Washington and found himself being accused of attempting to bribe Michael Bruce, a twenty-five-year-old University of Oregon halfback, who said that when he and his team went to Ann Arbor for an important game with the University of Michigan, he met with Lefty and another gambler, David Budin, a twenty-eight-year-old former basketball player, gambler, and card hustler, who later turned out to have been a paid government informer.

Bruce said the meeting took place in a hotel room and that he was offered $5,000 to make sure that his team—who were the underdogs—lost by eight points instead of six. Bruce said he pretended to accept Lefty's offer but immediately reported the incident to his coach.

Lefty has denied that he ever tried to bribe anyone. But when he took the stand before the McClellan committee, his lawyers advised him that if he answered one question—even an innocuous one—he would have to answer everything he was asked or be held in contempt and very likely jailed. His appearance before the committee was a fiasco.

THE CHAIRMAN: Are you known as Lefty?

MR. ROSENTHAL: I respectfully decline to answer the question, as I honestly believe my answer might tend to incriminate me.

SENATOR MUNDT: Are you left-handed?

MR. ROSENTHAL: I respectfully decline to answer the question, as I honestly believe my answer might tend to incriminate me.

THE CHAIRMAN: Mr. Rosenthal, according to this transcript of your testimony on the 6th day of January this year, 1961 [in the bookmaking arrest] . . . you were asked one question that says, 'You are also known as Lefty.' And your answer was, 'Yes, sir, it is a baseball nickname.' Is that correct?

MR. ROSENTHAL: I respectfully decline to answer the question, as I honestly believe my answer might tend to incriminate me.

THE CHAIRMAN: Did you ever play baseball?

MR. ROSENTHAL: I respectfully decline to answer the question, as I honestly believe my answer might tend to incriminate me.

MR. ADLERMAN: Mr. Rosenthal, were you formerly employed by Angel-Kaplan as a handicapper?

MR. ROSENTHAL: I respectfully decline to answer the question, as I honestly believe my answer might tend to incriminate me.

MR. ADLERMAN: Are you a professional gambler and layoff bettor?

MR. ROSENTHAL: I respectfully decline to answer the question, as I honestly believe my answer might tend to incriminate me.

MR. ADLERMAN: Do you know Fiore "Fi-Fi" Buccieri?

MR. ROSENTHAL: I decline to answer on the grounds that my answer may tend to incriminate me.

MR. ADLERMAN: Are you acquainted with Sam "Mooney" Giancana?

MR. ROSENTHAL: I decline to answer on the grounds that my answer may tend to incriminate me.

MR. ADLERMAN: Have you ever attempted to bribe any football players?

MR. ROSENTHAL: I decline to answer on the grounds that my answer may tend to incriminate me.

MR. ADLERMAN: Have you ever specifically tried to bribe any football players in the Oregon-Michigan games?

MR. ROSENTHAL: I decline to answer on the grounds that my answer may tend to incriminate me.

Lefty took the Fifth Amendment thirty-seven times.

◆ ◆ ◆

Lefty went back to Florida, but the heat was on. Robert Kennedy had pushed a bill through Congress prohibiting the interstate transmission of any gambling information, making Lefty's phone calls about team injuries, lineups, odds, and even weather conditions against the law and subjecting him to arrest.

In 1962, when the FBI's long-awaited crackdown on gamblers arrived and J. Edgar Hoover personally announced the arrests of hundreds of gamblers and mobsters all around the country, Lefty was among those arrested. Over the next year he was routinely arrested for bookmaking, handicapping, traffic infractions, using profanity, disorderly conduct, loitering, and gambling.

The FB planted two transmitters in his apartment. The court-authorized bugs, which were part of the Justice Department's crackdown on illegal gambling and the mob, remained in Lefty's apartment for a year and a day. (Lefty found out that he had been bugged only when Gil Beckley was indicted in a federal racketeering case and during the pretrial discovery motions one of Beckley's lawyers spotted the FBI affidavits acknowledging the bug in Lefty's house.)

Then the Florida State Racing Commission announced that Rosenthal's license to own racehorses or even enter a racetrack, a jai alai fronton, or a dog track anywhere in the state was being revoked. Despite the advice from his friends, Rosenthal insisted upon petitioning the Racing Commission for a hearing—which succeeded only in causing more publicity, all of it bad, for himself.

Eventually all of the bookmaking charges against Lefty would be dismissed or dropped. In fact, every charge— aside from a Miami traffic infraction—was dismissed without trial, until 1962, when Rosenthal was indicted in North Carolina for attempting to bribe Ray Paprocky, a twenty-year-old NYU college basketball player from New York. Once again, his main accuser turned out to be David Budin, the same government informant who said he had been present at the alleged bribery attempt in Ann Arbor—an episode that Rosenthal had never even been indicted for. In fact, the only charges that were filed in the Ann Arbor bribery case were against Budin, for registering under a false name at the Dearborn Inn.

In the North Carolina case, however, Rosenthal's lawyer, a local attorney familiar with the players and the court, told him that the North Carolina judge hearing the case had made it very clear that if Rosenthal insisted upon going to trial and was found guilty, he would be guaranteed a long prison term.

Lefty told his lawyers he didn't want to plead guilty. The negotiations between the prosecutors and Lefty's lawyers went on for more than a year. Finally, Lefty's lawyers said the prosecutors and judge would accept a no-contest plea from Lefty. Lefty wouldn't acknowledge the charge; he would simply not contest the accusations against him and accept the court's verdict.

6.♦

"You can't imagine the relief I felt just to get away from those maniacs."

By 1967, Frank Rosenthal's fight with the state of Florida ended—and the state of Florida won. Western Union stopped providing Lefty's Select Sports Service with the wire and—the crowning blow—the telephone company pulled their lines out of Lefty's house.

"At first I went back home," Rosenthal says. "I thought I could continue my betting back in Chicago. But I was wrong. I got to Chicago in time for the football season and I was doing okay, except it became clearer to me after every weekend that I should have been playing in Las Vegas instead of Chicago.

"I had a penthouse on Lakeshore Drive in Chicago and my beards in Las Vegas to make my plays for me, but I was getting frustrated.

"I'd ask my man in Vegas, 'What have they got on a certain game?' Meaning, what is the spread the Vegas bookmakers had on the game?

"My guy would check and call me back and he'd say, 'Seven.'

"I'd say, 'Take it.'

"Then he'd come back and say, 'It's now six and a half.'

"'Jesus!' I'd say, 'hurry up and get me the six and a half.'

"Two minutes later he's back again.

"'Now it's six,' he'd say.

"'SIX!'

"'What can I tell you, Frank? The line is moving.'

"This was going on week after week. Finally, I remember one weekend when I really liked the game. I eventually won the bet, but that was the day I decided that if I was going to make my living betting sports I couldn't do it long-distance. I'd have to go to Las Vegas. Take all my stuff and move out there, where I could sit down and watch the number until I was ready to pounce.

"On the day I left, Tony was supposed to pick me up outside the Belmont Hotel, drive me out to Fiore's farm to say good-bye, and take me to the plane. And of course, Tony was late.

"Buccieri had a summer home on Lake Geneva, Wisconsin. It was about an hour's drive from Chicago. It was a huge place with horses and gardens and a rifle and skeet range where Fiore entertained on the weekend.

"When Tony finally arrived he was more than an hour late. Tony was always late. He was late for his own wedding. Honest. But to be late for Fiore was dumb, because Fiore hated to be kept waiting.

"Tony finally shows up with two pals. One of them is in jail now. He was a really dangerous guy. A genuine tough guy. And I would have to say that he was about the meanest sonofabitch I ever did know. Ever. Ever. I'm talking about everybody I ever met.

"He hated me. Really hated me. With a passion. He hated everybody. He even hated Tony, but he was afraid of Tony. I don't think Tony knew how much this guy hated him, but I did.

"Tony ran the guy ragged. 'Do this! Do that!' Tony would insult him. I saw the guy get so frustrated in a hotel room where Tony was berating him, screaming at him, poking him in the chest, that the guy started pounding his own head into the wall by his ears. I was there. I saw it. Tony just laughed.

"By the time we finally got to Fiore's, there's hardly any time for even a cup of coffee. I think Fiore had given up on us. He was out riding on his horse. He had to come back and get off so we could meet for a few minutes before I had to leave. Mostly, I think, he just wanted to say good-bye. We hugged and I got back in the car and we headed for the airport.

"Now I'm hot at Tony because he was so late. He screwed me up with Fiore, and now I was going to miss my goddamn flight out to Vegas. Fuck! There were very few direct flights to Vegas from Chicago back then.

"He doesn't say anything, but he starts moving. We get on the freeway. First of all, as a driver, Tony was extremely good. That was one of his things. And by now, he's going about ninety-something miles an hour. We're in traffic. We're in and out of cars. I'm sitting next to him and I'm terrified.

"He's got the guys in the back and they're terrified. And wouldn't you know it, here come the sirens. The coppers.

"As soon as I heard the sirens I said, 'God damn it! Now I'm really gonna blow my goddamn flight.'

"He's calm as you can imagine. He chimes in, 'You ain't blowing shit. Just shut up!'

"The sirens are getting louder, but he doesn't even slow down. And now there are two cop cars chasing us. And we're racing. He stays ahead of the coppers for miles, skipping around cars, screeching tires, and all the time saying, 'Don't worry about it. You'll make your plane. Don't worry about it.'

"Finally, with the cops' cars still coming up behind us, he shoots into the airport and pulls up right in front of my terminal. He tells one guy to hurry up and get my bags checked. Then he tells the other guy to go up and hold the gate.

"The first guy jumped out of the car and went to the head of the line with my bags, and when the clerk said something to him, he said something back and the clerk backed down. Tony's other guy ran ahead to the gate and got them to hold it open for me.

"When I finally got on board and took off, you can't imagine the relief I felt just to get away from those maniacs."

◆ ◆ ◆

Lefty was on his way to Las Vegas, and so was his rap sheet. The Chicago Crime Commission was preparing to alert the Las Vegas police that Frank "Lefty" Rosenthal, a thirty-eight-year-old outfit bookmaker, handicapper, and layoff man, was about to arrive. The Crime Commission would routinely send the résumés of outfit members and their associates to Las Vegas as part of an unofficial intelligence-sharing program that had been going on for years. The Las Vegas police were informed that Lefty Rosenthal had at least a dozen gambling arrests and no convictions, had pleaded no contest in 1961 to the attempted bribery of a college basketball player in North Carolina, and had taken the Fifth Amendment thirty-seven times before a congressional subcommittee looking into connections between gambling and the mob.

"I'm not in Las Vegas a week before there's a knock on the door," Rosenthal says. "I remember I had the flu. It was the coppers.

"I let them in. 'What can I do for you?'

"'You're under arrest.'

"'What for?'

"'Burglary,' they say.

"'That's nuts!' I say. I'm genuinely amazed. I know I haven't done anything.

"'Don't get wise with us,' they say, and they cuff me. They walk me out of the hotel right through the lobby, and they take me over to Metro Police headquarters and into Gene Clark's office.

"Clark was sitting there. Chief of detectives. Real cold. A big strong guy. He said, 'You know, you don't appear to be as tough as your reputation.'

"'Mr. Clark,' I said, 'I agree.'

"'I'm not looking for your sarcasm,' he says.

"'I'm not offering any sarcasm,' I say.

"I see him nod to the detectives who brought me there and they leave the room. Now I'm in there alone and I've got my hands cuffed.

"'I want you out of this town by midnight tonight, and don't come back,' he says. 'We don't want your type around here. Do you understand me?'

"'I think I do,' I say.

"'So when are you leaving?'

"'I don't know,' I say.

"With that he gets up from his desk and comes around

behind me, and suddenly he grabs me by my throat and he starts squeezing. He squeezes so tight that I began to lose my breath. I got dizzy. I could feel I was going to faint. Then he released me.

"'You got the message, Lefty,' he says. He called me Lefty. 'Be out of here by midnight, because there are a lot of holes out there in the desert and you don't want to fill one of them.'

"When they let me go, I called Dean Shandell, a friend of mine, at Caesar's. He was a pretty big guy. Knew his way around. A top guy. I knew he was tight with the sheriff. I told him the story. He told me to meet him at the Galleria. It's now about eight or nine at night. I went to the lounge and we started to talk. I asked him: 'What's going on out here? Why did I get arrested for burglary in my own room?'

"At that moment we looked up and who should come in the place but Chief of Detectives Gene Clark and the two detectives who picked me up earlier.

"'You don't have a good memory, do you?' he says. 'The last plane out of here is about to leave.'

"Dean got up and said, 'Why don't you leave him alone?'

"'Mind your own business,' Clark tells Dean. 'This is from the sheriff.' And with that he arrests me again. After a night in the can, I was put on a plane for Chicago the next morning.

"After a few days calling around, I made arrangements to return. The sheriff told Dean they hassled me only because I had such a hot profile. The FBI and the Chicago cops said I had all kinds of affiliations, but at that point, the truth was, I was strictly freelance. So I went back.

"I moved into the Tropicana Hotel. I was spending all my time in the hotel room reading the newspapers. Or I'm over at the Rose Bowl Sports Book with Elliott Price. It was down the street from Caesar's, and it was a betting and booking operation. I was running my bets out of the Rose Bowl. Then at night I'd go to the Galleria, at Caesar's, and hang around with guys like Toledo Blacky, Hunchback Bobby, Jimmy Caselli, and Bobby Martin.

"I was doing well on Sundays. It was a great season. Monday was always a special day. Monday night was the ultimate. At that time my focus was keen. I was betting against the biggest bookmakers in the country and I was way ahead.

"That season, I won every game of Monday-night football, except one. After a while, the fun was in watching the line change and knowing it was because of me.

"I'd see the game open at six. Nice and stable. No secrets. The game shouldn't go below five or above seven. One point either way. But back then, when I was moving, I was able to move the spread on a game by as much as three points.

"I'd go home to watch each game. I'd turn off the phone. If I had a big wager on a game, I never watched with anyone. I watched it all by myself. I was too involved. I didn't want to be distracted.

"Meanwhile, I'd met Geri. She was a dancer at the Tropicana. She was the most beautiful girl I ever saw. She was tall. Statuesque. Great posture. And everyone who met her liked her in five minutes. The girl had fantastic charm. No matter where we went, people would turn around and look at her. She was that striking.

"When I met her, she was also a chip hustler. She was a working girl. She had a couple of guys who she went with, and she made about five hundred thousand dollars a year.

"I used to meet her after work, but the more I used to go out with her, the more I saw in her. I realized that I was changing my attitude toward her one night when I went over to see her dance at the Trop. When she came out I saw that she was dancing topless. Suddenly, it bothered me. I walked out. Later I told her that I saw her but that I had to leave before the end of the show.

"She didn't give it much thought. She just thought I was busy. I don't think it even dawned on Geri that I was beginning to feel differently about her.

"She used to dance and finish up whatever hustles she had for the night, and then she'd meet me at Caesar's. One night she said she had an appointment at the Dunes and that she'd meet me later.

"I don't know, but I just got curious. I wanted to see what she was up to. Who she was with. So I did what I had never done. I went over to the Dunes to see her in action.

"When I got there the place was hot. She was throwing pass after pass at the craps table, and the guy with her was stacking rack after rack. She must have pulled in sixty thousand dollars for the guy, judging by the racks of hundred-dollar chips he had in front of him. She looked up, and when she saw me, she gave me a dirty look. I knew she didn't like that I'd come by to see her. She rolled again and crapped out.

"Meanwhile, she had made the guy a small fortune. Of course, every time she made a pass I noticed that she was snatching little black hundred-dollar chips off his pile and dropping them into her purse.

"When the guy was getting ready to cash in the roll, Geri looked at him and asked, 'Where's my end?'

"The guy looked at her purse and said, 'You've already taken your end in there.'

"It's understood, after a girl makes a run like that for you, you give her five, six, seven grand. Geri hadn't picked up anything like that, even in hundred-dollar chips.

"'I want my end,' she said very loudly. The guy reaches for her purse. He's gonna empty her purse right there in front of us. But before he can do that, Geri leans over and grabs his chip racks and tosses them into the air as high as she can.

"Suddenly, the whole casino is raining hundred-dollar black chips and twenty-five-dollar green chips. They're falling and bouncing off the tables, people's heads and shoulders, and rolling along the floor.

"Within seconds everybody in the casino is diving for chips. I mean players, dealers, pit bosses, security guards—everybody's fishing for the guy's chips on the floor.

"The guy she was with is screaming and scooping up as many as he can. The security guys and dealers are handing him six and pocketing three. It's a wild scene.

"At that point I can't take my eyes off her. She's standing there like royalty. She and I are the only two people in the whole casino who aren't on the floor. She looks over at me and I'm looking at her.

"'You like that, huh?' she says, and walks out the door. That's when I realized I had fallen in love."

7.

"You've never been with anybody like me, have you?"

When Lefty met her, Geri McGee had been hustling in Las Vegas for about eight years. She owned her own house. She was raising an eleven-year-old daughter, Robin Marmor, whose father was Geri's high school sweetheart, Lenny Marmor. She supported her ailing mother, Alice, and her sister, Barbara, who had been abandoned with two young sons by her husband. Occasionally Lenny Marmor would visit Geri and their daughter for two or three days, usually to borrow money for a surefire business deal. Occasionally Geri's father, Roy McGee, a California auto mechanic, long separated from her mother, would visit.

Geri earned between $300,000 and $500,000 a year hustling chips and partying with high rollers. She made about $20,000 a year as a dancer at the Tropicana, and that job provided her with a work card, issued by the Las Vegas Sheriff's Office, showing that she was gainfully employed. Having a work card kept her from being harassed for hustling in a casino by Las Vegas vice cops and hotel security.

"Everybody loved Geri because she spread money around," said Ray Vargas, a former valet parker at the Dunes Hotel. "She hung around with another knockout back then. Evelyn. Geri was a blonde. Evelyn was a red-head. They were doing great.

"Geri knew you had to take care of people, and she did. I mean, everybody in Las Vegas who's got any brains is on the hustle. Nobody lives off their paycheck parking cars or dealing cards. That's the thing about Las Vegas. Everybody sharp who lives there is on the make. That's why they're there.

"And Geri got along because she gave everybody a few bucks whenever she scored. If she needed uppers to keep some butter-and-egg desperado awake, she got them. Mostly she got the johns to spring for the money, but what did I care? She always got me the money, and I needed it. My valet parking concession back then cost me fifty grand a year that I had to kick back to the casino manager just for letting me lease the place."

Las Vegas is a city of kickbacks. A desert city of greased palms. A place where a $20 bill can buy approval, a $100 bill adulation, and a $1,000 bill canonization. There are stories of dealers getting thousands of dollars in tips from lucky high rollers, and even comped high rollers are expected to make a laydown bet of a couple of hundred or thousand to repay the house for its courtesy. Las Vegas is a city where everyone takes care of everyone else. Maître d's at the big shows not only pay for their jobs but often give the men who hire them a percentage of their weekly tips. Smart girls like Geri tipped everyone in sight. She cast her money on the waters and expected it to come back tenfold.

"Geri was in love with money," Frank Rosenthal says. "To her, a night was a waste if she didn't go home with cash in her pocket. In the beginning, she treated me like I was a fucking square. One of her suckers. I was on the clock.

"I had to give her a two-carat heart-shaped diamond pin just to get her to start dating me. When we'd be out, she'd ask me for money for the powder room lady. I'd usually give her a hundred-dollar bill. I expected her to bring me back some change, but she never did. She never brought me back a penny.

"I mentioned it to her once and she said she lost it playing blackjack on the way back to the table. I knew she was lying. I didn't care about the money. I just didn't want her playing me for another one of her suckers. She had a Rolodex filled with their names. She knew guys all over the country. Clients. They'd call her up when they were coming to town. They were like friends. Some she drank with. Some she gambled with. Some she took on dates, and there were some where she went all the way. It all depended on what was there for her. If she didn't think she was going to see you again or make some money, forget it. You were gone.

"In those days, Geri was working all the time. She was carrying her whole family. She had a mother and daughter and sister and two nephews living in the house to support. She also had an ex-boyfriend who was the father of her kid. She was carrying him, too, especially after he got pinched for pimping in Los Angeles." Marmor's pimping charges were later dismissed.

♦ ♦ ♦

Geri McGee and her sister, Barbara, grew up in Sherman Oaks and went to Van Nuys High School with Robert Redford and Don Drysdale. Their father, Roy McGee, worked in gas stations and tinkered. Their mother, Alice, had been hospitalized for mental illness; when she was well, she took in ironing.

"We were probably the poorest family in the neighborhood," says Barbara McGee Stokich. "We baby-sat, raked leaves, fed people's chickens and rabbits. It wasn't much fun. When we were little kids we got all our clothes from the neighbors. Geri hated it more than anything.

"Geri started going out with Lenny Marmor in high school. He was the sharpest guy in school. He wore sunglasses indoors. Geri was only fifteen. She and Lenny used to dance together by the hour. Ballroom dancing. She was a great dancer. She only had to watch you do a step once and she could do it.

"They won silver cups and prizes dancing in contests all over the Valley and at the Hollywood Palladium. Geri won bathing suit contests and little modeling jobs. Nobody in the family liked Lenny, but he was always hanging around, acting like he was her agent. She didn't want us to see him in his dark glasses.

"Our dad really did not like Lenny. He tried to break them up. He went to talk to the school principal. My father always wanted to become a cop. One time my father got so mad at Lenny that he went to Lenny's house and beat him up.

"But Lenny was slick, and he convinced Geri that his own dad was cruel to him. He made Geri feel sorry for him right from back there when they were juniors in high school. So Geri started seeing Lenny on the sneak.

"In 1954, when Geri graduated, our aunt Ingram, my father's sister, who inherited a lot of money when her husband died, offered to send Geri to Woodbury Business School, which is where she had sent me two years earlier. But Geri didn't want to go to Woodbury. She wanted to go to UCLA or USC. Our aunt refused. She wouldn't do more for Geri than she did for me. So Geri said, 'No thank you. I don't want Woodbury. It's not right for me.' Instead, she got a job as a clerk in Thrifty Drugs. She didn't like it. Then she got a job as a teller in the Bank of America. She didn't like that either. Then she got a clerical job in personnel at Lockheed Aero Jet. The manager there really liked her. She got him to hire me to do steno for the engineers. I could take a hundred and eighty words a minute.

"She had an apartment and Lenny moved in, and he started taking her to Hollywood parties to meet people, and she kept on dancing and posing in bathing suit contests.

"In 1958, their daughter Robin was born, and Lenny talked Geri into moving to Las Vegas. He could talk her into anything. He used to say he was a professional pool shooter. He used to say he was a car salesman. But the truth is, I don't remember him ever working. He stayed in Los Angeles, but he said she could make real money in Vegas. Our mom moved out there with her to help keep an eye on Robin.

"When Geri first got to Las Vegas around 1960, she was a cocktail waitress and showgirl. Our dad would visit once in a while, but he got very upset when he saw what Geri was doing. It was very tough on Dad. He could see what was going on, but rather than lose a daughter, he had to accept her way of life.

"She was already seeing Frank in 1968, when I had to move in with her after my husband walked out. Geri was very generous with me. I couldn't have made it through that time without her. She had everything. She had blue-chip stocks. She had saved her money. But she knew it wouldn't last. She said she was over thirty. She talked to me about how it couldn't last.

"One day she and I were talking to a friend of hers named Linda Pellichio. Geri was telling us about the different men who wanted to marry her. There were men from all over who wanted to marry her. Guys in New York and in Italy. But she felt she couldn't leave. She had Robin and Mother and Lenny and our father. She wondered about whether she should marry Lenny. She told us that he had been after her about their getting married, but I told her Lenny had just been arrested in Los Angeles for pimping and that's why he wanted to get married all of a sudden. I told her Lenny only wanted to marry her because she had the money to keep him out of jail and pay his lawyers. But she knew that all by herself. She looked at me and Linda. 'What should I do?' she said. Linda Pellichio had the answer. I'll never forget it. 'Marry Frank Rosenthal,' Linda said. 'He's very rich. Marry him, get his money, and then divorce him.'

"Geri said, 'I can't marry him. He's a triple Gemini. All dualities.' Geri believed in horoscopes. 'Gemini is the snake. You've got to watch a snake.'

"Geri was also going out with Johnny Hicks at that time. She adored Johnny Hicks and he would have married her, except he had very rich parents. They owned the Algiers Hotel, and they didn't want him to marry her. He would have lost everything. The way it was, Johnny had a ten-thousand-dollar-a-month trust fund. I think he would have married her if he could.

"She started talking more and more about getting married. She didn't want to live the way she was living anymore. She said to me that she was going to find somebody to marry."

♦ ♦ ♦

Lefty Rosenthal had been married briefly in his twenties. He was skittish about getting married again. Geri did not exactly look like the sort of girl you took home to Mama.

She hardly seemed like someone who would ever settle down; every date was an adventure. "When we started going out," says Lefty, "she had been going with Johnny Hicks. He was about ten years younger than Geri. He came from a substantial family. They had owned the Algiers Hotel and the Thunderbird Casino. He liked to play the tough guy. Hung around downtown with a crew that used to beat up hookers. That kind of guy.

"Geri had been going around with him before I got there. They'd go out, and if somebody tried to pick up Geri or came on to her a little, Hicks liked to beat them up. Badly.

"He liked to kick people when they were down. A real tough-guy street fighter.

"One night I'm with Geri in Caesar's. We're there with Bert Brown, a gambling friend of mine, and Bobby Kay, the midget who ran the Galleria in Caesar's. Out of nowhere, Geri says, 'Let's go over to the Flamingo.' She says she wants to dance. She knows I don't dance, but she wants to go dance anyway. That's what it was like dating Geri. Okay? Okay.

"We get over there and we're sitting at a table on the aisle, and who walks in but Johnny Hicks and three or four guys, and one of them is this really good club fighter named Bates. As Hicks walks by my table I see that he gives me a bad look. He knows I've started dating Geri seriously. She's with me now. No more bullshit. By the look of him I know there's gonna be trouble, but there's nothing I can do.

"Now instead of staying seated and not starting a problem, Geri decides she wants to dance. I said, 'You know I don't dance, Geri.' So she gets up and starts dancing with Bert Brown.

"It's all fine until I see Hicks get up and tap her on the shoulder. Bert Brown backs off. I can see Geri and Hicks are talking, but I can't hear them.

"Now Geri starts dancing with Hicks. Suddenly, I see, he

puts his hands on her shoulders to sort of shove her roughly.

"I lose it. I remember I just started toward him. I remember flying and colliding with him and we both went down onto the floor. He was stronger than I was and he wrestled me around and got on top, and he got his hands and fingers and began tearing at my face. Some security guys and his own pal Bates got him off me and held him back. As he was being pulled off me, he kicked out and just missed my head by an inch.

"I was crazy. I went back to the Trop, where I was living, and went into my bag and got a gun. I was going to find the sonofabitch and kill him. You can see I was out of my mind.

"I went looking for Hicks. I had been bleeding badly from the face. Bobby Kay and Geri are pleading with me, but I don't care. Pretty soon Elliott Price and Danny Stein, from Caesar's, slowed me down, and they took me back to my apartment and I calmed down.

"What did I expect? Here I am going with one of the best-looking gals in the whole goddam state, if not the country. So help me God!

"She was. Boy!

"I was a fucking idiot. Naive. You know? And I'm saying to myself, 'What am I doing with this woman?' How did I get her?'

"You know, during this period, she once made a crack to me. It was very interesting. We were getting ready to go to bed. She was looking at me with a little smile. 'You've never been with anybody like me, have you?' she says, smiling. 'Have you?'

"I know she's right, but I asked what she means. 'Someone like you?'

"'You know exactly what I mean,' she says. 'You've never

been with anyone like me. Anyone that looks like me. Have you?'

"'Well, I'll tell you the truth, Geri,' I said. 'No, I haven't.'

"I thought about her right there and I knew she was right. I couldn't believe it was all mine. I had never been to bed or made love to somebody who looked like her.

"And she just looked at me and kept smiling."

♦ ♦ ♦

Frank and Geri were married May 1, 1969, by Justice of the Peace Joseph Pavlikowski.

"There was never any question," Lefty says. "I knew Geri didn't love me when we got married. But I was so attracted to her when I proposed I thought I could build a nice family and a nice relationship.

"Before we got married we talked about the fact that you can build or create a form of love, admiration, respect. What is love? I talked to her about that. But I wasn't fooled.

"She married me because of what I stood for. Security. Strength. A well-connected fellow. A well-respected fellow. Would probably make a good father. And she was getting older. She didn't want to chip-hustle anymore. Fuck around with her players. She wanted to be respectable. Quit her job at the Tropicana.

"When I was dating her, some of my friends warned me about her. They said, 'Listen, this girl will fucking empty you out. You don't know her background.'

"See, I was considered a square guy then. I was. And these were people who, I think, cared for me. And they were trying to tell me, 'Don't do it.' They'd see me with her all the time. I was really involved with her.

"Some of them knew her for a couple of years. I knew her

for a couple of months. But I was smarter than they were, I thought. I was the handicapper. I was this, I was that.

"And I could mold Geri. I don't give a fuck if she drinks too much. So what? I'll stop that in one day. I didn't know about alcoholism. How would I know about it? I never drank. All I knew about was handicapping and handicapping and handicapping. That's all I knew.

"At the wedding she got up and went to a public phone booth to make a call. When I went out to see if she was okay, I could hear her talking to Lenny Marmor. I could hear her telling him she had just married Frank Rosenthal. As she spoke, I saw that she was crying. I could hear her saying, 'Lenny, I'm sorry. I love you. This is the best thing I can do.' She's saying good-bye to the love of her life. She hung up the phone and she saw me. She told me it was something she had to do. I told her I understood that, but the past was now the past. We were now married. Life would be different. I took the drink out of her hand and we walked back into the wedding.

"So, we got married. Tremendous. It was a hell of a night. Maybe five hundred people. Her family. My family. Friends. Caviar. Lobsters. Cristal champagne for five hundred people. They erected a chapel in Caesar's Palace. I have no idea what the bill was. My wedding was comped."

8.

"He's not like a son; he is my son."

Lefty Rosenthal was forty-one. He had had enough of life as a freelancer. He was running a betting and booking office called the Rose Bowl and he had been arrested six times in a four-month period. He was tired of eighteen-hour days and continuous harassment by John Law. It was time to pack it in. Get a steady gig. Settle down. Of course, Las Vegas may be the only city in the world where settling down means going to work in a casino.

"In 1971 the pressure got to the point where Geri asked me to quit gambling and get a regular job," Rosenthal said. "Lend some respectability to the family now that we had a son. She wanted us to live a normal life. Geri felt squeezed out. She said Steven felt squeezed out. I felt I owed it to her to at least try to live a regular life for a while. She said, 'Take the same energy you're using betting every week and use it inside a casino.' I said okay and filled out a few applications. I had some friends at the Stardust and I got a job as a floor man. That's one step above a dealer. I got sixty dollars a day. I pulled an eight- or nine-hour shift. I was in charge of watching four blackjack tables."

The Stardust Hotel and Casino was built in 1959. It was the first high-rise casino hotel on the strip, and according to the Feds it had passed through several owners connected to the Chicago mob. It was famous mostly for having the largest sign in Las Vegas—with 932 electric bulbs in the *A* alone—and for being the home of the Lido Show. It was considered a grind joint—a place where players lost slowly and steadily, rather than spectacularly; the high rollers went to Caesar's and the Desert Inn.

"The guy they assigned me to my first night was Frank Cursoli, the blackjack manager," said Rosenthal. "Bobby Stella, a Stardust vice president who I knew from Chicago, took me over to Cursoli and introduced me. Cursoli gave me a few fucking crazy words about casinos and I didn't know what the hell he was talking about.

"Then, on my first night, I started getting paged over the loudspeaker. I couldn't pick up the page from where I was located, but I saw Cursoli's 'Who the fuck is this guy?' look, and he asks Bobby Stella: 'Who is this guy? What's this bull-shit with the paging?'

"And Bobby says, 'Take it easy. Take it easy. You don't know who he is. Relax.' In other words, Bobby's trying to get it across to Cursoli that I'm not the average hire.

"When I asked Cursoli about taking a break—my ulcer was beginning to act up—he gave me a fucking look. 'I'll let you know,' he says, like I'm an imbecile. I walked back to my station really pissed off. I wasn't used to having to beg somebody when I felt like a glass of milk.

"I saw Bobby Stella walking around. I got his eye. He walked over to the pit. I said, 'Hey, is this guy nuts, Bobby? What's his problem?' 'Relax, relax,' Bobby tells me and then he goes over to Cursoli and gets me a fifteen-minute break.

"At the end of the first shift, when my wife picked me up I couldn't stand up. My legs ached. I said, 'Geri, that's it.'

"But she convinced me to go back. And as I got into the industry I began phasing out my sports betting. By the end of the first year, I had reduced all my betting down to the NFL. I even quit college basketball.

"I never entertained the idea of working in a casino until my wife suggested it, but once I started working there I became intrigued. I never saw such a business where people were so anxious to give you their money. Give them a free drink and a dream, and they give you their wallets.

"One night I drove out to Henderson for a quiet dinner with someone. It was small place. It had one craps table and two blackjack tables. I saw a camper pull up and a fellow with a family got out and came inside. They were still thirty miles outside of Vegas, but it was their first stop.

"They stopped because there was a sign outside that said LUNCH, 49 CENTS—24 HOURS A DAY. The guy came in for a cheap lunch and started playing blackjack. He left behind twenty-four hundred dollars while I was sitting there. He never even got to Vegas. He just put his family back in the camper and went home."

Lefty never forgot it. He became obsessed with learning everything he could about the business. "I had a hundred questions, but no answers," he said. "The old-timers didn't want to tell me anything. To them, everything was a secret. I was going to have to learn on my own.

"What I learned was that there were no secrets. It was next to impossible for a casino not to make money. Some casinos had to win their money two or three times, because the people running them were so lazy or crooked.

"I saw casino managers laying back. They lived in a comfort zone. I could never be that way.

"My job was to hang around the pit, but on a busy night

I'd walk around on the outside of the pit behind the dealers and look at their backs and see if they were lifting their hole cards too high. Then I'd go over to them and say, 'That's a good-looking ten of spades you've got there.'

"I found out that it was a very common practice in casinos where they had a weak operation for one hustler to sit behind a weak dealer showing hole cards and signal his *compadre* playing at the weak dealer's table. They use head signals, eyes, hands, even impulse transmitters. Some of them were crossroaders—professional casino cheats—and they'd been photographed and listed in the Black Book. They'd come in wearing fake beards, wigs, phony noses. They'd have partners counting cards, spraying the roulette wheel, dropping baloneys onto a craps table, and using special magnets to get slot machine wins. They'd create any kind of diversion so one of them could slide card-dealing shoes onto a blackjack table—they can usually do this only with the help of the dealer and pit boss—and bang you out for a couple of hundred grand, which you never see again.

"I started looking for little signals. Clues. I learned that if a crapshooter's hands were not open after he tosses the dice, he could be palming baloneys. There are people so fast that it's not possible to see them put fake dice on the table. They work in teams and specialize. The person who slips in the dice can turn out to be a nice little old lady. It's usually not the shooter. The person who rolls the fake dice on the table usually leaves soon after. You can't prevent an expert getting bad dice on the table, but your pit boss or shift boss should be able to pick it up as the play begins.

"After a while you begin to learn all the games. You learn to be careful about distractions. People spilling drinks. Asking a dealer for a cigarette. Starting an argument with a dealer. Stopping a dealer and asking for change. I learned to spot a sub, a long sock sewn into a dealer's clothes where he can slide the chips he steals off the tables. One clue to a sub is that crooked dealers are constantly touching themselves. I looked to see if a dealer's boots were extended over his pants. Take off open-topped boots and nine times out of ten you'll find chips inside. The first week I worked in the casino, I caught a dealer slipping chips under his chronograph wristwatch.

"There were also turns, which is what they call people who help slot cheats. They're called turns because they turn the floor men away with questions like, 'Pardon me, can you tell me where the bathroom is?' while their partners cluster around the machines, blocking the view—and one of the crew opens the machine or places magnets inside that will spin off winners. It doesn't take long. A good slot man can get inside a machine in seconds.

"A few years later, when I was running the place, I got a call one night from Bobby Stella, Senior, my casino manager, who said we were getting murdered by some guy dressed like a cowboy. The kid was playing all six spots at the hundred-dollar blackjack table, and he's got about eighty grand in front of him.

"When I got over there I asked Bobby if he knew who the kid was. Was he a guest in the hotel? Did we have his name? Nobody had anything on him. That was very sloppy, very bad casino management. You get a player like that and the pit boss should be over there offering him free rooms, free drinks, free everything. He's got to be made to feel welcome as hell. He's the big man in the room at that moment, and you've got to stroke the guy so, first, he'll come back and lose, and, second, to give you time to find out just who the sonofabitch is and if he's straight.

"Let me tell you right now, there is no casino boss in the country who sees a guy come into his place and win eighty grand and not know, deep, deep down, that the bastard is stealing. I knew he was stealing. Bobby knew he was stealing. We just didn't know how he was stealing.

"We also knew he was being cute by the way he was betting. He was turning down what should have been good hands, and betting stiffs. He's throwing lavenders [$500 chips] after dumb plays and winning. He wasn't making enough normal mistakes to be on the up and up.

"I gave the orders to play him loose. I didn't want security breathing down his neck or a pit boss standing over the dealer's shoulder. I was looking for something. The first thing I saw was the way he was cutting his chips and fingering them. Before his bets he would hold a few in his hand and nervously work them in and out of his fingers like a professional dealer. So just from that I knew the sonofabitch was a pro. He was beating us and showing off for the crowd.

"I walked around behind the game and I saw that our dealer was weak. He wasn't cupping his hands tightly enough. He was lifting his hole card just a little too high when he had to stand pat. And that's just the kind of weakness crossroaders look for. They prowl up and down the aisles looking for weak dealers the way lions look for antelope. Bobby and I went upstairs to watch it on the Eye, and there we see this other guy hunched over the table behind the winner's dealer, and he's reading the dealer's bottom card and signaling his friend.

"I went back down and saw that the spotter was using some electronic device he had in his pocket. I immediately put through a page for Mr. Armstrong at BJ seventeen, which was a signal for a special security detail to surround the number seventeen blackjack table. I didn't want these guys to get away with any of that money.

"There was a large crowd gathered around the table, and we didn't want to have a problem, so we had one of the plainclothes security guys slide in very close to the winner, and while another security guy distracted the crowd for a second, our man pressed a small electronic zapper—a kind of stun gun—against the guy's chest and he crumbled to the ground.

"We scooped him up shouting, 'Cardiac seizure! Cardiac seizure!' and got him into a utility room around back. Security men made a thing about safeguarding his winnings. And the minute we got him off the floor, the games resumed as though he and his winnings had never even been there.

"We ripped his trousers and found the electronic device he was using to receive the signals. That was proof enough for me. I asked if he was a righty or a lefty. When he said 'righty,' a couple of the guards grabbed his right hand and held it against the edge of the worktable and another guard smashed it really hard a couple of times with a large yellow rubber mallet. 'Well, you're a lefty now,' I said. Then we brought in his partner and said his partner would get the same thing unless they both walked out of the Stardust and told all of their pals that our casino was now off-limits. They thanked us and apologized and said they'd tell everyone they knew. We took their pictures and got their ID and let them go. They never came back.

"The high rollers come from all facets of life. They're dentists, lawyers, open-heart surgeons, brokers, businessmen, retailers, manufacturers, all kinds of anonymous people. We didn't usually get real high rollers and whales like Adnan Khashoggi in the Stardust.

"But we had the Lido Show and Khashoggi liked it. At the time, the Lido was the biggest attraction in Las Vegas. We'd get a call from Caesar's and we'd get Khashoggi front-row seats. We'd accommodate and comp a celebrity or entertainer, whether they were staying with us or not. Khashoggi would usually come in with a party of twenty or eight and we'd comp him with iced Dom, caviar, everything.

"At the end of the night, he'd give us a lay-down bet, a courtesy bet for the hospitality. It could be for a few hundred or a thousand. He was a gambler and he could be beaten for between five thousand dollars and two million dollars. There was nothing like Khashoggi shooting dice. I'd stand there and watch. The man had unlimited credit.

"One time he went to the jewelry shop. Just like we'd go in and buy yogurt. He bought a hundred-thousand-dollar jewel for some girl. When he took out a credit card to pay for it, the poor clerk saw her sale evaporating. But when she checked his Visa card, it turned out that he had a one-million-dollar credit line.

"When Khashoggi would light on a casino, half the good-looking girls in Beverly Hills would get on planes. He was a hell of a player, but there were a few Asians who were right up there with him. Some even bigger. Guys who can come in and drop two, three, four million and then come back in a few months and do it all over again."

♦ ♦ ♦

Most of the people who worked at the Stardust felt there was more to Lefty Rosenthal's sudden appearance as a floor manager than a middle-aged man's desire to change his life's habits at his wife's request. "Lefty never really worked like a regular starting dealer," says George Hartman, a former Stardust blackjack dealer with whom Lefty began his casino instruction. "He knew all the top bosses in the place. He came in as a floor man. Within a week all kinds of people are treating him like he's a boss, even though his job title didn't justify it. The word got around.

"We always knew that Chicago ran the Stardust. Alan

Sachs was from Chicago. Bobby Stella, the casino manager, and Gene Cimorelli, the shift boss, were both from Chicago, and so were dozens of pit bosses, floor men, and dealers. The fact that Lefty was a Chicago guy just made it even plainer that he was a connected guy, but who's going to ask?

"The problem with lots of casinos back then was that no one ever really knew who owned them. I don't care what the mortgage says, the ownership of most casinos was so tangled and went back so many years with so many silent partners and half partners and fronts and point holders that nobody from the outside could ever figure it out, and lots of people inside never figured it out either."

Lefty's prominence and power at the Stardust were so clearly evident that within two or three months the Gaming Control Board agents began questioning whether Lefty should be required to submit an application for a key-employee license.

◆ ◆ ◆

Rosenthal had a work permit, but the difference between getting a gaming license and a work permit is the difference between a high roller and a nickel slots player. "A work permit and license both require an FBI fingerprint check," says Shannon Bybee, a member of the Gaming Control Board at the time, "but to get a gaming license to own or run a casino, we want to know everything, including everywhere you've worked and lived since you were eighteen years old. We do a net worth on you, check all your bank accounts and stock holdings and loans. We interview the bankers and brokers. We send investigators to check on assets, no matter where they are. We've sent investigators all over the world checking on an applicant's holdings, and the applicant has to pay for his own investigation up front."

Jeffrey Silver, counsel to the Nevada Gaming Control Board, was sitting in his office about that time when Downey Rice, a retired FBI agent from Miami, dropped by. "Downey was looking for some information that was relevant to some case he was working on in Florida," Silver said. "We started chatting and he asked me what was up, and I said not much, I was doing a routine workup on a guy named Frank Rosenthal who was coming up for licensing. Downey just sat there for a second and then he said, 'Oh, you mean Lefty.' I asked if he knew Frank Rosenthal and he said, 'I was one of the agents investigating him in Florida.' We've got a lot of material on Lefty.

"I had already received a preliminary workup on Rosenthal from our chief of investigations, but it was limited exclusively to Lefty's background in Nevada. There was not a mention of any problems in Florida or anywhere else. We're about to go into public hearings on the licensing and I find out about Lefty's background by accident.

"Downey then starts telling me how Lefty had been charged with bribing a basketball player in North Carolina and pleaded nolo, and he tells me there was another attempt to bribe a college player, and then he says there were congressional hearings where Lefty was questioned about all this. I'm sitting there numb. He asked if I had copies of the transcript. I said, 'Not yet.' He said he thought he had the transcripts in his garage, and I said I'd love to see the transcripts. A week or so later a parcel of those green government Senate hearing books arrived, and in it I find Lefty being questioned and asked very pointed questions about his activities.

"I took that and talked to the board's chief investigator and said let's look into Rosenthal some more, and we found that one of the athletes Lefty was supposed to have tried to bribe was now an attorney in San Diego. We got an affidavit

from him, and that's how the Lefty licensing case first got put together."

♦ ♦ ♦

"I wasn't in the pits more than three or four months," said Rosenthal, "when the Gaming Control Board comes down on me. Wow. Frank Rosenthal's in the pits. Shannon Bybee puts a full court press on me and tries to get me knocked out of the building. They were insisting that I would have to have a key-employee license if I was going to work at the casino, and my going for a key license in front of their kangaroo court was a waste.

"Meanwhile, I start to dodge and weave. I'm trying to sustain myself in the building any way I can, hoping to wait them out and get past the control board heat. So I changed jobs. I took a job in the hotel that didn't come under gaming regulations, so I wouldn't have to deal with the control board. I became an executive for the hotel's public relations department. I had cards made up. I was working PR, but believe me, I didn't miss much on the floor or in the pits.

"I wasn't supposed to be working in the pits. I wasn't supposed to extend credit. I'm not supposed to have anything to do with the games. But I'm in fact functioning as Bobby Stella's right-hand man. When people have questions for me, they would come over and we'd talk. You don't have to be in a pit to run a casino. And little by little, I'm quietly doing most of Bobby's work.

"Bybee was still trying to nail me. He couldn't stand it that I had thumbed my nose at the control board. The control board could make life very tough for a casino, and after a while, Alan Sachs, the president of the casino, was ready to fire me. He told people he didn't want to take any of the heat."

Sachs saw no reason to keep Lefty Rosenthal around. Rosenthal was smart. He was a good worker. But good workers are a dime a dozen. They're not worth a minute's flack from the Gaming Control Board. Eddy Torres, who owned the Riviera across the street, had tried to tell Sachs that Lefty was highly regarded back home in Chicago. But who wasn't? Sachs himself was the son of one of the outfit's first skim couriers back in the early days of Vegas. Sachs liked Lefty well enough. It wasn't personal. He just didn't need the trouble.

"Right in the middle of all this," Rosenthal says, "a friend of mine calls up. He's planning to come into Vegas for a visit. I'm a nobody. I'm trying to hold on to my job. And he's calling about staying in the hotel kind of incognito. Back then, the arrival in Las Vegas of a top guy like that was like a papal visit.

"Al Sachs knew the name, but he'd never met the man. And I felt an obligation—as a courtesy to Sachs, because of heat on the guy's name—to at least say: 'Is it okay if this guy stays at the Stardust?' If not, the guy himself had said he'd stay somewhere else. No big deal. I said, 'Al, the purpose of his coming here is just to visit for a few days. And he wants to see me when he can.'

"I remember Sachs kind of hesitated and said the following: 'No problem. And, Frank, don't you think I ought to show my respects and meet him privately?' I said, 'Yeah, Al, I guess you can. That's up to you. That's your call.'

"Al was very conscious of keeping himself very clean, and rightfully so.

"When my friend flew into Las Vegas he checked into the Stardust just like anyone else, except he was under a different name. Then he paged me and I went to his room and we talked and caught up on things for a little bit.

"Then I told him that Al Sachs, the hotel's president, wanted to say hello to him. He said to me—this was the kind of guy he was—he said, 'Why the fuck do I want to talk to him? I don't want to bother him. I don't want to put the heat on the guy.' He said, 'Forget about it, Frank.'

"I said, 'No, I think he'll be insulted. I think he feels he owes you that courtesy.' You've got to remember, the man at this time was a top guy in Chicago.

"So I convinced him that it was best for both sides to just shake hands. Sixty seconds and that's the end of it. I went back to the casino and I tell Sachs. I said, 'He's in his room.' And Al got all excited and made this underground meeting like you wouldn't believe.

"Here's Al's meeting: He went back into the rear of the Aku Aku kitchen, which was closed at these hours. There was no one there. Period. I had to bring my friend from the elevators through the empty Aku Aku dining room so he wouldn't be seen. I walked him through the swinging doors into the empty kitchen. There's Sachs waiting for us.

"I stood by the doors to make sure the man knew where it was, and as he walks toward Sachs, I see Sachs, about twenty feet away, rush up to him with both arms extended, and he gives my friend a big hug. Remember, Sachs is the president of the Stardust Hotel and Casino and he's never met this man in his life.

"I can hear both their voices as I'm walking away, because the kitchen is dead silent. And I hear Sachs say: 'Gee, it's a pleasure. I'm really happy. This is something I'll never forget.' And then he says, 'You know, I'm really delighted to have Frank around. I know he's just like a son to you.'

"My friend, real serious, says, 'You're wrong.'

"Sachs says, 'What do you mean?'

"And my friend says, 'No, he's not like a son; he *is* my son.' That was the last thing I heard. And then I kept on walking. After a while, things cooled off and I moved back behind the pits."

9.

"Tony had a way of getting under a guy's skin."

Tony Spilotro was ten years younger than his old friend Frank Rosenthal, but by 1971 their lives were on an oddly parallel course. Both of them were public figures, for all the wrong reasons. Both of them had been arrested many times, in Lefty's case for a series of minor infractions, in Tony's for a series of infractions considerably more minor than the ones he had actually committed. Both of them had handled the arrests by suing authorities. And as a result of the heat both of them chose to change their lives by going West.

Tony was still in Chicago in 1971, where he had quickly become the most likely to succeed in his own particular class of criminals. "After whacking Billy McCarthy and Jimmy Miraglia," Frank Cullotta said, "Tony rose up very quick. First he started working for Crazy Sam DeStefano as a collector. Crazy Sam was such a lunatic shylock that he once handcuffed his brother-in-law to a radiator, beat the shit out of him, had his crew piss on him, and then showed him off at a family dinner.

"Then Tony got assigned to Milwaukee Phil Alderisio, and I'd have to say it was Milwaukee Phil who groomed Tony in the outfit. Phil was a great earner. He's the first guy who figured out about shaking down sports bookies. Until Milwaukee Phil, only horse bookmakers paid the street tax. Phil changed all that and he started grabbing guys off the street right and left.

"For a while, around 1962, 1963, Tony became a bail bondsman. It's true. He could walk all around the courts in Cook County. Go behind the desks. Check the docket room. The outfit guys set it up for him. He worked with Irwin Weiner, on South State Street. Weiner used to bond out everybody. He bailed out Milwaukee Phil's guys, and Joey Lombardo's, and Turk Torello's.

"Now Tony had about six or seven guys booking for him out of different offices, and he had some loan-shark money on the street. One day Tony came to my house and gave me six thousand dollars from a score we had made. He told me, 'You know, Frank, this is a lot of money. Why don't you invest like me and go into the loan-sharking business?' He said, 'I have some money out on the street right now. I'm not asking you to invest it all, but why don't you invest, like, four grand on the street. You could be getting four hundred dollars a week and the four grand would always be there, and whenever you wanted it I could just pull it out.'

"Well, I didn't really feel like giving him four thousand, so I offered to give him two thousand. Tony said all right, but he said it was nineteen sixty-one and money was getting scarce, so that meant there was a big demand. He thought that was a joke.

"Anyway, I gave him two grand and he put it to work on the street. Every week I received my two hundred dollars cash. Plus, we had the accounts of loan sharks under us, and we used to get a percentage of what they were making, so it worked out pretty good. I spent money pretty good, too. I always liked brand-new cars. So I traded in my nineteen sixty-one Ford with the big engine and went to the Hope Park Cadillac dealer and got a blue Coupe de Ville. That's a car I always wanted.

"One night Tony took me to the North Avenue Steak House on Mannheim Road that was owned by the outfit. That's where Tony wanted to introduce me to some big shots. This was really the night I decided to move to another crew.

"Jackie Cerone was standing at the bar with Crazy Sam DeStefano and a blond broad. The three of them were drunk, and there's nobody as obnoxious as Jackie Cerone when he's drunk. When we walked in, I asked Tony who the loud bald-headed fuck was standing at the bar.

"I guess I said it sort of loud, because Tony told me not to talk so loud and explained to me who the two guys were. Just about that time, Jackie Cerone grabbed the cocktail waitress by the arm and told her to suck his prick at the bar. She said no and he gave her a crack in the face and ran her out of the joint.

"Then Crazy Sam DeStefano came over to us and started talking about how goofy Jackie Cerone was. Crazy Sam was also very drunk that night. Now Jackie Cerone comes walking over and asks Tony who his friend is, meaning me. Tony introduces me to Sam and Jackie. That's how I met Jackie Cerone.

"We only stood around for about an hour. They made all kinds of racket and noise in the place. This Jackie Cerone was a real, real ignorant man. Any girl that comes by, he'd pull her to him. He didn't care if they were with another guy or not.

"It was just uncomfortable being around him, because you had to be on your toes. You had to watch what you were saying. Meanwhile, we're standing there like goofs. Laughing along with Jackie and making him feel like a big man. Finally we left. We got in the car and went someplace else just to get away from them.

"I let my money ride on the street for about two more months, but I kept getting steamed up over the way you had to kiss their asses and be careful all the time, and about the beef over getting rid of my car. Tony really wanted to be an outfit big shot. I didn't.

"So finally I said to myself: 'Fuck this neighborhood! Fuck these guys!' I told Tony, 'I'm gonna start bumming east.'

"He said, 'What are you talking about?' So I told him I wanted to stay involved with his crew, 'but you guys ain't doing too much and I want to keep active.' We stayed close friends, but I told him I wanted more action and I started hanging on the East Side with a stickup crew."

♦ ♦ ♦

According to retired FBI agent William Roemer, who tracked Spilotro's rise during the sixties and wrote about it in his book, *The Enforcer:* "Tony had a way of getting under a guy's skin. He was a bondsman at the time, and I caught him tailing me when I left the gym. He was driving a green Oldsmobile. He was good. He stayed far behind, but I saw him make a couple of U-turns and I knew he was on me. I had him tail me to Columbus Park, where I waited for him in a deserted area.

"I knew what he wanted. He was trying to find out who I was meeting with, who my informants were, because we had been putting cases together against Sam Giancana and Milwaukee Phil and they knew we had inside informants. That's what he was doing for the outfit hanging around the court all day long.

"He lost sight of me for a while, but he kept looking. When he was about twenty feet from me, I pointed my gun at him and called out, 'Looking for me, pal?'

"He was startled, but just for a second. He came back real quick. 'Just taking a walk. Ain't this a public park?'

"I took a look at the guy. I didn't know it was Spilotro at that moment. He had on a fedora. The kind Sam Giancana used to wear. He was wearing a gray sweater with a tie, gray slacks, and black loafers. He was very, very short, but he seemed tightly wound. Muscular. Not a wimp. The opposite.

"When I identified myself and asked him for his ID, he said, 'None of your fucking business! I don't give a shit who you are, asshole, you don't have a right to question me unless you've got a warrant.'

"I said it was my business, and I grabbed his left arm, held it back, and yanked out his wallet. His driver's license identified him as Anthony John Spilotro. I should have guessed. I had seen him outside Sam DeStefano's house. I asked him about DeStefano and he said he never heard of him. I asked him why he was tailing me, and he said, 'Who's following you? I'm just walking in the park.' When I told him I didn't believe him, he said, 'I don't give a fuck what you believe.'

"That was Tony. Instead of going with the flow and conning me, trying to be nice, he kept giving me the wiseass answers. I even tried being nice with him. I told him he was still a young guy. He was a bondsman. He should pull out of all the bullshit he was involved with.

"'Yeah, like you, asshole,' he says to me. 'I see how you live. I seen your house. Big shot! Live in a little dump out there in the steel mills. Big fucking deal. I should live like you?'

"As I said, Tony had a way of getting under your skin. I

warned him that if I ever saw him anywhere around my house I would make it a personal matter.

"Still he keeps it up. 'Fuck you, asshole,' he says. I'm standing there in the woods with a gun on him. I'm over six feet and weigh two hundred and twenty pounds. If he's been tailing me he knows I work out boxing every day at the Y. Meanwhile, he's five five and a hundred and thirty-five pounds, and he's busting my balls in a secluded spot in the park. That was Tony. He dared you to murder him.

"I gave him a shove, pushed him back toward the parking area. 'Get the hell out of here, you little pissant,' I said, and he walked away, got in his car, and drove off.

"After that, whenever I talked to my friends in the press about Spilotro, I always referred to him as 'that little pissant.' Sandy Smith of the *Tribune* and Art Petacque of the *Sun-Times* and later John O'Brien of the *Trib* began using the name 'the Ant' when they wrote about him. I guess in those days 'pissant' was not proper for the public press."

♦ ♦ ♦

By 1970, Spilotro was appearing in the newspapers just about every day. He had made faces and mugged for the cameramen as he walked in and out of the Crime Commission hearings. He even insisted upon suing the police and the IRS for the $12,000 they had confiscated during a gambling raid. The police said the money was the proceeds of a gambling operation and the IRS had kept the money as a lien against possible unpaid taxes.

Spilotro lost the suit; to make matters worse, the legal action allowed federal agents access to his tax records. They wasted no time before bringing charges that Spilotro had filed a false mortgage loan application for his house when he said he had been employed by a cement company. The

IRS agents showed that he had claimed that his sole income that year, $9,000, had been derived from gambling wins only. There was no income reported from a cement company.

"Tony couldn't walk across the street without picking up a tail," Cullotta said. "The heat was on. Lots of his crew, me included, were on our way to prison and he was too, unless he got out of town. At my going-away party—I had been given six years for some robberies and burglaries and assaults—Tony said he and Nancy and the kid were taking a trip out West for vacation. He said he might move out to Las Vegas and that I should come see him out there as soon as I got out. I put it in the back of my mind and went to sleep for six years."

♦ ♦ ♦

In the spring of 1971, right around the time Frank Rosenthal started to think about going to work at the Stardust, Tony Spilotro rented an apartment in Las Vegas, and on May 6, 1971, a trailer van of Transworld Van Lines with a work crew pulled up in front of Spilotro's Oak Park house and began loading their van with the household's contents. A few minutes later, two cars of IRS agents pulled onto the street and began taking notes on what was being carted out of the house.

Spilotro immediately suspected that as soon as the van was loaded with his family belongings, the agents were going to seize the truck as a tax assessment. So he ordered the crew of Transworld Van Lines to unload the trailer and place all of his property back in his home. He then called his lawyer and sued the IRS; federal authorities had harassed him into leaving town, he said, and now they were interfering with "his constitutional right to travel and reside anywhere in the United States."

Within a week, prosecutors relented and Transworld Van Lines returned to repack and load eight thousand pounds of Spilotro belongings, including nine barrels of dishes, nine wardrobe cartons, forty-five cartons of household items, one crib mattress, four nightstands, a dining room table and six chairs, three TV sets, one sewing machine, a grandfather clock, three dressers, a divan, a love seat, six mirrors, six assorted chairs, four tables, and lawn furniture. According to the bill of lading, the items were valued at $9,900, and most were scratched or chipped.

On the bill of lading—in the space marked "Local Contact, person responsible for final payment"—the Spilotros wrote "Frank or Jerry Rosenthal."

◆ ◆ ◆

"Tony first came out to Las Vegas with Nancy for a visit," Frank Rosenthal said. " A little vacation. That was just before they decided to move here. He said, 'Let's take a ride.' We drove out of town into the desert, and we talked about what was going on back in Chicago.

"He said there was a lot of heat at home and he asked if I would have any objections if he moved out here. Why was he asking me? I think he was bullshitting me. He just wanted to cover his bases, so when the heat came down he could say: 'Jeezus, I asked you, didn't I?'

"During the drive I warned him that it was very different out here than it was at home. I told him that the local cops had a reputation for being very tough. I told him that a lot of people who got arrested out here could find themselves buried in the desert before they ever made it to court.

"Tony didn't say anything. I knew that if Tony did come out to Las Vegas, he had better be on his best behavior."

According to the FBI, when Spilotro arrived he did not

have the outfit's permission to start shaking everyone down and to start up the kind of loan-sharking operation that could jeopardize the mob's skimming of the casinos that was their primary source of income. "Tony was smart," retired FBI agent Bud Hall said. "He knew how far he could go with the outfit bosses back in Chicago. Joe Aiuppa, for instance, was a kind of don't-rock-the-boat kind of guy. Aiuppa didn't give a damn about Spilotro, but Tony knew that once he got out here, he would be left pretty much on his own."

◆ ◆ ◆

"When we got back to the house after the drive, it was obvious that Nancy and Geri had had a few drinks. They were both loaded. Tony went into his act. He started yelling at Nancy, 'You can't do this. You're embarrassing me. Frank's not going to want us around if you continue to act like this.'

"He was trying to bullshit me that everything would be okay. That the two of them would be on their best behavior.

"Well, a couple of weeks later they arrive permanently, and it was like a signal for the bureau. The heat began. They started watching him and me. And in a way, I don't blame them. They assumed—everybody assumed—that Tony had come to town with instructions from Chicago. That he was their muscle in town and I was the outfit's man inside the casinos.

"Nothing could have been further from the truth, but Tony took advantage of that incorrect perception. He went along with it. He encouraged it. He'd tell people, 'I'm Frank's advisor.' 'I'm Frank's protector.'

"Even Geri thought he was my boss. One day I walked into the country club with some executives and one of them said that my boss was in the corner. I looked over expecting to see one of the bosses from the Stardust, and instead there was Tony playing cards. When I really got annoyed the guy said he was only joking, but that was the perception in town right from the start.

"He was only in town two or three days before Sheriff Ralph Lamb gets ahold of me. He says, 'Tell your friend I want him out of town in a week.' I tried to speak up for Tony. I said, 'Ralph, I don't own this guy, but he'll behave himself. Give the guy a break.' It made no difference. He wanted Tony out of town.

"I gave Tony the message, but I think it was his birthday or something coming up, and anyway, instead of Tony leaving town by that weekend, his five brothers arrived. They were all legit guys. One was a dentist. But Sheriff Lamb picked them up as soon as they got to town and threw them in jail for a few hours.

"He kept Tony in the drunk tank overnight. That's a wet pit where they keep hosing you down because everybody in the place has lice.

"When Spilotro finally got out he was crazy. He's screaming, 'I'll kill that motherfucker.' But he calmed down. The truth was he had a perfect right to stay in town, and there was a truce, even though he and Sheriff Lamb were not what you could call friendly.

"I don't think Tony ever anticipated when he moved out here what was going to happen. I don't think he had a master plan. I think things just developed day by day and, most important, he was left alone to establish himself without interference."

◆　◆　◆

Tony, Nancy, and their four-year-old son, Vincent, settled into an apartment, and Nancy settled into being a Las Vegas wife. Lefty and Geri helped settle them: Lefty called the Bank of Nevada for Tony, and Geri introduced Nancy to her favorite hairdressers and manicurists at Caesar's Palace. Geri and Nancy became great friends. They shopped together, had dinner on the nights their husbands were busy (which was often), and played tennis three or four times a week at the Las Vegas Country Club, where Lefty managed to get them a membership.

In contrast to the elegant Rosenthals, with their expensive cars and house on the golf course, Nancy and Tony lived modestly. They drove inexpensive cars and bought a three-bedroom house on Balfour Avenue, a middle-income community. Nancy enrolled little Vincent in Bishop Gorman Catholic school, joined the PTA, and marched down to the local police precinct when her son's bike was stolen from in front of their house. Tony was a regular at Little League games, where he would sit in the stands or behind the coach with the other fathers cheering for their sons.

Tony opened a gift shop at Circus Circus called Anthony Stuart Ltd., and Nancy often worked there. Tony spent most of his time in the poker room at Circus or at the Dunes lending busted dealers money at loan-shark rates. It wasn't long before just about every dealer at the two casinos owed him money.

His loan-sharking, shakedowns, and crooked card games soon attracted so much attention that the Spilotros' Ozzie and Harriet act fell apart. Tony moved a cement block next to the rear wall of his house so he could look over the fence and see if he was being tailed that day. He usually was. Agents caught him partying late into the night with the youngest and most naive girls who hit town. Meanwhile, Nancy was arrested for drunken driving; on that occasion, she listed Geri's name—not Tony's—as the person to call in case of emergency.

♦ ♦ ♦

Tony wasn't in town two weeks before the Feds had him on a wire. The FBI in Chicago had alerted Las Vegas that he was on the way. They tailed him to one of his first meetings, in the middle of the desert, where he was asked to help get a connected meat company into all the big hotels. They then tailed him to a meeting with the leaders of the local culinary union. Later, those union officials had meetings with the main buyers at the casino hotels, and by the summer, all the hotels were buying their meats from the company.

"We'd pick him up every three or four months on general principles," said Las Vegas Metro Detective Sergeant William Keeton, "and bring him in on a complaint, and he'd grouse that people were just setting him up for a pinch, and then we'd let him go.

"But Tony liked publicity. He was a volatile type. Cocky. He could also be charming. The Chicago Crime Commission had sent us a picture of a guy whose head Tony had supposedly put in a vise. Every once in a while I'd look at it to remind myself about how dangerous he was. The guy's head was wedged to about five inches wide, and then Tony had put lighter fluid on his face and set it on fire. The eyeballs were bugging out.

"In September of nineteen seventy-two we picked him up on a nineteen sixty-three Chicago homicide warrant. He was being held without bail—normal in a homicide case—awaiting extradition back to Chicago. I guess Tony didn't want to spend the night in jail, because the next thing we know is that Rosenthal shows up in court at a bailing hearing for Spilotro. It wasn't the smartest thing Lefty could have done, but I guess he didn't have any choice."

♦ ♦ ♦

"Tony was only in town about a year when I got a call from him," said Frank Rosenthal. "He was in jail. 'You gotta vouch for me. You gotta do this for me,' he says. 'I need you as a character witness on a bond.'

"It turned out to be in connection with a homicide in Chicago back in nineteen sixty-three. I said, 'Holy shit, Tony, I'm working in the casino. I'm up for licensing.'

"I'm trying to get it across that it might not be the best move for me to go down to court and put myself on the line for him in a homicide bail hearing. It would be a red flag for the Gaming Control Board.

"'I need it bad,' he says. 'You gotta do it.'

"So, I went down to court. I vouched for him and he got out on ten thousand dollars bail. Tony swore to me he wasn't involved in the case. He was very convincing. The next day I scoured the papers to see if my name appeared in connection with the case. I was lucky. It didn't."

♦ ♦ ♦

"They took Spilotro back to Chicago to stand charges," said FBI agent Bill Roemer. "When he was arraigned, he pleaded not guilty and said that he had no idea where he was on the day of the homicide. He said he knew President Kennedy had been assassinated a week later, and he was going to use that date to try and reconstruct where he was on the day of the Foreman murder.

"He was very cute. He said he was going to ask his family to search through their records. He said he hoped they might find something that could prove he was not at the murder scene.

"Then, about a month before the trial, one of Tony's two codefendants, Crazy Sam DeStefano, gets shot and killed in his garage. Two fast shotgun blasts. Sam's wife and bodyguard just happened to leave about thirty minutes earlier to go see relatives.

"Tony had been worried about Crazy Sam. He had tried to get his case severed from Sam's. Sam had just been given three years for threatening a government witness in a narcotics case, and he had shown up for an earlier court appearance in a wheelchair, wearing pajamas and carrying a megaphone. Tony had been very worried that Sam was going to prejudice the jury. There were also reports that Sam had cancer and his fear of dying in prison was going to get him to double-cross his codefendants, namely his brother Mario and Tony. We heard that Tony had secretly appealed to the outfit's boss, Anthony Accardo, claiming that Mad Sam was going to take him down."

Spilotro beat the case. His sister-in-law Arlene, who was married to his brother John, took the stand. She testified that on the day of the murder, she and her husband and Nancy and Tony had spent the entire day together shopping for furniture and appliances, having lunch, and discussing color schemes. The jury dismissed the charges against Tony.

"I was there that day," said Roemer. "When the verdict was announced, Tony raised his arms up in triumph. Then he looked over at a group of us, law enforcement people, where I was seated. Spilotro had a big grin of scorn on his face. His eyes focused for a moment on me.

"As he exited the courtroom, now a free man, I stepped into the aisle. 'You're still a little pissant,' I said. 'We'll get you yet.' I said it very softly.

"Tony looked at me and smiled. 'Fuck you,' he said."

Part Two

TAKING THE ODDS

◆

10.

"You don't know what you're getting yourself into."

In 1971, when Frank Rosenthal went to work at the Stardust, the hotel-casino was for sale. "It was owned by the Recrion Corporation, which also owned the Fremont," said Dick Odessky, who was the director of public relations at the Stardust, "and the big shareholders were looking to sell it. They'd run the price of the stock way up, and they were all looking to get out. But the Securities and Exchange Commission had gotten suspicious and forced them to sign a consent decree not to sell their shares.

"It was like sitting there with a great big steak and not being able to eat it. If anybody tried to sell stock he would have been in big trouble with the court. So the only way the shareholders could get their money out was to sell the entire company.

"Del Coleman [the chairman of Recrion] represented the big investors, and there was tremendous pressure on him to sell out and make a killing.

"Even after Al Sachs took over as president of the Stardust, the pressure to sell the company continued. And right around this time, Allen Glick came along."

♦ ♦ ♦

Allen Glick was tougher than he looked. In 1974, when the thirty-one-year-old San Diego real estate developer suddenly became the second-biggest casino operator in Las Vegas history, many of the state's gaming regulators and casino owners were astounded. Glick's impact on the town until then had been minimal. He had arrived in Las Vegas only a year earlier, when he and three partners obtained a $3 million loan to develop a parking lot for recreational vans on the site of the bankrupt Hacienda Hotel casino at the low-rent southern end of the the Strip.

Glick's look and style—he was short, balding, and owlish—belied his tenacity. Few around him knew that the youthful, studiously mild-mannered Glick—who spoke so softly that he was sometimes barely audible—had spent two years hanging out of a Huey helicopter in Vietnam, where he won a Bronze Star.

"Vietnam taught me that life was short," said Glick. "I remember writing to my brother-in-law that I didn't think I was coming back. So when I did get back, I decided I didn't want to do what I didn't want to do. First, I really didn't want to be a lawyer. I had a bachelor's from Ohio State and a law degree from Case Western Reserve, but the thing I knew was that I didn't want to practice law. Second, I wanted to live in San Diego instead of Pittsburgh, where I was raised. A friend of my sister's got me a job doing some legal work for American Housing, the largest multifamily builder in San Diego, and Kathy and the kids and I drove out there. That started my education in real estate.

"By February of 1971, after about a year at American

Housing, I teamed up with Denny Wittman, a nice, wild guy, in a real estate development that involved large tracts of land and commercial building.

"I was first introduced to Las Vegas in 1972. Denny Wittman had heard there was a sixty-acre site at the southern end of the Strip that could make a great mobile home park. The only problem with the property was that the bankrupt Hacienda Hotel was sitting on it and the casino had three IRS tax liens against it. I don't know why, but I just had an idea that instead of tearing everything down for a parking lot, maybe we could raise the money and revive the hotel and casino. But Denny Wittman didn't want to invest in a casino. He was a religious guy. He had a problem with it, so he begged out.

"At the time I personally had twenty-one thousand dollars to my name, but with smoke and mirrors and Denny helping us inflate the value of everything our little development corporation owned, we were able to raise the three million dollars from the First American Bank of Tennessee, where we had been doing business before and had friends.

"I had to get a Nevada Gaming Commission license as the owner of a Las Vegas casino, and there I was, at twenty-nine or thirty, chairman of a Las Vegas casino. Within a day, everyone in town had a deal for me.

"About five months later, Chris Caramanis, who ran an air charter service the hotels used, said that the King's Castle in Lake Tahoe was also in bankruptcy, having been foreclosed by the Teamster pension fund, and he suggested we raise the money and take over King's Castle the way we did the Hacienda.

"That was how I met Al Baron, the assets manager for the Central States Teamster Pension Fund. Chris introduced me to him. I thought I was going to meet a banker type in charge of the assets of a multibillion-dollar pension fund.

Instead, I meet this gruff, cigar-chomping guy who looks at me and says, 'What the fuck are you doing here?' Al was very annoyed at the time because a deal that had been put in place to take the bankrupt King's Castle off the Teamsters' hands had just fallen apart.

"When he was told that I had raised the cash to buy the Hacienda, he asked, 'Do you have any money?'

"I said, 'No, but I might be able to borrow it.'

"Baron was so anxious to get the bankrupt King's Castle off the Teamsters' books that he said he would be back through Las Vegas in two weeks and I should submit a proposal.

"When he came back, I gave him the proposal and he got angry. 'I've got no time to read this,' he said. All he wanted was for me to raise the money for a mortgage and get the Teamsters out.

"Anyway, the deal never went through, but shortly after, I got involved in developing a large government office complex in Austin, Texas, that would house Internal Revenue, congressional offices, and various government agencies. This was a larger deal than we could finance with our usual bank loans, so I thought, let me call Al Baron. I called him three times, left messages, and he never called me back. Finally, after four days, his secretary said that I shouldn't bother calling him again.

"I said fine, but I wanted him to know that the government had contacted me and I needed to talk to him. He called back in three seconds. When I told him that I had been contacted by the government about developing a huge government building complex, he started cursing me up and down. He used every foul word and image you could imagine.

"But in between his cursing I must have gotten across that this was a federal government project and a great opportunity, because he finally said, 'Okay, you sonofabitch, fuck, submit the loan package.'

"Baron and the Teamsters loved this government deal I had brought them because it was totally legitimate and because Denny Wittman, our Austin partners, and I did all the work, and the Teamsters were the government's landlords.

"Then came the Recrion deal. I had heard that Recrion was for sale and that Morris Shenker, the owner of the Dunes, was in negotiation to buy the company from Del Coleman. It turned out that Shenker was offering Coleman only forty-two dollars a share. My accountants had gone through the numbers and realized that you could borrow whatever you needed to buy the Stardust and the Fremont and still have money left over to cover your costs.

"It was the deal of a lifetime. I immediately called Del Coleman in New York to set up a meeting. I grabbed the red-eye and met him in his town house on East Seventy-seventh Street first thing on a Friday morning. Del Coleman was a very sophisticated man, and I believe he was married or engaged to a famous model at the time.

"I told him I wanted to buy him out. I told him I already owned the Hacienda Hotel and casino and that my development company supported me in an offer which I knew was at least two dollars a share higher than Shenker had offered him. I said I needed some time to raise the money, but I was certain I would have no trouble doing so.

"Coleman said up front that he was already in negotiation with Morris Shenker. Actually, attorneys were typing up the papers at that very moment, but I didn't know that. He said if I had money to put up he would be obligated to tell the shareholders, which meant I would be in a position to make a public offer.

"He said if I was serious I could have until noon Monday to come in with two million dollars in a nonrefundable cash payment, and he would give me a hundred and twenty days to raise the rest of the money. I agreed to the deal, but I gulped. I had to give Coleman two million dollars cash by noon Monday, and even if I could raise it, here it was Friday afternoon and the banks were closed over the weekend. I called Denny Wittman. I said I had to borrow two million dollars. He knew what was involved and he offered to let me use two five-hundred-thousand-dollar CDs our company had in the First American Bank in Nashville, Tennessee. He then said maybe I could get a million-dollar letter of credit from the same bank, where we had a very good relationship.

"I called Steven Neely, the bank president, and told him what I needed. 'You're crazy,' he said. I told him it was the deal of a lifetime.

"'If you're serious, you gotta get down here tonight,' Neely said. I hung up and called the airlines and found that there were no more flights heading anywhere near Nashville that would get me there in time.

"I took a car to Teterboro airport in New Jersey and chartered a Learjet to get me there. I had no money, but I gave the charter service a credit card, and thank God I had enough credit to cover the trip.

"When I landed in Nashville, Neely saw me get off the Lear and asked me where I got the plane, and I said a friend lent it to me. I didn't want to say I had just melted my credit card. We went to his house and worked all night setting up the holdings and collateral for the letter of credit.

"Wittman flew in the next day. He pledged everything I needed, and the bank gave me the letter of credit, and it was all completed by Sunday morning. I flew back to New York.

"I called Coleman from the airport. 'Del, I've got your money now and I don't want to wait until Monday morning.'

"'You've got two million dollars?' he said.

"'It's in my briefcase,' I said.

"I went over, we filed the escrow papers for the money, and Coleman said on Monday morning he would notify the SEC and stop trading in Recrion stock.

"I flew back to San Diego on Monday morning, got there before dawn, and began putting together lists of possible investors. I called Al Baron, because the Teamsters held the mortgages on the Stardust and Fremont, plus I knew they had liked the government office development I had brought them. I thought they might want to get involved in the package.

"When I told Al Baron what I had done and that I was now going to bid on the Recrion stock, he said, 'Listen to me, I'm giving you the best advice you've ever had—walk away from this thing. Call the deal off. You have no idea what you're doing. You don't know what you're getting yourself into.' He said there was no way he was going to get involved in the mess I was creating. Looking back, I realize he gave me all the red flags he could.

"Since the Teamsters looked bad, I had investment people try and find me other sources of money. One of the L.A. people came up with a guy named J. R. Simplot, an Idaho investor, who was interested. I went to meet him. He was very low key. He was wearing a two-hundred-dollar suit. He said he had some hotel interests and he would give me the money, except he wanted fifty-one percent of the deal.

"I had no idea who he was. When I got back to the office I called Kenny Solomon at the Valley Bank and asked him to check out somebody named Simplot. He said he didn't have to check him out. He said Mr. Simplot could give me the sixty-two-point-seven million dollars just by writing a check on his personal account. Simplot was the largest potato grower in the United States, and there probably wasn't a McDonald's french fry that didn't come through him.

"But I wasn't interested in giving up control of the company. So I called Al Baron back and said that in the morning he was going to hear that I was a partner with J. R. Simplot and that we were going to buy out Recrion and take over the Teamsters' interest in the Stardust and the Fremont.

"Baron said, 'Don't do anything until I call you back.' He calls me back. He says, 'Come to Chicago for a meeting.'

"'Why should I?' I said. 'Are you going to give me the loan?' He said he still didn't know.

"The next day I flew to Chicago to the pension fund office, where I met Al Baron. 'Now that you're in the ball game,' he said, 'you've got to come up to bat.' He then explained how the system worked.

"He said you had to know a pension fund trustee, because only trustees could make loan proposals. He said the trustees then turned the proposals over to the asset manager for due diligence, and then the applications went to an executive committee, which might or might not recommend, and then the proposal went to a vote of the full board.

"Baron then took me on a tour of the building and introduced me to Frank Ranney, who was coming back from lunch with Frank Balistrieri. Baron told me that Ranney was the Teamster trustee from Milwaukee and a member of the three-man executive committee that oversaw all loans west of the Mississippi, which meant Las Vegas.

"Baron said that Balistrieri could be my link to Frank Ranney. Balistrieri was a very quiet, very dapper man. He said he would be happy to help and the next time he was in Las Vegas we would meet.

"The next time I met Balistrieri he came into the Hacienda. We discussed the loan and the application package and he said he would help me. He told me that after I submitted the loan package in Chicago, I should drive over to Milwaukee, where I could meet his sons. I didn't exactly know how or where Balistrieri fit in, but the things I didn't want to think about I didn't want to think about, and Baron had said Balistrieri was my primary link to Frank Ranney, the trustee and member of the executive committee pushing my loan.

"After I submitted the package I went to Milwaukee, where I met his two sons, John and Joseph. They were both attorneys. Balistrieri said that he would like his sons involved in the operation in some way. He said Joseph had helped him run dinner theaters and was very knowledgeable about entertainment and might serve that kind of function at the Stardust. I didn't commit myself. I always said we could discuss it once I closed the deal on the place.

"When I got home I called Jerry Soloway. He's an attorney with Jenner and Block, a firm I had used. I asked him to check on a guy named Frank Balistrieri. I told him what I knew and hung up. I was due at the offices of the Gaming Control Board. Shannon Bybee, one of the board members, had said he had a 'funny feeling' about my buying one of the largest companies in the state after having been there only one year, and asked if I would do him the favor of taking a lie detector test. My lawyer said it was uncalled for and unnecessary, and Bybee agreed, but he said he would sleep better if he knew I was totally clean. I knew I was clean, so I wound up taking the kind of two-hour test they use on capital crime cases, and I passed like a breeze. That's what convinced Bybee and got me the gaming license I needed to be able to buy the place.

"A couple of days after taking the lie detector I get an emergency call from Jerry Soloway. He sounded hysterical. He wanted to make sure Frank Balistrieri was the right name. I said yes. He said, 'What are you doing with him?'

"I told Jerry I had been out to dinner with him. That he had been to see me at the Hacienda. That I had been in restaurants with him. That I had been to his home, met his sons, been to their law firm.

"Soloway went crazy. He said I couldn't be seen with Balistrieri. He said Frank Balistrieri was identified by the FBI as the Mafia boss of Milwaukee. He said my gaming license could be jeopardized with my just being seen talking to such a notorious organized-crime figure.

"I told Jerry he had to be wrong. I had met Balistrieri in the Teamster pension fund offices. He had just come back from lunch with Frank Ranney, one of the pension fund's trustees.

"He said he didn't care where I'd met Balistrieri, the man was the organized-crime boss of Milwaukee.

"I didn't sleep very well that night. The first thing I thought was, what would have happened had Jerry told me this before I took the lie detector test? Then I remembered I had been talking to Balistrieri just about every day on the phone discussing the progress of the loan arrangements. I had also been seen with him all over the place.

"On the other hand, I didn't feel there was anything I could do. What was I going to tell him? I know you're the head of the Mafia in Milwaukee, so don't help me get the loan? I was now very, very wary, but I felt I could maneuver it.

"The next time he called me, he was happy. He said we had gotten the approval of the executive committee for the sixty-two-point-seven-million-dollar purchasing loan, but Ranney had said there was a debate about the second part of the loan for sixty-five million dollars. Bill Presser, the Cleveland trustee, was resisting the second part of the loan. We needed the additional money to renovate and expand the Stardust.

"Balistrieri said he wanted to meet me in Chicago about the second part of the loan. I was terrified of being seen with him. But I wanted the loan application to go through. He said he wanted to meet me at the Hyatt Hotel near O'Hare Airport. I went. When I got to his room he said that the executive committee was now considering the second part of my loan—the first twenty-million-dollar installment to begin the renovations. The rest would come a little later, and that would be used to expand the Stardust and build a luxury guest tower. This had all been worked out and agreed to in principle, since the properties needed extensive work to stay competitive with the market.

"Bill Presser was still opposed, Balistrieri said, and there were only two weeks left to pass the entire loan package. I see now that he was building up the pressure.

"Then he reminded me about the promise I had made about his sons getting jobs with the new corporation, and I said that we'd work it out as soon as the deal went through. Balistrieri then asked me to go with him to Milwaukee and see his sons.

"I agreed. The next day we met in his sons' law offices, and Balistrieri said he would like to have something formalized. Balistrieri then left the room and his sons, Joe and John, discussed an agreement, actually an option agreement, in which for twenty-five or thirty thousand dollars, I don't even remember, they would have the right to buy fifty percent of the new company if and when I decided to sell.

"'Without this,' one of the sons said, 'you're gonna get turned down tomorrow.'

"I asked if we could talk about it later, after the deal.

"They said no.

"I'd already sworn to the Gaming Control Board that I had no partners. I knew the Balistrieris would never get licensed.

"I said I'd like to do it, but I'd signed with the state that I had no partners. They suggested I postdate the option.

"I asked if they thought they could get licensed, and they said they both felt licensing would be no problem for them. I began to sense these people were living in a fantasy. They didn't seem to know who they were or what baggage they carried. Or they didn't know that I knew and were simply carrying off a charade. Whatever it was, I felt like Alice in Wonderland.

"I said that I would sign it, but they had to promise they wouldn't do anything with the option. They agreed.

"That night I changed my mind. I called Joe and said I can't go through with the option agreement. If the control board comes back and finds out about it, everything will be jeopardized. I'll lose it all.

"I said if the deal was contingent on the option, as much as I would hate to, I would have to step away from the deal. I said I respected his dad and was grateful for what he had done, but I couldn't jeopardize everything I had, including the Hacienda. I said I didn't have a problem with retaining them as lawyers—I eventually retained them as counsels for fifty thousand dollars a year—but that option could destroy everything.

"A few minutes later, he calls me back. He says, 'My dad is going to call you and say he's "Uncle John." He wants to talk to you.' Uncle John! He had never used code names before. Why? I didn't know and I couldn't even act surprised, because I didn't want them to know I knew who they were.

"Balistrieri called, identified himself as Uncle John, and said, 'You can't back out.'

"I said, 'I can't do it the way it is.'

"'Are you sure?' he asks.

"I said, 'Yes, and I'll just have to take the consequences.'

"'You disappoint me,' Balistrieri said. He sounded very sad.

"His son Joe then calls back and says they'll rip up the option and we'll work something out after the deal goes through.

"I told him not to rip it up, but to send it back to me. I had already shredded my copy and I didn't want another copy floating around and finding its way to the control board.

"'You don't trust me?' Joe said, almost hurt.

"I told him it wasn't a matter of trust. It was business. He said he would send me the copy, but of course he never did.

"A week later or so the loan went through. It got a full-board approval. The board's discussion of my loan took no more than two minutes. At the end, Bill Presser, the Teamster boss from Chicago, who had been the most reluctant of the trustees, said, 'Good luck,' and that was that.

"I had gotten the sixty-two-point-seven-million-dollar Teamster loan in sixty-seven days."

◆ ◆ ◆

On August 25, 1974, over 80 percent of the Recrion shareholders tendered their stock to Allen Glick's company, Argent. The company name was an acronym for Allen R. Glick Enterprises and, of course, meant "money" in French, a language in which no one connected with the deal was fluent.

"I was euphoric," Glick recalled. "Joe Balistrieri called and said his father was coming into Chicago and wanted to have a celebration dinner.

"I said I didn't think it would be a good idea, but Joe insisted. He said, 'You can't tell my father no.'

"I didn't even want to be seen in an out-of-the-way restaurant with him, but we wound up in the Pump Room at the Ambassador Hotel in Chicago. He was well known in the place. Waiters, captains, they all came over. He was ordering Dom Pérignon. All through dinner I'm thinking, if the FBI was tailing him tonight, my life in Las Vegas is over.

"Toward the end of the dinner he said if I had any questions concerning the loan—especially the additional sixty-five million dollars for renovations and expansion—I should talk to him and only to him. I shouldn't try and discuss anything about what we had done with other trustees or union officials. He said the two of us had established a successful pattern that's the pattern that should remain established.

"Then, as we were leaving, Frank said to me, 'You've got to do me a favor, Allen. There's a guy living in Las Vegas; he's working for you now. It would be helpful if you give him more recognition. He can help you.'

" 'Who?' I said.

" 'I can't tell you now,' he said.

That was the end of the evening.

"One week later I got a call from Uncle John. He said he wanted me to meet the guy he had mentioned to me. I was in La Jolla, and Balistrieri said, 'He'll come to see you there. I want you to give him a promotion. More money. Okay?'

"I asked, 'Who is it?'

"He says, 'His name is Frank Rosenthal. If you don't like him, you can call me up and I'll straighten him out.' He said there were people on the fund who would look very favorably on the rest of my loan application if I were to promote Rosenthal. When I hesitated just a little, I could hear the tone of his voice change. He sounded annoyed. After I agreed, he asked me to meet with Rosenthal as soon as I could.

"I phoned Rosenthal right after I talked with Balistrieri. He said that he was expecting the call.

"Rosenthal came to La Jolla. He came to my home. He told me that Al Sachs was a moron. He told me that there was a lot of potential in the company. He was very good. Plus, he was very smart. He may be the devil—which I personally think he is—but he's very smart.

"I told him I knew about his expertise in gaming and that I would appoint him as my assistant or as an advisor. At first he was very conciliatory. He said he understood and he would do as I said and that he appreciated the promotion and that he would do his very best.

"He asked me to acknowledge his promotion through a memo, and asked me for a raise. I gave him the memo and the raise.

"The next day I checked with the chairman of the Gaming Commission. I learned that Rosenthal was a genius with numbers, a master handicapper. He knew all the casino games. I also learned he would probably never get a license."

◆ ◆ ◆

Frank Rosenthal returned to Las Vegas with a new job description and a raise from $75,000 to $150,000 a year. He immediately began to make changes in the operations of the casino. "Almost all of the executives viewed him as the man with all the authority," Glick said. "He was supposed to clear everything with me, but he didn't. At the outset, when I questioned him about these things, he wasn't disrespectful. But every day I would hear that he had taken a little more power. I heard that when he walked through the casino, dealers used to jump to attention. He would fire a dealer for not standing with his hands folded before him, even at an empty table. He hired whoever he wished. He changed certain purveyors. Without clearing it, he changed the car rental company, the advertising company, and he tried to bring in his own ticketing agency for the Lido Show.

"When these things were brought to my attention I would either stop them or rescind them, but he was hard to stay ahead of. While I was unraveling one thing he did, he'd be in the kitchen telling the chefs how to cook.

"I was commuting between my home in San Diego and Las Vegas, and whenever I would get to town I would hear all the stories about what he did while I was away. Then, for a few days, I would have almost daily confrontations with him. I saw him in operation. He was the kind of man who held out his cigarette and expected it to be lit. He could be withering with people. He did not curse. He did not raise his voice. But you'd rather get hit in the mouth than have him harangue you.

"He designed himself an office that Mussolini would envy. It was four times larger than any office in the place. He didn't like the wood paneling he had ordered and had it all ripped out and replaced. It was all ego. He wasn't satisfied being a boss behind the scenes; he had to let everyone know it.

"Finally, in October 1974, I called him into my office. I had just arrived from California. It was a Monday. Again, I'd learned that certain things had gone on in the casinos over that weekend, and I felt that this was the time to terminate his position.

"I met him in the coffee shop of the Stardust, which was called the Palm Room.

"I said, 'Let's go to the back of the coffee shop. I want to explain a couple of things to you.'

"I told him what I had told him on repeated occasions—that he had to control his activities and that he was supposed to work within the parameters of what I had outlined to him in our meeting in September in California.

"I said that on repeated occasions he had lied to me, that there was subterfuge, and I learned that he had even instructed my secretary to tell him on a daily basis what my movements were, where I was going and what I was going to do. I said that I found that intolerable.

"He looked surprised. He asked if my secretary had told me that. I said yes. And instead of apologizing for spying on me, he said that he was going to fire her.

"That's when I realized I wasn't dealing with a normal man. We were in the back of the coffee shop. It was a closed section. He hesitated for a second and then he got up and he walked away from the table. Then he came back to the table. I could see his blood pressure rising.

"He said, 'I think it is about time that we have a discussion, Glick.' He referred to me by my last name. He had always called me Allen. But he called me by my last name as in setting the stage.

"He said, 'It is about time you become informed of what is going on here and where I am coming from and where you should be. I was placed in this position not for your benefit, but for the benefit of others, and I have been instructed not to tolerate any nonsense from you, nor do I have to listen to what you say, because you are not my boss.'

"I began to argue with him and he said, 'Let me just cut you off right here.' He said, 'When I say you don't have a choice, I am just not talking of an administrative basis, but I am talking about one involving health.

" 'If you interfere with any of the casino operations or try to undermine anything I want to do here, I represent to you that you will never leave this corporation alive.'

"I felt like someone had just arrived from an alien planet. I was a businessman and everything I had conducted was in a businesslike manner, and this was almost totally a different subculture. I didn't know what to make of it. In respect to the conversation that I had had with Jerry Soloway in regard to Frank Balistrieri, I realized that I just entered into a trap.

"I told him I wanted him out of the hotel. He said, 'I hear what you are saying, but I want you to listen to me carefully again. When I said you will not leave this corporation alive, I meant the people that I represent have the power to do that, and much more. You should take me very serious. You are an intelligent individual, but don't test me.'

"After I recovered, I was in somewhat of a state of shock. I called Frank Balistrieri and I said, 'You got me into something I did not bargain for, or I would not have accepted anything like this.' I said, 'I felt that the appointment of your sons as corporate counsel was done in a businesslike manner, and I have no problems with that, but I do have problems with this.'

"I related to him the conversation I had with Rosenthal and he was very conciliatory. He said he would get back to me. But just remember, he said, the only one I was to talk to about this matter was him. Frank Balistrieri. If anyone else approached me and I talked to them, I would be doing it irrespective of his wishes. He was very firm. I did not pursue it with him.

"Within a few days Balistrieri called back. He explained to me on the phone that he understood the situation, but at this time there was nothing he could do about it and that I should heed Mr. Rosenthal's advice and keep him in that position.

"I discussed Rosenthal's mention of 'partners,' and I said that I bought this corporation through my own efforts, acknowledging that he helped me get the pension fund loan, but there were no partners.

"But Balistrieri said, 'What Mr. Rosenthal told you is accurate.'"

♦ ♦ ♦

For several months, Glick fenced with Rosenthal. He was afraid to confront him, so he tried to limit his activities. He excluded him from meetings. He tried to keep him out of the loop. He countermanded his orders. He rejected his suggestions. And finally, one night in March 1975, Allen Glick's wildest nightmare came true. He was having dinner in the Palace Court Restaurant in the Stardust when Rosenthal called. "He said there was an emergency. I had to join him at a meeting. I asked what emergency. He said he couldn't tell me over the phone, but I had to meet him. I said I'd rather not. I said we could deal with whatever it was in the morning.

"Then he said, 'It's an emergency and you don't have a choice.'

"I said, 'Okay, where is it?'

"He said, 'Kansas City.'

"I thought that was ridiculous. I told him I couldn't get there before three or four in the morning. He said, 'We are going to come and get you, or you are going to come voluntarily." He said he would meet me at the airport. The corporation had a couple of Lears at the time, and by two thirty or three in the morning I landed in Kansas City.

"Rosenthal was waiting for me with a car at the airport and introduced me to the driver, Carl DeLuna, a really gruff, vulgar man. Rosenthal referred to him by his nickname, 'Toughy.'

"We then took a circuitous route to wherever we were going, because I noticed that we were passing the same places time and again. It took about twenty minutes. Round and around, and no one is saying anything. Finally we got to a hotel. We go up to the third floor. It's a suite with a connecting door that is only partially open to a connecting room.

"The suite was pretty dark. As I walked in I was introduced to a white-haired older man named Nick Civella. I had no idea who Nick Civella was. He turned out to be the Mafia boss of Kansas City. I put out my hand to shake and he said, 'I don't want to shake your hand.'

"There was a chair and an end table with a light on it. He told me to sit down. I saw Rosenthal leave the room. I was in there with DeLuna and Civella, except I could hear people moving in and out of the room through the interconnecting door of the suite, but that was to my back.

"Civella called me every name under the sun and then he says, 'You don't know me, but if it was my choice you'd never leave this room alive. However, due to the circumstances, if you listen, you may.'

"When I said the light was bothering my eyes, he said he could accommodate me by pulling my eyes out. Then he said, 'You reneged on our deal. You owe us one-point-two million dollars, and you're gonna let Lefty do what he wants.'

"I was amazed. I said I didn't know what he was talking about. I meant it.

"He looks at me and says, laying a gun on the table, 'You're going to start telling me the truth right now or you're not leaving this room alive.'

"He asked about my agreement with Balistrieri, and when I said I didn't have an agreement with Balistrieri, he said, 'What?' Kind of surprised. He said he wanted to know about the agreement he had been told I had with Balistrieri.

"I said the only agreement I had with Balistrieri was about hiring his sons, and I told him about the option, but I explained that the option was voided and we were going to work something out now that the deal had gone through.

"Later, I found out that Civella did not know about my

deals with Balistrieri—about hiring his kids and their fifty percent option. He thought Balistrieri had been given a one-point-two-million-dollar cash commission for getting me the loan. Since Civella felt he had also helped get me the loan through his trustee—Roy Williams, the Teamster boss of Kansas City and the next president of the entire union—he too was entitled to one-point-two million dollars.

"Balistrieri had told me never to talk to anyone else about our arrangement, but I felt under these circumstances I had no choice. I also began to see why Balistrieri insisted I never talk to anyone else.

"Civella was a tough guy but a smart man. When he asked me questions I could see that he was putting things together. All of a sudden, something rang a bell and he got up. He said I still had a commitment to him and he wanted the money paid.

"When I said that I didn't know how the corporation could pay him this money, he said, 'Let Lefty handle that.'

"He said that because he did not like me, he was going to personally see to it that I did not get the additional Teamster loans for renovation and expansion.

"Then he said, 'Get him outta here,' and told DeLuna to take Lefty and me back to the airport and 'drive down to Milwaukee and yank that fancy-pants sonofabitch out of bed and bring him here.'

"This time it only took us five minutes to get back to the airport from the hotel, and all the while DeLuna was griping about how he had to drive all the way to Milwaukee to pick up Balistrieri, as though Balistrieri were a sack of laundry.

"When I met Rosenthal the next morning I told him that I could not accept Civella's conditions about paying him money and having partners, and Rosenthal said that I was really no longer in a position of authority. He said I could no longer determine my destiny.

"When I told Balistrieri about my meeting with Civella and told him about the threat to cut off our additional loans, Balistrieri said there was nothing he could any longer do to help me. He said the pension fund matters were now out of his hands."

11.

"Do you know who I am? I run this town."

When Tony Spilotro got to town in 1971, Las Vegas was a relatively quiet place. The bosses had been making so much money from their own illegitimate enterprises, such as illegal bookmaking, loan-sharking, and casino skimming, that there was a concerted effort by the mob to keep the town clean, safe, and quiet. The rules were simple. Disputes were to be peaceably settled. There were to be no shootings or car explosions in town. Bodies were not to be left in car trunks at the airport. Sanctioned murders took place out of town or the bodies disappeared forever in the vast desert surrounding the city.

Before Tony arrived, mob matters were so benignly administered that Jasper Speciale, the biggest loan shark in town, operated out of his Leaning Tower of Pizza restaurant, and his waitresses moonlighted as collectors after they finished work. The town's petty criminals—the drug dealers, the bookies, pimps, even the card cheats—were operating for free. Las Vegas was an open city: mobsters from different families around the country needed no permission to wander into town, extort money from high rollers, work a credit scam on a casino, and go home. The kind of street tax imposed by the outfit back home was unheard of.

"Tony stopped all that," said Bud Hall Jr., the retired FBI agent who spent years eavesdropping on Spilotro's life. "Tony changed the way business was done in Las Vegas. He took over. The first thing he did was bring in some of his own men and impose a street tax on every bookie, loan shark, drug dealer, and pimp in town. A few, like a book-maker named Jerry Dellman, resisted, but he wound up shot dead in a daylight robbery in the garage area behind his house. Nobody tried to hide the body. It was a message that there was a real gangster in town.

"Tony understood very quickly that he could run Las Vegas any way he wanted, because the bosses were fifteen hundred miles away and didn't have the same kind of street ears in Las Vegas that they had back in Elmwood Park."

♦ ♦ ♦

"When Tony first moved to Las Vegas, very few people even knew who he was," Lefty said. "I remember we had this re-ally arrogant guy, John Grandy, in charge of all construction and purchasing. Nobody fucked with John Grandy. If peo-ple asked him for anything, he'd say, 'Why the fuck are you bothering me? Get lost!' I handled him with kid gloves.

"One morning Tony was coming in to see me. Grandy was there giving orders to three or four workers who were putting together some blackjack tables for dealers. He had a bunch of construction material in his arms, and he looked over and sees Tony coming up to me, and he says to Tony, 'Hey, come here! Hold this! I'll tell you what to do with it later.'

"I'll never forget this. The stuff weighed about thirty or forty pounds. Tony was so surprised he held it a second before shoving it right back.

"'Here,' Tony said, 'you hold it, not me. Who the fuck do you think you are? The next time you talk to me that way, I'll throw you out the fucking window!' Quote unquote.

"Grandy looks at me. I look at Tony. Tony is fuming. And Grandy does what Tony says. Grandy takes the stuff back and doesn't say shit. Tony says he'll meet me down in the coffee shop and he leaves.

"When Tony's gone, Grandy says, 'Hey! Who the fuck's that guy? Who's he think he is?' I said, 'The guy doesn't work here. Never mind who he is.'

"But Grandy knows something's wrong. He goes down into the casino and spots Bobby Stella and drags Stella to the coffee shop to look for Tony.

"'Bobby, who's that fucking guy over there? Who the fuck does he think he is?' Grandy's getting all riled up now.

"Bobby saw he was pointing to Tony and tried to calm him down. 'Slow down. Take it easy.'

"'What do you mean, "slow down"?'

"Bobby says, 'That's Tony Spilotro.'

"Grandy just stood there and said, 'Holy shit! Holy shit!' He apparently knew the name but not the face. He went right over to Tony and apologized four or five times. 'I'm very, very sorry. I really didn't mean to insult you. Things were a little bit busy and I didn't know who you were. Would you accept my apologies?' Tony said yeah and looked the other way. Grandy ran."

♦ ♦ ♦

Frank Cullotta got out of prison after doing six years for a Brinks truck robbery, and Spilotro flew to Chicago for his coming-out party. "I had 'Free At Last' on my birthday cake," Cullotta said. "Everyone came and they all gave me envelopes, and at the end of the night I had about twenty thousand dollars, but mostly it made me feel great that so many guys were with me and liked me. I was still on paper [on parole], so I couldn't leave Chicago right away, but Tony said that as soon as I got off paper I was supposed to come to Nevada.

"By the time I got there, Tony was already running the town. He had everybody on the payroll. He owned a couple of guys in the sheriff's office. He had guys in the courthouse who could get him grand jury minutes, and he had people in the telephone company to tell him about phone taps.

"Tony had the town covered. He was in the papers all the time. He had broads coming around in Rolls-Royces who wanted to go out with him. Everybody wanted to be around a gangster. Movie stars. Everybody. I don't know what the fuck's the attraction, but that's the way it was. I guess it's a feeling of power, you know. People feel like, well, these guys are hitters, and if I need something done, they'll do it for me.

"He knew I was a good thief, and he said we could make good money. Tony always needed money. He went through cash fast. He liked to bet sports and he never stayed home. He was a sport. He always picked up the check. No matter if there were ten, fifteen people with us, he'd always pick up the check.

"He told me, 'Look, get a crew together. And, whatever you gotta fucking do with the guys, you got my okay. Just give me my end. You've got carte blanche out here.'

"I sent for Wayne Matecki, Larry Neumann, Ernie Davino, real desperados like that, and we started putting the arm on everybody. Bookmakers. Shylocks. Dope dealers. Pimps. Shit, we'd strong-arm them. Beat them. Shoot their fucking guard dogs. What did we care? I had Tony's okay. In fact, half the time Tony'd told us who to grab.

"Then, after we'd rob them and scare them, they'd run to Tony for protection to get us off their backs. They never had any idea it was Tony who sent us over to rob them in the first place.

"We made good money turning over houses. It was all cash and jewelry. I'm talking about thirty, forty, fifty thousand dollars in twenties and hundreds laying in dresser drawers. One time I found fifteen thousand-dollar bills next to a guy's bed. Now, where the fuck am I gonna get rid of them? Thousand-dollar bills are hard to get rid of. Banks want your name if you try and cash them. So I pushed them at the Stardust. I handed them to Lou Salerno, and he shoved them in the drawer and gave me back fifteen grand in hundreds.

"How do you think I put up the money for my restaurant, the Upper Crust? I got the money in two days. Me and Wayne and Ernie hit two maitre d's' houses and got over sixty thousand dollars. Maitre d's take twenty-dollar bills from people looking for good tables all night. Well, we took the twenties back. One of the guys also had a thirty-thousand-dollar Patek Philippe watch, and we sold it to Bobby Stella for three grand. Bobby gave it away as a present.

"We'd get our information from the casino people. Bell captains. The registration desk. The credit clerks. Travel agency people. But our best sources were the insurance brokers who sold the people the policies of the stuff we were robbing. They'd give us the information on everything. What kind of jewels the people had and how much they were insured for. Where in the house the stuff was located.

What kind of alarm system. The people had to put all that info down on their policies when they got insured.

"If the doors and windows and alarm systems were a pain, we'd go right through the wall. Going through the walls was my idea. I invented it. It's very simple. Almost all the houses out in Vegas have stucco exterior walls. All you need is a five-pound sledge to make a hole big enough so you can get in. Then you use metal shears to clip away the chicken wire inside the wall they use for lathing. Then you bang away a little more until you break through the interior drywall, and you're inside the house.

"You could only do this in Las Vegas, because the houses were stucco and they have high walls around them for privacy. People have pools and things outside, and they like to live private lives. Nobody knows their neighbors. Nobody wants to know their neighbors. It's that kind of town. It's the kind of place, if people hear a noise from the house next door, they tune it out. We did so many of these jobs that the newspaper started calling us the Hole in the Wall Gang. The cops never knew who we were.

"'Mean fucking pigs,' Tony'd say, proud of us. 'Look what I have created out here.'

"We had it down. We'd be in and out of a house in three to five minutes tops. And whenever we did a job, we had a guy in a work car outside with a scanner picking up police calls. We even had a descrambler so we'd get the FBI. Tony gave us the descramblers and the police frequencies.

"But no matter how well we were doing, we always needed more money. Burglary money goes quick. We always had to divide it four ways—me and my two guys, and then Tony would always get his end. On a forty-thousand-dollar job, Tony would get ten grand. For sitting home. He got an equal end every time.

"Sometimes, if we needed cash and things were slow,

we'd do straight robberies. We took the Rose Bowl out like that. At that time the Rose Bowl was owned by the guy who owned Chateau Vegas, and Tony gives me all the information and then says, 'You're gonna need a guy with a clean face.' So I imported a kid from Chicago with a clean face, a guy that nobody knew. We couldn't use a known guy because we weren't supposed to be doing robberies like this in the first place. If the bosses found out Tony was doing armed robberies in the middle of town, he wouldn't have been here long. But nobody back home knew we were doing burglaries and robberies. That was our little secret.

"The old broad who ran the Rose Bowl and her bodyguard came out into the back parking lot just like Tony said they would, with a bag of money. She walks toward her car. The bodyguard is just standing there watching her. The new kid I brought to town walks right up to her, flashes a gun, and grabs the bag out of her hand.

"The guy she had watching her tried to be a hero, and my kid whacked him with the back of his hand and the guy's on his ass. My kid was real rough. He's in jail now on something else. He's doing forty years.

"The kid runs the block parallel to the Strip. There's a chapel over there. Ernie Davino was waiting for him. Larry Neumann was in the parking lot, right nearby, as a backup if the kid needed help. When the kid jumps into the car with Ernie, Larry has already gotten in back. And as they're coming off the street, I'm coming off the street. We were four blocks away cutting up the money when we could hear the police just starting to show up at the Rose Bowl parking lot.

"Looking back I see how crazy we were. Here we were in Las Vegas with a million ways to make a dishonest buck, and Tony's got us out here doing house burglaries and armed robberies and 7-Elevens. It was dumb."

♦ ♦ ♦

All booming industries create jobs, and the Spilotro operation was no exception. Within a year Spilotro was providing work not just for his own crew but for dozens of law enforcement officers who tailed him, bugged him, and attempted to ensnare him in elaborate stings. At one point, Spilotro was betting $30,000 a week at a bookmaking operation that was actually an IRS sting; he was attracted by the fact that it offered better odds than any other book in town. When the IRS agent operating the sting had the nerve to ask Spilotro for collateral, Spilotro greeted him with a baseball bat. "Do you know who I am?" Spilotro asked. "I run this town."

Spilotro had moved his jewelry store front from Circus Circus to West Sahara Avenue, just off the Strip. The Gold Rush Jewelry Store was a two-story building complete with platformed sidewalk and fake hitching posts.

"We got the necessary probable cause and dropped a mike in the ceiling of the back room of the Gold Rush," said Bud Hall. "The front room was strictly for selling rings and wristwatches. Upstairs, Tony had antisurveillance devices, telephone scramblers, battleship binoculars so he could see if he was being watched from a mile away, and shortwave radios that picked up police calls and were even able to unscramble the bureau's frequencies. Tony got our frequencies through some Metro cops he had on his payroll. He also had an electronics expert from Chicago, Ronnie 'Balloon Head' DeAngelis, who would fly into town every few weeks and sweep the place for taps and bugs. We always got our best stuff right after DeAngelis left. 'Balloon Head says the place is clean,' Tony would proudly announce, and everyone would relax.

"Tony was a totally focused human being. He woke up in

the morning knowing exactly what he was going to do that day. He'd get dozens of calls at the Gold Rush. He had all kinds of financial deals going on at the same time. He had different groups, hundreds of people, a million schemes, all of them in various stages of development. And even though most of them never panned out, he still had to put in a sixteen- to eighteen-hour day trying to put the deals together.

"It would have been difficult doing what Tony did if he had secretaries, a filing system, Xerox machines, and the free use of a phone. But Tony did it all off-the-cuff and kept it all in his head. The only things he ever wrote down were telephone numbers, and he used to write them down in the tiniest little handwriting that made them unreadable without a magnifying glass, and when we'd get ahold of them, we found he would transpose the numbers or write half or three-quarters of each number backwards.

"Listening to someone on a wire every day," Bud Hall says, "is different than being around them all the time socially. It creates a strange relationship between the person listening and the subject. You're listening to their lives, and pretty soon you're inside their lives. I don't mean that you get to like them, but you get to be able to tell by the sound of their voice what their moods are and where in the room they might happen to be. There are times when you can almost lip-sync what they are going to say before they say it. You come to know them so intimately that you almost become a part of the person.

"Tony was the smartest and most efficient mobster I had ever seen. I think he was a genius. His biggest problem was that he was surrounded by people who were always screwing up. That's all we kept hearing him say over and over. He'd harangue his crew about their incompetence and how he had no choice but to do things himself if he wanted them done right.

"If you talked to him on the phone, all you had to say were three or four words and he would have digested the purpose of the call, and the call had better be about business and it had better be in his interest.

"Tony had no capacity whatever for casual conversation. He could be congenial. Cordial. Likeable. But you couldn't waste his time. He lost his temper faster than anyone I ever knew. There was no slow burn. He went right from being nice to being a screaming, violent maniac in a second. There was no way to prepare for him. I think the speed with which you were suddenly under attack was as terrifying as the thought of having Tony mad at you. However, once it passed, it passed. He forgot it. He went back to business.

"He lived a completely separate life from Nancy. They shared their son, Vincent, but that was about it. He slept in his own room on the ground floor of their house behind a locked steel door. When he got up in the morning, around ten thirty or eleven, Nancy stayed out of his way. He'd make his own coffee, and when he picked up the paper on the front step or off the walkway, he'd look up and down Balfour Avenue for surveillance.

"When he was ready to leave, there was no 'good-bye' or 'see you for dinner.' He'd just get in his blue Corvette sports car and routinely go around the block a few times, checking for tails. It could take him forty-five minutes to drive the ten minutes between his house and the Gold Rush because Tony would automatically dry-clean himself of tails by driving through shopping centers, stopping at green lights, moving through red, making illegal U-turns, and then checking his rearview mirror to see if anyone was following.

"After all that time I spent listening in at the Gold Rush and at his house, I decided that he had what we called in the marines 'command posture.' When he talked, people listened. When he entered a room, he was always in charge. But in charge of what? That was his problem.

"One day we picked up that Joe Ferriola, one of the Chicago street bosses, was trying to get a relative a job as a dealer at the Stardust. Tony asked Joey Cusumano to take care of it. Cusumano, one of Spilotro's top guys, hung around the Stardust passing Tony's messages back and forth so much that many of the casino's employees thought he worked there.

"A week passed and Tony got another call from Ferriola's people that she was still unemployed. Tony had a fit. Cusumano checked back and found the casino wouldn't hire her as a dealer because she had no experience and would have to go take a six-week course at dealer's school.

"Tony then tells Joey to ask Lefty, who was pretending to be the Stardust's food and beverage director at the time, to get the kid a job as a waitress.

"A few days later, Joey comes back and says that Lefty doesn't want to hire her because he doesn't think she's good-looking enough to be a Stardust cocktail waitress, and besides, she's got bad legs.

"Spilotro exploded and he did something he should have never done—he called the Stardust himself. He got hold of Joey Boston, an ex-bookmaker Lefty had hired to run the Stardust Sports Book.

"Tony shouldn't have called the Stardust himself, because now we at the FBI had a tape of Spilotro asking a top executive of the Stardust casino to get a job for a Chicago capo's relative. That's exactly what we had been waiting for. It made for the kind of direct link between the mob and a licensed casino that neither side would ever want made public, the kind of connection that could jeopardize a casino's license and call into question just who really owns the casino and who might be serving as a front."

Ferriola's relative eventually went to work as a security guard at one of the other Las Vegas hotels. But the story of how Tony Spilotro, the most terrifying mobster in Las Vegas, could not manage to get a job at the Stardust for the relative of a Chicago capo did not help his reputation back home.

◆ ◆ ◆

"I was around Tony all the time and he was always worried about people listening in," says Matt Marcus, a 350-pound illegal bookmaker who took a lot of Spilotro's action. "We'd be in the Food Factory on Twain Street, a place he had a piece of, and he'd communicate with body language. He'd lean back and shrug and twist his head and frown. He drank tea all the time. Not coffee. He always sat with the tea bag hanging out of the cup, leaning and shrugging and twisting and frowning. He was positive the next person passing by would be the FBI. He was always changing cars. The intell unit was always checking his license plates. They'd go right up to the cars and take down their numbers."

"Tony seemed to get a real kick out of matching wits with the FBI, but he wasn't stupid," Frank Cullotta said. "Whenever he had anything to say we'd go for walks in empty parking lots or on the side of the road in the desert. When you said something to him, mostly he'd just make faces, or frown, or smile and get across what he meant for you to do. Even when he did talk, he'd always cover his mouth with his hand in case the feds were using lip-readers with binoculars."

At one point, the FBI became so frustrated with its telephone taps and its once-promising Gold Rush microphone that they installed a surveillance camera in the ceiling of a back room behind Cullotta's restaurant, where they suspected Spilotro was having some of his key meetings.

"We got a tip something was up there," Cullotta said, "and we went up behind the false ceiling and tore it out. It was like a small TV camera and it said 'United States Government' or something, and its serial numbers had been scraped off. I got really pissed. I wanted to trash the damn thing, but Tony made us call Oscar and give it back. I think he liked the idea of the feds coming over with their hats in their hands to get it back."

When the FBI saw that over two years of electronic surveillance had failed to snare Spilotro, they sent an undercover FBI agent, Rick Baken, into the Gold Rush, using the name Rick Calise.

As part of the ruse, Baken had first curried favor months earlier playing cards and losing to Tony's brother John. During their card games Baken let it slip that he was an ex-con and jewel thief who desperately needed cash and was looking to unload some stolen diamonds at a great price. The bureau had, of course, given Baken the backup necessary to verify his criminal past in case Spilotro checked. But even after meeting Spilotro, Baken found that Herbie Blitzstein, Tony's go-fer, always kept him away from a direct conversation with Spilotro.

After eleven months of this futile and dangerous undercover work, the feds became so frustrated that they tried a desperation move. Wearing a wire, as usual, Baken approached Spilotro directly and said that he had been picked up and questioned by the FBI and threatened with prison unless he talked about Spilotro's illegal activities.

To Baken's surprise, Spilotro suggested they visit his attorney, Oscar Goodman.

The next thing Baken knew, he was in a defense attorney's office wearing a wire and pretending to be a crook. Goodman listened to Baken's story for about fifteen minutes and gave him the names of several lawyers to call.

Goodman later had a great time playing up the incident just enough to make it appear as if the FBI had tried to violate the attorney-client privilege by eavesdropping on a potential defendant and his attorney.

♦ ♦ ♦

As time passed, Spilotro spent less and less time with his wife, Nancy. When they were together, they fought—and the FBI listened. She complained that he had lost interest in her. She accused him of affairs. He was never home. He never talked to her. In the morning, the FBI recorded the sound of silence as Tony made his coffee and Nancy read the newspaper. Then he would leave for the store without even saying good-bye.

Sometimes Nancy had to call him at work to relay a message; according to Bud Hall, Tony was always rude. "She'd say, 'I don't know if this can wait, but so-and-so called.' 'It can wait,' Tony would say, sort of sarcastically, and just hang up. Or he'd say, in an exasperated tone, 'Nancy, I'm busy,' and hang up. He was never gentlemanly with her, and she'd whine to Dena Harte, Herbie Blitzstein's girl-friend, who managed the front of the Gold Rush. Nancy would tell Dena whenever Tony beat her up or whenever she suspected Tony was fooling around with this one or that one, and Dena kept Nancy informed about what Tony was doing.

"There was one time when Dena called Nancy at home and said, 'The bitch is here.' Nancy jumped in the car and tore over to the place and started screaming at Sheryl, Tony's girlfriend, calling her a no-good cunt right there in the middle of the store.

"We could hear the screaming on the wire, and then Tony comes out, and then we hear Nancy screaming for Tony to stop hitting her. He was really beating her up. We got worried that he was going to kill her. It was a mess. So we called nine-one-one and said we were in the Black Forest German Restaurant next door, and said someone was being assaulted in the Gold Rush. We couldn't tell the cops who we were because at that point it looked like Tony owned Metro, and we didn't want to blow our surveillance. The police got there in a few minutes, and everything calmed down."

"Nancy had her life and Tony had his," said Frank Cullotta. "Hers was mostly playing tennis and running around in white outfits. She had Vincent and Tony's brothers and their families. Once a week Tony'd take her out to dinner or something. But she wasn't afraid of him. She would scream and yell at him and drive him crazy.

"Once, he told me, she tried to kill him. They were having an argument over something and Tony knocked her across the room. She came up with a loaded thirty-eight cocked at his head. 'I'll kill you if you ever hit me again,' she said. Tony said, 'Nancy, think of Vincent.'

"'I saw death,' he told me after. 'We talked until she put down the gun and then I hid all the guns in the house.'"

♦ ♦ ♦

"Sheryl was about twenty, but she looked younger," said Rosa Rojas, who was her best friend. "She was a Mormon from northern Utah, cute and fresh. When Tony first met her he used to call her his country girl. She was so naive that when he asked her out, she said she'd only go if she could bring her friend.

"Sheryl and I were both working in the hospital where he was going for his heart problem, which was how they met. They'd go to restaurants, but he never put the make on her. He held her at a distance for a long, long time.

"Before he got too close he found out everything there was to find out about her. He had Joey Cusumano ask about where she was from, who her friends were, how long she lived where she lived. He wanted to know everything he could know about her before he got involved or felt he could trust her.

"It was a long time before she knew who he was. She began to suspect something was strange, because every time they went out, they were tailed by cops in plain clothes. Tony's brother told her that there were some legal problems and that Tony was being trailed because of the legal stuff. Tony used to tell us that we were going to read things about him in the newspapers, but he said the newspapers weren't always right.

"It was only after a long time that Tony and Sheryl started going to bed together. He was a gentleman always. Very quiet. Very reserved. I would see him mad sometimes, but I never once heard him curse or use bad language.

"Eventually, he bought her a two-story condo around Eastern and Flamingo, a two-bedroom place for about sixty-nine thousand dollars. It had everything. Refrigerator. Blinds. A washer-dryer. There was a garage and small patio and a sliding door that led into the downstairs, and upstairs they had the bedrooms and a large room that had all of the stereo and TV equipment you would want. That's where they spent most of their time—watching ball games and listening to music.

"Tony was very generous. He used to leave a thousand dollars a week in a bear-shaped cookie jar in the kitchen. He never mentioned money and it was never mentioned that he was keeping her, but when he bought her a full-length mink coat Sheryl felt he had finally committed himself to her. She had really fallen in love with him.

"She didn't know he was married for quite a while. When

she found out, it was very hard. She believed the only reason she and Tony weren't married was because Tony was a very strict Catholic and would have trouble leaving his wife. For a while, Tony even had Sheryl learning to be a Catholic. He gave her religious books to read. He knew the Bible.

"He never ever said anything bad about his wife. They had been married in the church and it was a difficult situation. On top of that, Tony loved his son. Vincent meant everything to him. Vincent was his soul. Tony would always get home at six thirty in the morning so he could be there to make breakfast for Vincent. Sheryl said he would do that even if he was in bed at her place.

"Eventually, Tony bought a car for her. It was a new Plymouth Fury. It wasn't a showy car.

"When Nancy found out what was going on, things got a little tough. Sheryl had stopped by the Gold Rush to see Tony. She was wearing a diamond studded S necklace that Tony had given her, and when Nancy came in and saw Sheryl wearing the S necklace, Nancy went wild and she reached for it.

"I got there just at that time and I found the two of them wrestling on the floor. Sheryl managed to hold on to her S. Tony came out of the back room and broke up the fight so Sheryl and I could get away.

"In the end, when it was over between Tony and Sheryl, he wouldn't return her calls. Sheryl was really crazy about him, but maybe she pushed too hard. He was having a lot of problems with the cops when they broke up, and maybe he was trying to spare her.

"His brother John used to tell her not to try and reach him. 'Don't call him,' he'd say. 'Spare yourself.' But she'd see him making his court appearances on TV and she saw that he was gaining weight and didn't look good, and she used to blame Nancy for not taking care of him. Sheryl used to make sure he ate the right food, and her refrigerator was always filled with fruits and salad and the kinds of healthy food that were good for people with heart problems.

"After she and Tony broke up she got a job doing cocktails at night. Tony wasn't happy about it. But she had grown accustomed to his lifestyle. She needed the money. Then she got into dealing blackjack. She worked in the old MGM, at Bally's. She had a prime shift and made excellent money. She started meeting high rollers. She wised up. She learned and started looking around for another rock to stand on."

♦ ♦ ♦

"One day we're in the back of the My Place Lounge, in the parking lot, and Tony tells me to kill Jerry Lisner," said Frank Cullotta. "Jerry Lisner was a small-time drug dealer and hustler.

"Tony said: 'Frankie, you gotta take care of this guy. He rolled. He's a rat.'

"I told Tony that Lisner would be hard for me, because I had just beaten him out of five thousand quaaludes and he and his wife didn't trust me.

"And Tony got all mad. 'I'll go kill the motherfucker,' he says. 'Just get him over here.'

"I told him it wasn't that I didn't want to do it; it was that Lisner was worried about me. It would be hard to get close enough to get him.

"'I want it done now!' he said. 'Now and quick!'

"That was all he said. He walked inside the joint. We were all being followed all the time, so I got in my car, went home and packed a bag, drove all the way from Las Vegas to Burbank airport in L.A., where I took the next flight for Chicago. Nobody even knew I had left town.

"In Chicago I got ahold of Wayne Matecki. We left the next night using fake names on a flight for Burbank, got in my car, and drove back to Las Vegas.

"We went from the airport to my condo, the Marie Antoinette, where I thought I'd take a chance and call Lisner. I say to myself, 'Let me give it a shot. See if he's home.' He is. I say, 'I've got a mark, a real good one. Somebody we can take for a lot of money.' I tell him the guy is in town. I'm talking a great score.

"He tells me to bring the guy over. We use a work car where we've got a police scanner and a twenty-five-caliber automatic. I didn't have a silencer so I made half loads—I half-emptied the bullets so they wouldn't make as much noise.

"I left Wayne in the car with the scanner and I went inside. I told Lisner I wanted to talk with him before the guy came in. I want to make sure that there's nobody in the house. I know his old lady works. I know he's got two sons, but he was always complaining that they were pains in the ass.

"As we're walking into the house I'm asking, 'Are you sure nobody's home? You positive? Where are your kids? Where's your wife?' He's telling me that there's nobody home, and I'm telling him I want to make sure before I bring the guy inside.

"We're walking around inside and I say, 'I hear a noise,' and he's saying it's nothing. I looked out the living room toward the pool and I closed the blinds. We're walking together and we're coming out of the little den area and I pulled the stick out and popped him two times in the back of his head.

"He turns around and looks at me. 'What are you doing?' he says. He takes off through the kitchen toward the garage.

"I actually looked at the gun, like, 'What the fuck have I got? Blanks in there?' So I run after him and I empty the rest in his head. It's like an explosion going off every time.

"But he doesn't go down. The fuck starts running. It's like a comedy of errors. I'm chasing him around the house, and I've emptied the thing in his head.

"I catch him in the garage. And as I catch him in the garage, he hits the garage door button, but I hit him before it goes down. I can see he's getting weak. I drag him back into the kitchen.

"I've got no more bullets. I'm thinking, what am I going to do with this guy? I grab an electric cord from the water cooler and I wrap it around his neck and it breaks. I was going to the sink to get a knife and finish this thing when Wayne walks in with more bullets.

"Lisner is still gasping. He says, 'My wife knows you're here.'

"I emptied the gun into his head. In the eyes. And then he just went down, like he deflated, and I knew he was gone.

"Now I wanted the house to be clean. I had blood all over the place. Blood was all over him. My worry was that I'd leave a print in the blood somewhere on his body or clothes.

"I hadn't worn any gloves because Lisner wasn't dumb. He wouldn't have let me in the door if he saw me wearing gloves. So I made sure I didn't touch anything. The only thing I knew I touched was the wall, when I hit him near the watercooler. And there, right away, as soon as he went down, I wiped everything clean real fast.

"But there was the danger of my prints on his body, so I grabbed him by the ankles and Wayne opened the sliding door, and I dragged him to the pool and slid him, legs first, into the water. He went in straight, like a board. Like he was swimming.

"I knew by soaking him in the pool the blood would dissolve and any of my prints on the body would disappear. I looked down as he floated there and I saw the blood starting to come up.

"Then Wayne and I looked through the house. I wanted to make sure the guy wasn't recording my conversation with him in the house. I looked downstairs and Wayne went upstairs. I found his phone book and took it.

"We got back to my place and I took a shower with kitchen cleaner to get rid of any blood trace. Then we got rid of our clothes. We cut them into shreds, put them in a bunch of bags, and drove out into the desert, depositing them all over the place.

"Wayne took a taxi to the airport and went back to Chicago. I then drove by the Lisner house, but there was no activity. So I drove over to the My Place Lounge. As I was pulling up, Tony pulled up with Sammy Siegel.

"I asked him if he had a minute.

"We walked to the side.

"I said, 'It's done.'

"He said, 'Done?'

"I say, 'I just took care of it.'

"He said, 'Did you get rid of everything?'

"I said, 'Yeah. I put ten into him and I threw him in the pool.'

"He looked at me and said, 'Fine. As of this day we'll never talk about this again.' We never did."

◆ ◆ ◆

"I was driving Tony to a place about sixty miles out of town for dinner, because between his heart and my licensing problems we didn't want to be seen together in town. All the way out he's telling me about how he's under constant surveillance and how he's just trying to make a living and live a quiet life. All I can do is 'yes-yes' him. Tony wasn't telling me all this because he wanted an argument. He didn't seem to put together the fact that he might have been making enemies of various people with the fact they they would secretly pass the word around about what he was or wasn't doing. I don't think he understood, right or wrong, that when you're as hot as he was, every cop in the state had your picture up on their bulletin boards. Later, his lawyers found that the federal strike force had pictures of Tony and his whole family, and friends, even their lawyers. The agents and prosecutors had Tony's picture on a dart board and nasty comments written in under most of the snapshots. That's what happens when you're the target. There isn't a cop in the state that doesn't know who you are and isn't looking to either put you in jail or shake you down.

"When we got to the restaurant outside town, two of his guys were already waiting. They had taken a booth in the back.

"We had just sat down when a guy comes over to the table. 'Mr. Rosenthal,' he says, 'let me introduce myself to you. I'm the owner of this property. I've seen your picture in the paper and I wanted you to know we're all rooting for you. How's the service? I hope you enjoy your dinner.'

"I told him everything was fine and thanked him, except I felt awful that he spotted me. Then, instead of going away, he turns to Tony. 'And Mr. Spilotray'—he pronounced Tony's name with an A—'can I introduce myself to you?'

"Tony stands up and puts his arm on the guy's shoulder and sort of walks him about twenty feet away, just out of earshot.

"I can see Tony's shaking the guy's hand and I'm watching the guy's smiling face and then I see he goes white and turns around and walks into the kitchen.

"When Tony sits down he's all smiles.

"'What the hell did you tell that guy?' I asked him.

"'Nothing,' he says.

"What happened was that Tony walked the guy away and said: 'My name isn't Spilotray, you motherfucker. You never saw me in your life. And Frank Rosenthal wasn't here either. And if I hear you telling anything to anybody, this place is going to become a bowling alley and you're gonna be in the fucking racks.'"

♦ ♦ ♦

Spilotro was wired, he was tailed, he was harassed, he was arrested, he was indicted. But he was never convicted. In his first five years in Las Vegas, there were more murders committed than in the previous twenty-five. He was indicted in the murder of a Caesar's Palace box man named Red Kilm, but the case never got to trial. He was suspected of killing Barbara McNair's husband, Rick Manzi, who was involved in a drug deal that went sour, but nothing ever came of it. Spilotro would walk into court waving and smiling, with his lawyer, Oscar Goodman, as the television cameras ground away. Says Frank Cullotta: "The more reporters Oscar saw, the further away he'd park his goddamn car so he'd have more time to be interviewed. Tony swore by Oscar. In all the years he was out there, he never spent more than a couple of hours in jail waiting for bail. When I'd warn him about Oscar, who as far as I was concerned was a publicity hound, Tony'd just nod and chew on his thumb. He used to chew on the cuticle of his right thumb. If you looked at it sometimes it was all raw and chewed away.

"Later on, when Oscar got rich, Tony'd look up at the big

brick building Oscar built on Fourth Street and say, 'I built that building.' Like he was proud of it. But I never understood why Tony liked Oscar so much. The guy was a lawyer. He made a fortune off Tony. I could never trust a man who wears a fake Rolex."

12. ♦

"That's one of the problems with marrying a ten, or even a nine."

After two or three years, Lefty's marriage looked like a bad bet. Geri had given birth to a son, Steven, whom she adored; but she found the domestic life Lefty wanted her to live far too restrictive, especially since he refused to play by the rules he expected her to follow. Lefty was working day and night at the casino, and Geri began to suspect he was seeing other women. She told her sister she had found receipts for jewelry and presents in his pockets when she took his suits to the dry cleaners. When she accused him of fooling around, he told her she was crazy. He accused her of being drunk and taking too many pills.

So Geri started going out. Sometimes she'd stay out all night. Sometimes she'd disappear for a weekend. On more than one occasion Lefty hired private detectives to track her down. He would turn up at her favorite bars and demand that she come home immediately. Finally he threatened to divorce her. He met with her in Oscar Goodman's office and produced affidavits attesting to her addictions to alcohol and pills. He made it clear that her days of power and wealth were over and that she would lose custody of her son as well.

"Geri didn't want to lose everything," her sister, Barbara Stokich, said, "but Lefty would only take her back if she agreed to have another child and make a greater effort at staying away from the pills and liquor. I know Geri didn't want to have another child, but that was the only way she had to keep from getting thrown out on the street. She used to tell me he was a very powerful man. That he owned the judges and courts. That she wouldn't stand a chance against him.

"So she gave in and they had Stephanie in 1973, but that didn't solve their problems. In fact, in many ways it made things worse, because Geri always resented being forced to have Stephanie. Steven was wonderful. He was a boy. Geri loved having a boy. But being forced to have a child and for that child to be a girl—a girl in competition with her daughter Robin—made Geri very upset. She could never warm to Stephanie. And I don't think she ever forgave Frank for making her go through the second pregnancy."

◆ ◆ ◆

"I knew things weren't going all that well at home," says Lefty, "but I didn't know how bad they were for quite a while. Geri was still hard to figure. Some days she'd wake up happy, and other times you couldn't be around her. Everything you said was a fight.

"She didn't like it when I got on her about her drinking, and she didn't like it when I got on her about letting

Steven, who was seven, beat up on Stephanie, who was only three.

"Geri just adored Steven. She spoiled him rotten. He was her prize. A beautiful Gerber baby. She favored him over her daughter.

"Also, Geri was very strong minded. She didn't give a damn what people said or saw. And the people who knew us both tried to keep what they knew to themselves.

"For instance, I didn't know the hypnotic powers Lenny Marmor still had over Geri long after I married her. I knew they had to remain in touch because of Robin, but I didn't know that when Geri would go to Beverly Hills for a shopping trip with Allen Glick's wife, Kathy, she'd meet Marmor there.

"Geri and Kathy would take off in the Argent Lear once or twice a month. A limo would pick them up at the airport in Burbank, and they'd go to some store and start browsing. After a few minutes, Geri would just walk out. She wouldn't even tell Kathy where she was going. She would just disappear and then, three or four hours later, she'd find Kathy somewhere, either at the airport or somewhere, and they'd fly back together. No explanation. No nothing.

"Kathy Glick would tell her husband, but Allen, out of fear of getting involved or whatever, wouldn't tell me. So I really didn't know what was going on. Geri knew that no one was going to give her up, and she was right.

"Two of my closest friends, Harry and Bibi Solomon, two of the straightest people I've ever met in my life, finally tipped me off. Occasionally they would go out with Geri if I was working. One night, I made a reservation for them at the Dunes Hotel. It was the top restaurant. Music. Dancing. Gourmet food.

"Later, Harry came to me and said he had a confession to make. He was that kind of guy. He said, 'I know you're not going to forgive me, but I'm going to tell you anyway. I should have told you sooner. I've been busting ever since.' I said, 'Come on, Harry, get to the point.'

"He said: 'Let me tell you what happened. We were having dinner, and the music was playing. And a fellow came over to the table and asked Geri to dance, and I told the guy to hit the road. I said to her, 'What are you, crazy?' She said, 'Mind your own business,' and she gets up from her chair and walks over to the table where this guy was sitting and she says, 'I'll accept that dance.'

"Harry went bananas. He didn't know what to do. He asked for the check. When Geri finished the dance, Harry said, 'Geri, I'm not going to tell Frank about this. I will never be at your table again without Frank being present.' Geri didn't care. She thought they were nuts.

"Geri had always lived her own life. She didn't want to change. Looking back, I think the only real reason she stayed with Lenny Marmor all those years—and remember, this is a guy who never even sent her a birthday card—was that Lenny never tried to stop her from doing anything she wanted to do.

"That was his power over her. He didn't care what she did—as long as she made money. And I think Geri preferred that to somebody like myself who was always after her about this and that and the other thing.

"When Geri was hustling out here, Lenny didn't say, 'Stop! I love you. I don't want you doing that anymore.' No sir. Lenny let her do whatever she wanted. He didn't care. Drink? Sure. Take pills? Okay. Lenny never told her not to do anything, because she was making money.

"Then I come along, and probably for the first time in her

life, there's a guy laying down rules. Well, Geri never took to anybody's rules but her own."

♦ ♦ ♦

"Geri was a stoned gypsy rat," Tommy Scalfaro, who worked as Lefty's driver, said. "Her attitude depended upon her drug supply. When she took Percodan, she was friendly and warm. She'd want to give you money. She couldn't do too much. She had the kids all dressed and looking good.

"When she ran out of Percodan, she was mean. It was 'motherfucker' this and 'motherfucker' that. She'd start arguments with Lefty. It could really get ugly.

"She'd scream that Lefty was fucking this one or that one, and she was going to go out and do it too. 'I saw you with Donna,' she'd yell. 'I saw you rubbing asses with Mary,' she'd say. 'You keep that up and I'm going to go out and do some of that too.'

"Who the hell knew what she was doing? Lefty wasn't home all that much anyway. He was running the casinos and trying to stay ahead of the control board over his licensing. He was very fastidious. Everything had to be perfect. He was obsessed with getting his jackets and suits to fit perfectly. Once a week he would go back to his tailor and the guy would cringe. Lefty was always bothering him about a quarter of an inch or an eighth of an inch on his left side. Lefty adjusted his collar, sleeves, cuffs all day long.

"He had more suits than you can imagine. He had a closet thirty feet long and it was lined with suits. Then he had slacks and shirts and sweaters, and every one of them had to be perfect.

"And here he was married to a pill freak. He had a Percodan prescription for his ulcer, and she would send me to the pharmacy to get it refilled every two weeks. But he hardly ever touched them.

"When I first met Geri I could see she was going to be trouble. She kept referring to Lefty as 'Mr. R.' and started asking me questions. I could sense that she was getting me prepped to run her errands. In fact, right off the bat, she started suggesting that I go to Burger King and get her kids hamburgers. Pick up her dry cleaning. She'd not only send you on errands, but she'd try to belittle you in the way she'd give you your orders.

"If I hadn't put my foot down, she would've had me running all over town. I beefed to Lefty and she hated me from then on, but I didn't give a fuck.

"Geri would go to the malls. She'd go to California and shop. The maid and the maid's daughter raised the kids.

"Lefty spent all his time at the casino or meeting with people from the casino. A couple of times I had to pick him up at three in the morning and drive him to a 7-Eleven, where he'd meet with people from Chicago.

"He'd still be in his pajamas, and he'd jump out of our car and jump into the other guy's car. I didn't want to look too close, but sometimes it looked like Lefty was giving the orders, and sometimes it looked like he was taking them."

◆ ◆ ◆

"About a year after Allen Glick took over the corporation he had a party at his place in La Jolla," Lefty said, "and Geri and I went. There were about three hundred or four hundred people there.

"He had six Learjets taking people from Vegas to San Diego. This from a guy who had to borrow seven thousand dollars in pocket money from me when he first took over the company and the checks hadn't come through. He paid me right back, by the way.

"For the party, he gave me the use of two jets just for my friends.

"When we got there, it turned out Glick had me sitting next to him, and Geri was on my other side.

"On our way up there I had told Geri: 'No fucking drinking.' We had been jamming about her drinking problem for a while, but I didn't know what I was up against.

"At that point in my life I didn't drink, really. I didn't know that it was something some people couldn't control. I didn't know about uppers and downers. I was really very naive. I was a square. But I insisted we go to the party and she not have one drink. No booze. 'This is business,' I said. Oh yeah, oh yeah.

"So the party starts, and here comes a waiter with a tray and Dom Pérignon champagne, and she takes a glass. I say to myself, 'You bitch.' There are three hundred people there. I don't want her to get loaded and make a scene.

"She drinks the glass down. I'm looking at her, but she doesn't say shit to me. She doesn't acknowledge I'm even looking at her.

"Someone asks her to dance. She got up and danced. Then I saw the drink hit her. No one else could see it, but I knew her so well I could see the drink bang in.

"After the dance, she comes and sits down, and the waiter comes around again with the tray and she nods. The waiter puts a glass of champagne in front of her.

"I whisper to her: 'Listen, bitch, you put your lips to that glass, I'll knock you off that chair.'

"She looks at me and says, 'You don't have the guts.'

"'Yes I do,' I say.

"Now, I notice that Glick is looking at me, but he can't

hear what we're talking about. I said to her, 'I don't care how much of an embarrassment it causes, and I don't care if it costs me my job, but if you put that glass to your lips, you're going off that chair.'

"She grabs ahold of the glass with her hand. She holds it in her hand. I saw what was coming, so I leaned over and told Glick that I didn't want to upset him, but could he try and convince Geri to put down the drink, because if she didn't, I was probably going to have to do something that I would regret for the rest of my life.

"I told Glick, 'Allen, if she touches that drink, I'll have to knock her on her ass.'

"Glick got white. 'If she stonewalls me,' I told him, 'she's going down.'

"Glick says, 'Geri, will you do me a favor and listen to your husband?'

"She released the drink and turned to me under her breath and said, 'You sonofabitch, I'll get even with you for this.' You can imagine what a great party that turned out to be, but I don't think anyone knew. Geri was a great actress and a drunk. She held it. She didn't stumble around.

"When I married Geri I heard all the stories. But I didn't give a fuck what she did. 'I'm Frank Rosenthal,' I said, 'and I can change her.'"

◆ ◆ ◆

"They had lots of terrible fights," Barbara Stokich says. "They were both very strong willed and refused to back down. He used to threaten to take Steven away because of her drinking, but then they'd make up and he'd buy her a nice piece of jewelry.

"I remember she told me after one of their fights that she would rather die than give up booze. She loved it whenever

Frank had a glass of wine. He'd relax. She'd relax. I know, Frank started drinking just to please her, but he had ulcers and he couldn't really drink."

♦ ♦ ♦

"One day Tony had been to my house for a meeting," Lefty said. "He was about to leave, and he was dialing the phone to have one of his guys pick him up. Geri was about to take Steven and Stephanie somewhere, and she volunteered to give him a lift.

"Tony asked me if it was okay, and I said, 'Sure, go ahead.' I didn't think another thing about it.

"Then a week or so later, Tony called me up. He said he wanted to meet me. He was very serious. We made a date for about midnight or one in the morning. I picked him up at a certain corner and we began to drive around. We used to do this a lot before the heat got too tough.

"He said he had a story to tell me. Something he was really disturbed about. Something he'd seen when he'd been in the car with Geri and the kids. I didn't know what he was going to say. He was so solemn. Here's a guy who has done all kinds of things, and he's upset. I'm driving with my heart in my mouth. I'm swallowing muscle.

"He said that he'd gotten into the car with Geri and the kids, and Steven started picking on Stephanie. Kid stuff. Nothing serious. Then all of a sudden, Stephanie cried out, 'Mommy, help! Mommy, help!' Tony glanced into the back seat and saw that Steven was punching Stephanie really hard.

"'Geri,' Tony said, 'can't you stop that?'

"'It's not serious,' Geri said.

"Stephanie is screaming in the back seat. Tony turns around, and Steven has Stephanie on the floor in the back of the car and he's hitting her with his fists. Finally, Tony said, he had to force Geri to pull over and stop the fighting.

"Tony made me swear not to give him up to Geri, but he said he had to tell me what he saw. He said it was sick. It was like Geri was getting pleasure out of seeing her own kid get hurt."

◆ ◆ ◆

One night, Rosenthal took Geri to a dance at the country club. She looked beautiful. She was charming. "I was so proud of her," Lefty said. "She attracted attention wherever she went. She was that much of a knockout. It's one of the problems with marrying a ten, or even a nine. They're dangerous.

"Anyway, we're at the club, and a young executive I had hired, a smart, good-looking kid, walked up and complimented me on something. I don't even remember what. Then he turned to Geri and he said, 'Mrs. Rosenthal, you are the most gorgeous woman I have ever seen.'

"She thanked the kid. I smiled. I thanked him too. Sometimes Geri did that to people. She came on just a little bit. She encouraged him. Still, that kid had some balls. I fired him the next day."

13.

"He didn't have a clue about what they were doing or how they were doing it."

Allen Glick was now the second-largest casino owner in Las Vegas. He shuttled between Las Vegas and his home in La Jolla—a Norman-style mansion with tennis court and pool and a car collection that included a Lamborghini and a Stutz Bearcat with mink carpets and upholstery—in a Beechcraft Hawker 600. His office, on the Stardust penthouse floor, was decorated in purple-and-white, and there he sat, giving interviews about his brilliance as a businessman. He even told the press about his ability to keep still, barely moving, for extended periods. "I'm highly disciplined," he said.

Down the hall, Frank Rosenthal was the town's most important gambling executive—no matter what his job title. He had negotiated a $2.5 million contract. He planned to introduce a sports book at the Stardust, and he appeared before the state legislature as an expert witness. He was the first to allow women blackjack dealers on the Strip, and he doubled the blackjack drop in a year. He hired Siegfried and

Roy and their white tigers away from the MGM Grand by offering to build them a dressing room designed to their specifications; he threw in a white Rolls-Royce as a bonus. "The truth is I had bought the Rolls for Geri," Lefty said, "but she preferred the little Mercedes sports car, and it was just sitting in the garage, so I gave it to them." The two flamboyant magicians became the hottest and longest-lasting act in Las Vegas history.

But life in the Argent Corporation was far from peaceful. Instead of being lionized by the press, Glick was ridiculed as a conduit for Teamster money. Instead of being saluted for his innovative casino management, Rosenthal was constantly diverted by problems over his licensing. Crisis followed crisis. Glick and Rosenthal must have hoped that things would settle down and get better once the crisis of the day was solved—but there was always a new crisis the next day. The constant friction between the two men was the least of it. Rosenthal had been selected by the mob as the man to run the casinos, but his combativeness over his licensing problems attracted far more scrutiny than anyone wished. Allen Glick had been chosen as a mob front because he was thought to be squeaky clean; but even squeaky clean people have pasts. In 1975, Glick's San Diego real estate operation filed for Chapter 11, and Glick defaulted on a $3 million loan he had used to buy the Hacienda. Then a former real estate partner of Glick's turned up to threaten the entire setup at Argent.

The only thing that was working well was the skim. And for a long time, for the mob bosses back home, that was all that mattered. For years, skim money had been coming from the Stardust and Fremont casinos; the reason the mob needed a straight-arrow naif like Allen Glick in place was to keep the money coming.

The practice of skimming—the illegal siphoning off of

casino cash, cash that is not reported as tax or as corporate income—is probably as old as the first casino count. In the late forties and fifties, after Bugsy Siegel opened the Flamingo, the skim was used to secretly repay the original mob boss investors, who wanted their dividends in cash to avoid FBI and IRS problems.

There are dozens of ways to skim a casino, and most of them were in place long before Glick and Rosenthal took over. There were ticket skims, food and beverage kickbacks, theft from the count room. But amazingly, the slot machines had been largely untouched because of a serious logistical problem: the difficulty of hauling coins. One million dollars in quarters, for instance, weighs twenty-one tons. But as slot machines were becoming a larger and larger part of the casino gross, there had to be a way to get at that money.

So George Jay Vandermark was hired to run the slot machines at the Argent. Vandermark was perfectly qualified for the job: he was known as the greatest slot cheat who had ever lived. According to Ted Lynch, an acquaintance of Vandermark's, "Jay would take four months off a year and just go up and down the state opening slots. All he had to do was look at a machine and it would give up the drop. He loved doing it. I've seen him open ice machines at gas stations just for the pleasure of seeing the quarters roll out."

Vandermark was so well known as a crossroader and slot machine cheat that he was listed in Bob Griffin's Black Book, a who's who of casino cheats used primarily by casinos. In fact, when one of the Fremont casino executives first saw Vandermark walk into the casino, he attempted to have Vandermark thrown out; he reversed himself when he was told that Vandermark was his new boss.

One of the first things Vandermark did after taking over at Argent was to eliminate the controls that safeguarded the proper reporting of all cash pouring into the casino count room. He centralized slot supervision of all four Argent casinos and had the coins hauled from the Fremont, Hacienda, and Marina to the Stardust, where they were counted daily.

Vandermark also cut down on the number of auditors who were supposed to double-check that the wrapped and stacked coins corresponded in weight and value to the number of loose coins that had originally entered the count room.

When one auditor complained to Vandermark that he was being cut out of a critically important fiscal safeguard, he was told that it was none of his business.

The auditor later told the Gaming Control Board that he immediately went upstairs to complain to Argent treasurer Frank Mooney that he suspected Vandermark was stealing. According to the auditor, Mooney simply told him: "Do the best you can under the circumstances."

Among the innovations Vandermark brought to the Stardust was to rig the slot machine meters to falsely record one-third more in wins than were actually being paid out.

It was a brilliant stroke, because when the slot machines were emptied and the coins taken to the count room, the electronic scale used to weigh the coins had been rewired to underweigh the coins by one-third.

Vandermark now had one-third of the entire slot machine coin count available to skim, since the slot machines had been rigged to indicate that players had taken that amount home with them as wins.

But there was a problem: how to remove tons and tons of coins from the tightly guarded count room, let alone the casino. But Vandermark had a solution: he created auxiliary banks on the floor of the casino, where the skimmed coins were exchanged for paper money by slot machine change clerks. The auxiliary banks circumvented normal casino procedure: the paper bills were never taken to the cashier's cage to be counted in with the rest of the casino's paper money. Vandermark had small metal doors built into the side of the auxiliary banks so that after the clerk had slid the bills into a locked compartment inside the bank, Vandermark's men could open the door from the outside and take the bills away in large manila envelopes.

The manila envelopes from the auxiliary banks in each of the Argent casinos were then taken to Vandermark's office. Then the money was handed over to special couriers who made regular trips transporting the cash between Vegas and Chicago, where it was distributed to Milwaukee, Cleveland, Kansas City, and Chicago.

The Argent skim was blatant. No one sneaked around in the middle of the night with cash hidden under his shirt. People who worked in the count room and cashier's cage knew all about it. On one occasion, after the electronic scales were rewired, the switches were installed in back so that by flipping them the scale would underweigh the coin count by either 30 percent or 70 percent. During a particularly hectic day, one of Vandermark's guys flipped the wrong switch, and suddenly the scale was underweighing the coin count by 70 percent. Vandermark suddenly noticed how high the final count had become and realized what had happened. He screamed, "You dumb son of a bitch, you're gonna get us all in trouble. We can't steal that much."

The more experienced casino executives, who suspected that some kind of skim was in place, were experienced enough to understand that it was not in their interest to pursue such matters.

They well knew that even an unintended implied threat to security of the skim could be fatal.

♦ ♦ ♦

Edward "Marty" Buccieri, a distant cousin of Fiore Buccieri, was a pit boss at Caesar's Palace. An ex-con and former bookmaker, he had met Allen Glick when Glick first tried to buy the King's Castle in Lake Tahoe in 1972. Buccieri introduced Glick to Al Baron and Frank Ranney, the Teamster fund officials who later became instrumental in Glick's purchase of the Stardust in 1974. In 1975, after the skim had begun pumping out shopping bags of cash to the mob bosses who had arranged for the loan, Buccieri began harassing Glick. He wanted a finder's fee, and he asked for $30,000 to $50,000. "Buccieri had been pissed at Glick for years," Beecher Avants, the Metro homicide chief at the time, said. "Buccieri told anyone who listened that he first got Glick the pension fund loans and then Glick aced him out. Here was Glick owning four casinos, three hotels, jet airplanes, houses all over the place, while Marty's standing on his feet in the pit at Caesar's for an eight-hour shift."

One afternoon in May, Glick and Buccieri met at the Hacienda Hotel. Once again Buccieri raised the question of a finder's fee. The conversation escalated, and Buccieri grabbed Glick by the throat and threatened him. They were separated by security guards.

"I remember Glick coming back to Stardust afterwards," Rosenthal recalls. "He was red in the face. All excited. 'I need to see you,' he says. 'It's an emergency. Do you know Marty Buccieri?' I didn't know the guy. I knew his name at the time, but I didn't know him personally. I knew he was a distant relative of my friend Fiore Buccieri, maybe third cousins or something. But I had never met him.

"Glick's all upset. Very unusual for him. He says, 'Frank, I'll never let this happen again. And you have to help me.'

"I asked him what happened, and he goes on to tell me about Marty grabbing him by the throat and shoving him. I asked him why Buccieri would do such a thing, but Glick just wanted to describe what happened. He gave me some horseshit answer as to why, but it wasn't very clear. Later I sensed it was because Buccieri thought he'd been stiffed."

A week after the incident, Buccieri was about to start his car in the Caesar's Palace employee parking lot when two men armed with .25-caliber automatics with silencers shot him five times in the head.

"I went to talk to Glick about the murder," said homicide chief Beecher Avants. "Glick had one of those very opulent offices with a lot of mirrors. He had the latest electronic stuff all over the place. Shelves with books and plaques all over. Electronic stock market quote machines. Expensive lamps, bowls filled with flowers. It was a chairman's office. There was no place you could sit where you couldn't see yourself in a mirror. Glick was one of those very small guys who hid behind a very big desk.

"Glick said that he had had a 'disagreement' with Buccieri, but he denied that Buccieri had attacked him physically.

"As he talked, Glick sat very still. Very controlled. You'd get a businessman's answer to everything you asked. He was like a zombie. A nonperson. And the mirrors all around the room were reflecting the same nonperson. After a while I began to wonder which of these guys was the real Glick.

"Lefty was a different story. Lefty's office didn't have any mirrors. It was absolutely spotless. There was nothing on his desk at all. Behind the desk he had this poster with a great big 'NO!' taking up the top nine-tenths of space and a little 'yes' crammed down at the bottom.

"Lefty was standing behind his desk, and the only thing moving was this pencil, which he kept fiddling with. Lefty was one of those guys who didn't want to tell you anything, but he always had to let you know that he knew a lot more than he was ever letting on."

Beecher Avants and the homicide division spent months attempting to pin the Buccieri murder on Tony Spilotro, whom they had spotted a week before the murder talking to Teamster pension fund officials in the Tropicana coffee shop. Meanwhile, the FBI knew within days that Frank Balistrieri in Milwaukee had ordered the murder. According to a top informant in Milwaukee, Balistrieri had become convinced that Buccieri was a rat, and he went to the bosses in Chicago for approval for the hit. The murder was assigned to Spilotro and his crew. According to the informant, Spilotro angrily insisted to Balistrieri that Buccieri was not an informant; but he carried out the assignment anyway. He imported two shooters, one from California and one from Arizona. None of them was ever charged with the murder.

The FBI had most of it right. What they had no way of knowing at the time, but found out later, was that Marty Buccieri was killed because he posed a threat to Glick, and Glick was the mob's front man. A threat to Glick was seen as a threat to the bosses and the skim. Since preserving the sanctity and safety of the skim would never be given as the reason for killing Buccieri, the erroneous story that he had become a government informant was leaked within the mob by the bosses who ordered it. Even Spilotro, the man assigned the murder by Chicago, never knew the real reason behind Buccieri's murder.

◆ ◆ ◆

Six months after Buccieri's death, on November 9, 1975, a wealthy fifty-five-year-old woman named Tamara Rand was shot five times in the head and killed in the kitchen of her house in the Mission Hills section of San Diego. It was a professional hit. The killers used a .22-caliber with a silencer; there was no sign of forced entry and nothing was missing. The body was found by Rand's husband when he got home from work.

"The morning after the murder, I began getting calls from the press," said Beecher Avants of Metro homicide. "It turned out that Tamara Rand had just been to Las Vegas and had an argument with Allen Glick.

"Shades of Marty Buccieri! You can't have an argument with this man and not wind up somehow getting yourself killed. It turned out Rand had claimed to be some kind of a limited partner of Glick's and had gone to court to ask for a piece of the Stardust.

"She was a tough lady. She had flown into town in May to file her suit, and when she got back to San Diego she told her niece that she had had an argument with Glick. She also said that she had been threatened—but exactly who had threatened her was not clear. Her niece said she shrugged the threat off: "She was more interested in getting all her ducks in order for the lawsuit."

Glick had been quietly fighting Rand's claims that she was a partner in the Stardust for years, but her sudden mob-style murder pushed an obscure financial-page dispute onto the front page.

Glick found out that Tamara Rand had been murdered when he got off the Argent jet in Las Vegas and was greeted by reporters and TV cameramen asking his reaction to the murder. After expressing shock, he jumped into an Argent limousine and fled the scene. The next day the Argent public relations department issued a statement saying that while Glick had known Rand and had fond memories of her as a friend, he had no other comment.

The newspapers found their comment elsewhere. They discovered that a couple of months before her murder, Rand had escalated her civil actions against Glick by filing criminal fraud charges against him. And she had won an important and dangerous victory in court: she and her attorneys were given access to corporate documents pertaining to the Teamsters pension fund loan.

A week after the murder, the *San Diego Union* reprinted a letter Rand had written seven months before she was killed, detailing her relationship with Glick. It was not flattering. It accused Glick of living like royalty, of flying friends to football games in the company plane, of surrounding himself with a "parade of toys."

The publicity surrounding the murder—capped by an article in the *Los Angeles Times* reporting that Glick was one of several people being questioned in connection with it—forced Glick to appear before reporters at the Stardust executive offices to issue a statement countering the allegations.

"For the past two weeks, and in recent days," Glick began, "I have been the subject of one of the most malicious characterizations based upon utter falsehoods, devious innuendos and criminal-sounding inferences for no other reason than news sensationalism.

"I feel compelled to respond to these unconscionable attacks, not only because of the emotional stress caused my family, but out of respect for the over 5,000 Argent employees and my many associates and friends.

"To allow these recently publicized falsehoods to go unanswered by me would be a betrayal to the integrity of my family, my friends and the Argent Corporation.

"Two weeks ago a woman was found dead in her home in San Diego. Mrs. Rand was a past business associate of mine and most recently party to a lawsuit filed against a company I was active in, as well as me personally.

"The characterization and innuendos that I was connected with or had any knowledge of this terrible tragedy is an irresponsible and unethical practice of a public media.

"To infer that a business disagreement would in any way be related to a savage murder is contemptible. I am appreciative that certain members of Mrs. Rand's family have come forward to personally express their indignation at the false accusations.

"To associate me or any department or employee of my company with so-called 'organized crime' is false.

"The truth is I have never been convicted or guilty of crime greater than a traffic violation. The truth is that Argent operates three Las Vegas hotels and four casinos. The truth is that I was unanimously approved for licensing to operate these hotel casinos after an exhaustive and extensive investigation. . . . The truth is that I have tried to live a low-keyed social life based on a wholesome family relationship.

"Instead of recognizing these truths," Glick went on, "there have been continuous distortions by certain members of the news media.

"I have no newspaper, magazine or television station to openly use in a response to combat these false allegations, but I do have one fact on my side which cannot be distorted, maligned, nor falsified when it be known—that is the truth that Allen R. Glick has never, nor will ever be associated with anything other than what is lawful."

◆ ◆ ◆

According to the FBI, Tamara Rand was murdered to protect the skim; her murder was ordered by Frank Balistrieri. When Mrs. Rand won the right to subpoena documents relating to the Teamster loan to Glick and Argent, it was clear to Balistrieri the law case had to be stopped.

So Balistrieri took another trip to Chicago. This time he told the outfit bosses that Tamara Rand was on the verge of jeopardizing the entire setup. If the Teamsters' books on the Argent loan were to be subpoenaed, it was only a matter of time before individuals were subpoenaed. Rand was going to bring Glick and everyone else involved with the project down.

A Milwaukee informant later told the FBI that Balistrieri told the Chicago bosses, "We don't want any grief. We've got to keep the genius with a clean image. He will be messed up if she gets her lawsuit going."

No one was ever indicted for Rand's murder.

◆ ◆ ◆

And the skim went on.

It is estimated that Vandermark managed to skim between $7 million and $15 million out of Argent between 1974 and 1976, a sum that does not include what was skimmed from the Stardust's Race and Sports Book, credit department, or food and beverage accounts. There was no department under the control of the corporation's financial reserves that wasn't infiltrated by associates of the bosses back home.

For the men who arranged the loans, the casino skim was the equivalent of striking oil. The money came pouring out every month. In Glick's first year of operation, between August of 1974 and August of 1975, Argent reported a net loss of $7.5 million. This was startling news to Glick, since the corporation's total revenue was up $3.4 million, to $82.6 million during the same period. Glick was so out of the loop that he attributed the Argent casino losses to additional interest payments that hadn't been anticipated, higher depreciation and amortization costs, advances to subsidiaries, and even increased operating costs and expenses. "He didn't have a clue about what they were doing or how they were doing it," Bud Hall says.

14. ◆

"If you excluded everyone with something in their backgrounds from getting licensed, you'd probably have to terminate fifty percent of the people in this town."

"**A**fter I was fired at the Stardust, I got a job writing a column for the *Valley Times*, and I used my columns to drive Lefty and Glick crazy," Dick Odessky, the Stardust's ex–public relations director, recalls.

"I didn't make much money, but I had a load of fun. Here was this hundred-million-dollar corporation, one of the biggest in Las Vegas, surrounded by controversy.

"By the end of 1975, after just one year in operation, their chairman of the board was being questioned about his connections to two mob murders and whether he had the mob's influence in getting the Teamster loans, and the guy he had hired to run the casinos was so afraid he couldn't pass the test to get licensed that he was masquerading in any job title he could while pulling all the strings behind the scene.

"I still had lots of friends in the company, and there were lots of leaky faucets. One day I got a call from a woman who said Rosenthal walked into the pit and pointed to everyone around and fired them.

"She had given me good stuff about Argent and Frank before, but it had all been uncheckable. Now I had something I could check, and when I did, I found out that it was true.

"Lefty had done just what the woman said he'd done. It didn't make sense. That could have been enough for the control board to force him to go up for licensing. But he didn't seem to care. That's how bold and secure he felt about his position.

"Still, there were some guys on the control board who were on his case. In fact, two of them came by and wanted to know about my relationship to Frank. I told them that I didn't have any. I had been fired.

"'What about when he worked for you?' they asked.

"I told them he never worked for me. It was ludicrous.

"Then they showed me some cards that identified Frank Rosenthal as an assistant to the director of public relations. Since I was in charge of PR they assumed that he had worked for me. Instead, he had just had the cards printed up, thinking that would take care of everything.

"The agents went back with their report, but typically, nothing came of it.

"On another day I was tipped off that two control board agents were questioning Bobby Stella in the Stardust when he stopped them and said they'd have to talk to Rosenthal. He took them upstairs to see Lefty.

"The story I heard was that when the agents got to Rosenthal's office and started asking him the questions, Lefty stopped them.

"He asked his secretary to dial a number, and after talking for a few minutes, handed the phone over to one of the agents.

"'Commissioner Hannifin wants to talk to you,' Frank said, handing them the phone.

"The agents were shocked. Phil Hannifin was their boss. He was one of the strictest control board members. He refused to allow his agents to call him after office hours no matter how urgently they felt they might need his attention, and here was the man they saw as the biggest unlicensed gambler in town able to call Hannifin at home.

"Hannifin got on the phone and started screaming at the agents. He reminded them that there was an order at the control board that no agents were allowed to go into the Stardust without first clearing it with him personally.

"Hannifin chewed the agents out, and it made them so furious that they spread the rumor that Lefty's personal connection to Hannifin was allowing him to operate without a license.

"It was a serious enough rumor for me to call Hannifin for a comment. He denied that any such thing had ever taken place. He never chewed out his agents, he said, and certainly never in front of Frank Rosenthal in Rosenthal's office. I gave Hannifin credit for that."

◆ ◆ ◆

While Hannifin refuted the story told by the disgruntled agents, rumors about Rosenthal's close relationship with Hannifin had a basis in fact. Hannifin's admiration for Lefty's gaming expertise was well known. It was Hannifin's idea to allow casinos to have sports books, and he enlisted Rosenthal in the campaign; in the process, Hannifin became an admirer. "Back then you couldn't run a race and sports book in a casino," Hannifin said. "They were usually on the outside, and they had lots of problems. There was past-posting and the state never got a full count. There were two and three sets of books. You'd have a guy with a chalk-board, a phone line, and a lease, and at the first sign of trouble he was gone. I always felt it would be better if we brought the sports book into the casinos and that way we could regulate them. Lefty probably knew more about the sports book than anyone in Las Vegas, and I asked him if he'd help explain the advantages to the state legislature of getting the Gaming Commission to approve sports books. He loved the idea. I had him fly up to Carson City a half dozen times and testify. He was great. He liked getting on the stand and he was brilliant on the subject. He stood up and sold the system."

Lefty Rosenthal says, "Hannifin was onto something with bringing the sports books inside the casinos. In 1968, when I first got here, there were only two or three sports books in Vegas where you could bet sports. But there was about to be a revolution. Television was about to start covering sports, and every year after the first Superbowl in 1967, the interest in betting sports quadrupled.

"Before then, there was no Monday-night football. Most sports books were devoted to horse bettors, and the places looked more like stables than what you see today. They were very inhospitable places. Sawdust joints. Most of them had the old chalkboards. There were no amenities.

"So when we got the okay, I knew exactly what to do. I had spent my life in those places and knew what they needed. I can't tell you the hours I spent going over the design, just the hours going over the right kind of seat to buy, the space, height, the boards, the TV screens. I wanted them to be like theaters.

"But I'm working with people who didn't know what I was talking about. There had never been a sports room like this before.

"It was nearly nine thousand square feet with room for

six hundred people, including two hundred and fifty individually lighted theater seats with their own desks and dimmer controls for our regular players.

"We put in a bar measuring nearly a quarter mile of inlaid wood and mirror and the largest projection-lighted board system in the world. We had a forty-eight-square-foot color television screen, and since horseplayers were still our biggest bettors, we had entry boards for five separate racetracks covering a hundred and forty square feet. It was the largest and most expensive system of its kind anywhere, and we had it all. Quinellas, exactas, futures, daily doubles, and parlay betting, along with the regular win-place-show bets.

"I was in a great position. The sports books began making money for the casinos and, therefore, for the state. In some circles I was golden. I had a shot."

♦ ♦ ♦

Phil Hannifin was genuinely grateful to Lefty Rosenthal for his help. He told him he would vote to license him. And he gave Lefty Rosenthal some sound advice. Keep a low profile, he said. Lay low. You'll have a better shot at getting your license if you stay in the background.

But in June 1975, an article about Allen Glick appeared in *Business Week*—and it was the nail in the coffin. "Glick is the financial end," Lefty was quoted as saying, "but policy comes from my office."

No one could believe it. The Gaming Commission had tried for months to catch Lefty running the Stardust, and he had repeatedly insisted that he was simply the executive assistant, or the public relations person, or the food and beverage chieftain. Whenever an investigator showed up, Rosenthal would vanish from the casino. Now here was

proof, in black-and-white: Rosenthal made policy. If he made policy, the consequences were clear: he would have to apply for a gaming license. Naturally, Lefty claimed he was misquoted. No one believed him. "The real question is should he be licensed," said Robert Broadbent of the Clark County Gaming and Licensing Board. "And if he shouldn't, why not? And if he is not licensed, and cannot be licensed, should he be there?"

Around the same time, Rosenthal made another mistake. "Allen Glick asked me to check out the Hacienda," he said. "He wanted me to evaluate it from top to bottom. I did, and my report back to Glick was very negative. There was malfeasance and mismanagement. There were glaring violations of the Gaming Commission's rules."

Lefty decided he had to get rid of a Hacienda executive. Lefty didn't know about the executive's friendship with Pete Echeverria, chairman of the state's Gaming Commission. "I should have known, but I didn't," says Lefty.

"When the man was fired he told everyone that Pete Echeverria would take care of Frank Rosenthal good and quick. I heard the threat after the fact. I paid no attention to it."

◆ ◆ ◆

Peter Echeverria was a fifty-year-old attorney who boasted that he had "never rolled a set of dice, played a hand of twenty-one, or put a dollar on a wheel" in his life, but he felt that "gambling was an essential part of our state economy and it should be run like a real straight, honest business."

A former state senator who had worked on the State Planning Board, Echeverria had been raised in Ely, Nevada, had graduated from the University of Nevada and Stanford Law School, and had been practicing real estate invest-

ment law for twenty-five years when Governor Mike O'Callaghan chose him for the state's top gaming post in October 1973.

"I knew that Echeverria was going to be my nemesis, and I got ahold of Phil Hannifin," Rosenthal said. "I got him in the coffee shop at the Stardust. I asked him about my possibilities going for a gaming license as a key employee. I told him about my past, everything. If it was hopeless, I told him I had no problem in backing off. I'd take another position. I said, 'I'm talking to you as a friend.' I said I had a lot of respect for him. 'Can I go before the control board and get a fair hearing in view of my background?'

"That's all I wanted to know. Can I get a fair shake? Now, Hannifin was a tough guy, and he said, 'Here's what I'll tell you.' He said, looking me in the eye, 'I'll vote for you with a clear conscience.'

"I'm looking at a Christmas present. The key license would allow me to be at the top of the corporation officially. I'd be able to avail myself of stock options. Everything.

"Hannifin gave me a fifty-fifty chance at passing. Echeverria had been putting the pressure on Hannifin and the control board to get me to come up for licensing.

"If I had a shot I had to go for it. The opportunity was too great. Argent hired a private detective firm—all ex-FBI agents—and they received a hundred thousand dollars in front to find out everything they could about me. I wanted to know everything the control board investigators would know if they tried to take me down.

"The FBI guys did an incredible job. They were tough. They wouldn't take the assignment unless I gave them my approval that if they came up with anything serious against me, they could take it to the authorities.

"I began to feel pretty good. Even the Justice Department

had finally gotten around to officially dismissing the Rose Bowl charges against us, and they dated back to 1971.

"I went to Glick and said I was filing for a key employee's license.

"But a couple of weeks before the hearing, Hannifin stopped coming by. I didn't hear from him. I couldn't get him on the phone. I'd call twice a week and he was never there. One night I got his wife. She said he'd return my call, but he never did. I had a feeling I was going to be double-dealt.

"The control board hearings were held in Carson City, which was very usual and inconvenient. We had to fly up there with two or three Lears so we could accommodate my lawyers and most of my witnesses, who lived and worked downstate in Las Vegas.

"The hearings were held in a huge room. I remember watching Linda Rogers, Oscar Goodman's secretary, wheeling in a cart with stacks of my material on it."

The hearings took over two days on the second-floor state office building in Carson City. Lefty was asked about everything—about Eli the Juice Man, about his alleged bribery of the North Carolina football player, about his relationship with Tony Spilotro. "Lefty answered the Commission's questions at great length," said Don Diglio, a columnist for the *Las Vegas Review Journal*, "sometimes at too great a length."

According to Diglio, when Lefty responded to questions he got so wound up that he could not stop himself from going on and on with his explanations and justifications. When asked about his relationship with Spilotro, for instance, Lefty began a long rambling monologue: he said he had known Spilotro since Spilotro's birth, that their parents had known each other, but that since moving to Las Vegas they had nothing to do with each other socially or professionally.

"I recognize," Lefty testified, "that with all the adverse publicity and the allegations against Tony—and I state to you that I do not agree with them. I have read where Mr. Spilotro was here to watch out for me, over me, and every other thing. I recognized that I was getting into a very sensitive area of gaming, and I became familiar with the control board, the commission, and the business as a privileged industry.

"But then I also recognized my right or my family's right, the fact that I was married and fortunate enough to have two healthy children, that I better get with it.

"I have tried to do that from the very day that I walked into the Stardust. I think my records, I think the chair"—and here, according to Diglio, Rosenthal looked pointedly at Hannifin—"would agree that my record has been such that I am nearly perfect—or close to perfect.

"I think Tony recognized that. Tony came to Nevada on his own. He has the right to choose to live with his family wherever he wishes. I respect that right. I think he respects mine.

"Tony has avoided Frank Rosenthal and I have avoided Tony, to the point where I cannot recall Tony Spilotro walking into an Argent property. I just can't. If you ask me, 'Frank, did you have any arrangement or agreement with Tony about not meeting?' the answer is absolutely not. I think it was respect, and I appreciate the respect."

Rosenthal defended himself for five hours; the full hearings took two days. Allen Glick testified too, and he admitted that he hadn't known all of the details about Rosenthal's background when he hired him. But, he said, he had been pleased with Rosenthal's work and would make the same decision today. "If you excluded everybody with something in their backgrounds from getting licensed," Glick told the board, "you'd probably have to terminate fifty percent of the people in this town."

"During the second day of questioning," Jeff Silver, the control board's chief counsel, said, "it was apparent that Lefty did not have enough answers for the questions we were asking. I asked one of the board members, Jack Stratton, if they were going to deny the poor guy a license anyway, why put him through all these questions? We stopped the hearings."

On January 15, 1976, after the two days of hearings, the control board made its recommendation to deny Lefty his license.

♦ ♦ ♦

"When the other two board members voted to deny my licensing," Lefty said, "Hannifin refused to vote on the record. But after the other two members gave their speeches and asked that the vote be unanimous, he went along.

"After the hearing Hannifin came over and stuck his hand out. 'I'd like to apologize to you and your family,' he said, 'but I did what I had to do.' I know Hannifin felt bad. He knew I had been dealt a bad deal, but he was just a little school teacher and parole officer by profession, and the governor owned him.

"A week later, my lawyers and I went back to Carson City to appeal the board's ruling, but it was obvious Echeverria was going to slam us. As soon as my lawyers began to make their arguments, you could see him very ostentatiously put up his arm and look at his watch and yawn. It wasn't much of an appeal. The commission backed up the control board unanimously."

"I should have been licensed," Lefty says. "Hannifin had

my file, my entire file, and there was nothing in that file that should have kept me back from being licensed as a key employee. There were guys licensed in town you wouldn't believe. But that's not my business. I can't point to anybody else. I had to convince them that I was okay.

"But meanwhile I had run four casinos. No one had four casinos. No one in town had the kind of floor responsibility I had. If the food was not right at the Stardust or something was happening at the Fremont, I had to be there. I had people trained to call me at all hours. Many's the time I'd have to get up and go back to one of the casinos at three in the morning.

"I remember I kept hearing that the short-order cook at the Stardust was serving terrible stuff. The complaints got to my office. They said that he didn't scramble the eggs. He'd just send them out wet, no matter what the waitresses and customers wanted.

"One day I got up at four in the morning and went to the restaurant. I sat down and ordered scrambled eggs and told the waitress she was fired if she told the cook I was placing the order. When they came out they were wet. I got up and went into the kitchen and fired him on the spot. Boy, did I get trouble from the union for that.

"But I couldn't tolerate incompetence. I was very rigid. Stupid. I think it came from years of handicapping. From years of gathering information eighteen hours a day, poring over fifty pounds of papers a day, talking to sources all over the country. It's a kind of obsessional business, and I see now that I took those same work habits into a more social environment."

The commission's refusal to license him was supposed to be the end of Lefty Rosenthal at the Stardust. Lefty was to be out of gaming. No more masquerades behind different job descriptions like public relations director or food and beverage director. He was given forty-eight hours to clear out his desk. And he did. On January 29, 1976, Lefty moved out of his newly refurbished office at the Stardust and went home. The next day control board investigators learned that his $2.5 million ten-year contract was still in effect.

Part Three

CRAPPING OUT

◆

15. ♦

"Fuck it. Drill it open."

Lefty Rosenthal had no intention of either quitting or
giving up. He established a war room at home and embarked on a dual campaign—first, to continue to exert as
much influence as he could over the casinos, and second, to
start a series of legal battles with state gaming authorities
to challenge the power of the state to even issue gaming
licenses. These highly publicized and increasingly bitter
court cases went on for years. They seemed to take on a life
of their own. From local courts to state courts to state appeals courts to U.S. district courts to U.S. appeals courts and
all the way to the U.S. Supreme Court, Lefty led a parade of
legal maneuverings. He won some. He lost some. When he
won, he moved back into his offices at the Stardust. When
he lost, he moved out.

"Lefty loved it," Murray Ehrenberg, his Stardust casino
manager, said. "He handicapped his lawsuits the way he
handicapped football games. He started reading. He started

researching. He started driving his lawyers crazy. He was in his element."

It started out simply. In January of 1976, when Lefty was first ordered out of the Stardust, he continued to run the casino. Murray Ehrenberg and Bobby Stella were still in place. He hooked up the red telephone between his bedroom and the Stardust pit. Before his dismissal, thousands of dollars of Argent money had been spent to hook his home to the casino's electronic system, including the Eye in the Sky surveillance cameras; he was able to watch every table game in the Stardust on television sets in his house.

"We knew he was watching," Shirley Daley, a retired Stardust waitress, said, "because all of a sudden Murray or Bobby would start criticizing you about the kinds of petty stuff that could only have come from Lefty—like if a waitress took too long to bring up the drinks, or if a dealer didn't call out for the pit boss when he changed a hundred-dollar bill."

"He was supposed to be out," Ehrenberg said, "but he was still giving the orders. One night, I remember, Lefty called all of us to his house. There must have been fifteen cars parked outside. Gene Cimorelli. Art Garelli. Joey Cusumano. Bobby Stella Sr. Every casino boss in the joint was there.

"What happened was that I had caught one of the blackjack dealers stealing about sixteen hundred dollars, and I wanted to fire him. But Bobby Stella wanted me to let it go. I didn't want to give the guy any grief, just tell him to get lost. But Bobby went to bat for him. We were standing around in the living room while Lefty listened to both of us. We had pit bosses and shift bosses there because they had seen it happen. After listening to everybody, Lefty went along with me. Bobby got very upset. He didn't want the guy to be fired, but Lefty slapped him right down.

"Lefty said, 'Bobby, do you want to talk to the animals?' Bobby knew what Lefty meant. Bobby used to run crap games for Momo Giancana. He shut right up."

♦ ♦ ♦

Allen Glick became so concerned about Lefty's meetings with the casino staff that he confronted them. "They all denied it or said the visits were purely social," Glick says. "Finally I hired a private detective agency to follow them. I wanted to see how often these 'social meetings' took place.

"Right after I got a report back from the private investigators, I got a call from Frank Balistrieri. He was very agitated. He said he wanted to meet with me. I was surprised, because during this period, obviously, I had had very limited contact with him. He said it was so important that he was coming to Las Vegas personally. He said he'd call me as soon as he got to town.

"We met in a suite at the MGM Hotel. Balistrieri was there along with a man I didn't know. I could tell he was nervous when I walked in. He said this was a difficult trip for him to make. It was something he didn't want to do, but something he was asked to do, because of how well he knew me.

"He said that I had committed an act that he and his associates not only frowned upon, but it was about the worst thing in his estimation that I could do. 'But for me,' he said, 'you wouldn't be here. You would have been killed.' He said if I ever did anything like what I'd done again, he could not guarantee my safety.

"I still didn't know what he was talking about until he tossed the private detective's report on the table. It turned out that the detectives I had hired to watch the meetings at Lefty's also worked for Tony Spilotro, and they had given Spilotro copies of everything they had given me."

♦ ♦ ♦

Within a few weeks, the control board caught on to Lefty's midnight meetings and Eye in the Sky peekaboo maneuverings, and they said that Argent's own gaming license was in jeopardy if Lefty continued to flaunt the control board's ruling. As a result, Lefty began to concentrate most of his energies on the legal battle for reinstatement.

In February of 1976, he and his lawyer, Oscar Goodman, brought a federal suit against the Nevada Gaming Commission charging that it was an unconstitutional body and that its decision against him was arbitrary and capricious.

He then brought another suit against the control board in Las Vegas District Court, challenging the board's power to deny him the right to make a living. Lefty said his record in Nevada was clean and he had long ago paid whatever debt he owed to society. His plan was to legally challenge the Gaming Commission and force it either to give him his license or ease up on its enforcement, just as he had forced Hannifin and the control board members to ease off back in 1971, when Shannon Bybee had wanted to yank his work card.

Gaming Commission chairman Pete Echeverria was outraged that Lefty would challenge the gaming authorities in court. He said that Lefty should never be licensed, as far as he was concerned. "In my three and a half years with the state Gaming Commission," Echeverria said, "I have never found an applicant whose background was so repugnant." Echeverria said Lefty was denied licensing because of his "notorious background and associations, and just because you pay a debt to society, that doesn't entitle you to a Nevada gaming license."

Oscar Goodman fought back, claiming that Echeverria and the control board "violated just about every concept stated by the due process clauses."

Goodman said, "Frank Rosenthal is a modern-day Horatio Alger. He is without peer in the industry." He said that Rosenthal had been told about the charges against him only six days before the hearing convened.

"Mr. Rosenthal did not have an opportunity to face one live witness," Goodman said. "He faced reports that were fifteen years old. The time has come in Nevada that somebody in Mr. Rosenthal's position is entitled to fairness."

♦ ♦ ♦

With Lefty now spending more time at home, life around the house became very tense. Lefty and Geri harped at each other all day long; their already fragile relationship fluctuated between plate-tossing brawls and icy standoffs during which they barely spoke. Geri's drinking—which she always denied was a problem—made matters worse.

"Frank had always been very generous," Geri's sister, Barbara Stokich, said. "Now he started to complain about everything she did. She didn't cook his lamb chops right—he had a special way he liked her to do his lamb chops. She didn't pay enough attention to the kids. Geri was no bargain, but Frank could be very trying too."

"Geri started putting on a show," Lefty said, "and I didn't like it. If there was a birthday party for one of the kids, for instance, it wouldn't be at home like in the past. Now she'd have it at the Jubilation or the country club, and it would be outrageously lavish. I enjoyed the family moments, because they were about my family, but I didn't enjoy the phony lavishness."

Their most strenuous battles usually resulted in either Lefty or Geri slamming out of the house.

"When Lefty was partying everyone in the town knew about it," Murray Ehrenberg, his casino manager, said. "The word got around. Lefty was out with this one and that one, and Geri would hear about some dancer getting a ten-thousand-dollar bracelet or even a car, and there would be hell to pay.

"I think it was Lefty's generosity with his girlfriends that drove Geri the craziest, not the fact that he had girlfriends. It was like all his little presents should go to her, not some lead dancer or showgirl. She'd hear about it at the manicurist. The hairdresser. She'd pick it up from her friends. I mean, it was no secret.

"And I think part of why he did it so openly was to drive her nuts. But then they'd make up and he'd give her another diamond necklace or ring, and things would be quiet for a while."

When Geri stormed off for a night or a few days Lefty never knew where she went. He always suspected that she went to Beverly Hills to meet up with the man he thought of as her Svengali, Lenny Marmor. He also suspected that she saw her ex-flame Johnny Hicks, the Las Vegas tough guy with whom Lefty had gotten into the brawl on the Flamingo dance floor back in 1969.

Barbara Stokich believes that Geri stayed in the marriage only because of her fear of losing custody of Steven. And, of course, her jewels. Barbara said Geri valued her jewels as though they were children. Whenever Geri was feeling depressed, she would go over to the Las Vegas Valley Bank's Strip branch and ask to see their three safety deposit boxes.

In the privacy of a small viewing room, Geri could go through her jewels piece by piece. Counting them. Fondling them. Trying them on. Geri had over $1 million in jewelry in the safety deposit boxes. Some of her favorite pieces included a flawless round diamond valued at $250,000; a large star ruby valued at $100,000; a large flawless 5.98-carat pear-shaped diamond ring valued at $250,000; a diamond dinner ring set valued at $75,000; a couple of diamond-and-opal Piaget watches valued at $20,000 each; and a pair of diamond earrings by Fred valued at $25,000.

There was another place Geri went for solace in this period: the Spilotro house. There she and Nancy would drink vodka and share their domestic woes. Geri would complain about Lefty. Nancy would complain about Tony.

Geri also took her complaints to the only man she felt had influence over her husband—Tony Spilotro. She'd meet him at the Villa d'Este, a restaurant owned by Joseph "Joe Pig" Pignatelli. "They'd be at the bar or in a booth," said Frank Cullotta. "She always drank vodka on the rocks. I'd watch him nod his head and try to reason with her. I'd be across the room watching them and they'd be talking for an hour sometimes, and then she'd get up and leave. I knew how long they talked because I had business with him and I could only go talk to him after she left."

◆ ◆ ◆

In February of 1976, shortly after Lefty had been ousted from his post, the auditors claimed they called Frank Mooney, the Stardust's secretary-treasurer, to tell him that the slot machine coin-counting scales were off by one-third. Mooney later told the Securities and Exchange Commission

he didn't remember getting such a call, but it was the first signal that there was trouble in the Stardust count room.

At the time, Glick's attention was focused on raising $45 million in additional Teamster money for his planned renovations and on hiring a replacement for Lefty—the latter a task made considerably easier by the fact that he was told whom to hire. Allen Dorfman, the pension fund's chief financial advisor, had summoned Glick to Chicago. Frank Balistrieri had told Glick that Dorfman had a replacement for Rosenthal in mind.

Dorfman, an athletic fifty-three-year-old ex–gym teacher, had been left in charge of the pension fund in 1967 when his close friend Teamster president James R. Hoffa was sent to prison. Dorfman had gotten close to Hoffa through his father, Paul "Red" Dorfman, a Teamster business agent who had friends in the outfit and helped Hoffa take over the union.

The younger Dorfman was barred from having any official position in the union because of a 1972 conviction for taking a kickback to arrange a pension fund loan. Still, he controlled the pension fund's billions in 1976, when Glick went to see him. Through mob associates all around the country, Dorfman secretly controlled many of the fund's trustees, and he used his Amalgamated Insurance company as a cover. Amalgamated even occupied the second floor of the pension fund's Bryn Mawr Avenue building near Chicago's O'Hare Airport, where it employed about two hundred people and made over $10 million a year just processing Teamster disability claims. Dorfman also handled the insurance for companies seeking pension fund loans.

Glick said that after meeting with the pension fund lawyers upstairs, he went to Dorfman's second-floor office where Dorfman informed him that Lefty's job would go to Carl Wesley Thomas. Thomas was a politically connected

and experienced forty-four-year-old casino executive. It was a surprisingly pleasant suggestion.

Carl Wesley Thomas was one of the most highly respected casino executives in Nevada. In his conservative business suits and his steel-rimmed glasses, Carl Thomas looked more like a Carson City banker than a Las Vegas casino boss. He had moved to Las Vegas in 1953 and had risen, in ten years, from blackjack dealer in the Stardust to minority partner at the Circus Circus casino, which was owned at the time by Jay Sarno, one of the great casino impresarios. In addition to Circus Circus, the town's first kiddie-friendly casino, Sarno built Caesar's Palace, the most successful casino in Las Vegas history. Sarno was a great friend of Allen Dorfman's and had used Teamster pension fund loans to build both casinos.

Gaming officials throughout the state breathed a sigh of relief when they heard that Carl Thomas was going to replace Frank Rosenthal at Argent. There was no question among them that Allen Glick had made a brilliant, purifying choice for his troubled corporation.

What Glick did not know about Carl Thomas—what almost no one in the state knew about him—was that in addition to his impeccable reputation as the first of the new breed of Nevada casino executives, Carl Thomas was also the greatest casino skimmer in America at the time.

He and the tiny crew of casino executives he took everywhere had devised such deft methods of siphoning millions of dollars out of casinos that no one ever even suspected there was money missing. Sometimes Thomas and his guys skimmed for the owners; sometimes they skimmed for the secret owners; and sometimes they skimmed the money for themselves.

Carl Thomas had learned at Circus Circus, where skimming the casino was part of his job. The practice had started under Sarno even before Thomas got there and had been established to repay the fees on the Teamster pension fund loans. Back in the early 1960s, the skimming of casinos was a relatively common practice, and Thomas proved so able and discreet that he soon became casino manager. During this period, Sarno introduced him to Allen Dorfman, who was in Las Vegas at least once a month, on the prowl for entrepreneurs looking for Teamster loans to build new casinos.

Thomas and Dorfman became good friends, and in 1963, Dorfman invited Thomas to Chicago for his fortieth birthday party. There were about three hundred guests at the party, many of them from Las Vegas, but in the middle of the affair, Allen Dorfman made a special point of introducing Thomas to Nick Civella. Civella, Thomas learned, was one of the men to whom the skim was delivered, and Thomas soon found himself meeting secretly with the mob boss whenever Civella came to town.

◆ ◆ ◆

"Let me tell you a little bit about skims," said Frank Rosenthal. "There is no casino, in this country at least, that is capable of defending itself against a skim. There are no safeties. You can't prevent a skim if a guy knows what he's doing. On the other hand, there's two kinds of skims. One is what we call bleeding. And that's horseshit. You've got a guy who's a twenty-one manager. He's going to knock out his three hundred dollars, four hundred dollars a night. That's bleeding a casino. That only takes two people—the manager and a runner, the guy who runs the chips back and forth from the cage to the games. Now when you get into the organized skim, you're talking about something very, very sophisticated. You couldn't do it in my day unless the whole casino was corrupted. This isn't a question of standards, rules, and regulations set down by the control board and the commission. Because those fellows, they didn't have a clue. An organized skim calls for at least no less than three people. At a high level. You cannot do it without. You just can't do it. If there's a way, I'd like someone to tell me how, because he would have an exclusive patent on it."

◆ ◆ ◆

Dennis Gomes, the twenty-six-year-old chief auditor for the control board, had learned from informants who worked at the Stardust that there was something going on with the slot count. Gomes had always been curious why Argent would have ever hired anyone as notorious as Jay Vandermark to run the slot machine operations. It was not unusual for casinos to hire crossroaders, card mechanics, and dice cheats. What better way was there to catch a crossroader than to use other crossroaders familiar with the routines? But it was very unusual, perhaps even foolhardy, to put a world-class crossroader like Jay Vandermark in a position of fiduciary responsibility.

Gomes was certain Argent's slot operation was being skimmed. But he needed help. As the board's chief auditor, he was in charge of a handful of accountants who kept routine tabs on casino tax payments and fees. Nobody at the control board was even looking for second and third sets of books. Dennis Gomes did not even have an investigative auditor who could use the casino's own figures to unmask fraud or worse. The control board had never bothered to fill that position.

Gomes decided to change all that, and he put an ad in the *California Law Journal*. "I just did it," he said. "To this day I don't know why."

Dick Law, a bored twenty-eight-year-old CPA and a non-practicing attorney, answered the ad. Law, who had been a philosophy major in college, thought the job would be a challenge. He was hired.

Law and Gomes began digging into the Argent slot machine books and compiling and cross-referencing the data and the lists of people and jobs with the names of organized crime figures.

"Everything we found," Gomes said, "led to something else."

Gomes and Law started making unannounced audits of the Argent casinos. They found a number of small-scale scams—two-person arrangements in which a casino slot employee with a slot key would rig the machines to hit jackpots for a second person, an outsider, who would simply walk up and win the money.

Then Gomes began monitoring the auxiliary banks on the Stardust casino floor and comparing the number of plays shown on the machines with the totals listed by the Argent auditors. Huge discrepancies began to emerge. Clearly the only purpose for such banks was to circumvent sending the slot machine cash into the count room and cashier's cage, where it could come under the scrutiny of people not in on the skim.

Gomes and Law became even more suspicious when they discovered that Argent's other casinos, the Fremont and Hacienda, sent their slot revenue to the Stardust for tabulation, despite the fact that they had their own count rooms.

On May 18, 1976, Gomes, Law, and two Gaming Control Board agents walked into the Stardust cashier's cage and demanded to see the books. The cage employees were stunned.

"We waited until five o'clock," Gomes said, "because we

knew that the control board would be out of town. We had snitches inside who had told us there was a special fund set up and that they were siphoning slot money out of the casino.

"When we went in we asked for the special fund. The shift boss turned white and said he didn't know anything about any 'special fund.' He called the slot manager at home. The slot manager said he didn't know anything about a special fund either. I got on the phone and said, 'Listen, you asshole, I don't care what you call it, I want to see where the money that isn't kept in the coin room is kept.'

"We finally got to two steel cabinets behind the change booth. We asked for a key and they finally found one, but it only opened one side. It was filled with coins. Somehow, nobody could find the key for the other side. Finally, I told the slot manager he better get me a key or we were going to drill it open.

"'Fuck it,' he said. 'Drill it open.'

"So we drilled it open and inside we found stack upon stack of hundred-dollar bills. And when we checked, we found that the coins were nowhere to be found in the general ledgers. It was all skim, and it was being held there until the change girls converted it to paper at the auxiliary banks."

One of the Fremont employees later told Gomes that the Toledo Company scale fixer who had quit the scale company and gone to work for Vandermark at the Fremont, had gotten a call from Vandermark shortly after the raid at the Stardust and was told: "Clean it up. They've hit the Stardust."

As a result, the Fremont's auxiliary bank was dismantled and the parts stored in the hotel's basement before Gomes's four-man raiding party could finish their work at the Stardust and ride downtown to the Fremont.

"While all this was going on we kept trying to reach Jay Vandermark," Gomes said. "Vandermark had been in the casino when we arrived, but at the first sign of trouble he had ducked out through the kitchen and was hiding out at Bobby Stella's house."

Vandermark spent the night at Bobby Stella's house, and the next morning flew to Mazatlán, Mexico, under an assumed name. Anyone who inquired after him at the Stardust was told that he had gone off for a few weeks' vacation.

♦ ♦ ♦

The raid of the Stardust uncovered the biggest slot skim in the history of Las Vegas and sent the hotel into complete chaos. Glick at first called the charges of skimming nonsense and then charged that he was the victim of "embezzlement by ex-employees." The Gaming Control Board agreed: "We are not talking about skimming," one of the control board members said, "because for that we would have to show that management participated. We are looking for the possibility of embezzlement."

The word "embezzlement"—rather than "skim"—was worth millions of dollars to Allen Glick: the casino's license would have been revoked if the control board had decided that Argent's management had participated in the skim.

The control board did issue a subpoena for Vandermark, even though there wasn't the remotest possibility that a man who had fled under an assumed name and was hiding somewhere in Mexico was likely to turn up.

"After the raid," Dick Law said, "it was apparent that everyone knew what was going on at Argent, but no one wanted to do anything about it. The investigations followed. I tried connecting Argent and Glick to the mob. I knew it was there. I had accumulated every check ever written to Glick's Saratoga Development Corporation. I had a wall-high stack of documents. It was clear to me that Glick might have known about the skim.

"But what did Glick do? He kept up the facade that he did not know about the skim, and he even insisted upon applying for the insurance that covered the loss against embezzlement. I think he eventually collected something.

"Meanwhile, the control board kept asking me where my report was and I kept giving them bits and pieces while I tried to tie up the mob and Argent. I knew it was there. I just had to prove it."

♦ ♦ ♦

Carl Thomas began to work at the Stardust a couple of months before the casino was raided by Gomes and Law. "It was complete chaos," he later recalled. Thomas discovered—to his amazement—that in addition to Vandermark's slot machine count, there were a dozen different skims going on, and he dutifully reported all of them to Civella.

"I was appalled at what was happening," Thomas later said. "I wanted to tighten everything up. I told Nick it was like having a bucket with twenty holes going every way. They had a prepaid advertising contract of three hundred thousand dollars—you paid for the advertising before you actually got it. . . . The food and beverage was a joke. . . . Race and sports bookmaking was a shambles. . . . It looked to me there could have been anywhere from four hundred to five hundred thousand a month missing out of the race and sports bookmaking alone. . . . Some room clerks were taking reservations and when a person paid in cash for the bill, they'd pocket the money and destroy the record that the person had even stayed there."

Thomas also told Civella about a casino theater ticket scam, where the cash for at least six hundred tickets a night was being stolen because the seats assigned to those tickets had never been listed as even existing on the theater's blueprints or construction plans. Thomas suggested they stop all the money leaks, and Civella agreed with everything he recommended—except for the theater seat ticket scam. "Let the theater alone," he told Thomas.

"As far as skimming the money was concerned," Thomas continued, "I wanted to take the money out of the boxes, the cash money—no fill slips, no food and beverage, no entertainment; just one way, out of the money boxes. Nick thought it was a good idea. He said everything takes time.

"Next I asked Allen Dorfman to come in. I said there was a major problem and it was just a matter of time before there would be another huge investigation like the slot investigation going on. . . . Sometimes I couldn't work for the FBI agents running all over the place. . . . We had agents in there constantly. I asked Dorfman, number one, how did I get in that mess, and how could I stop it? And he said the same thing, time will take care of it.

"Dorfman also agreed as to the method of skimming I proposed. Using the cash boxes may be old-fashioned, but there are no records. There is nothing you have to sign. Just take cash. You walk out with it. It is not like signing a contract and getting a kickback—I had never done anything like that. Plus, with money coming out of a box you have pretty good control of it. It may be two men involved, period. . . . Every table has a box. It is put into a steel container. At the end of the shift the security guard puts a key in the steel container and pulls out the box and takes the box to the count room. The boxes are there until the count team comes in the following day and counts the money. If you have a key, you can pull the box out, open the drawer, take the money out, and lock it back up. There is no record. No fill slip."

◆ ◆ ◆

In the six months that Thomas ran the Argent casinos, he was able to put his men in place and establish the skim at the Fremont and Hacienda, but he never gained control of the Stardust. He tried firing the people Lefty had hired, but Lefty resisted.

"Tony Spilotro was the guy who first spoke to me about Carl Thomas taking my job," said Lefty. "He was trying to make points with Allen Dorfman and wanted my vote. I didn't know Carl very well, and when I asked Tony why, he said, 'This is a favor for me.' I didn't think Thomas was qualified enough. I thought he had too much bullshit and not enough knowledge.

"But Tony kept pushing. 'Frank, it's me, Tony, talking. You understand? This is important to me. This is your buddy talking; I'm asking for a favor.'

"So I threw in my weight, and Carl got the job replacing me.

"Anyway, one of my conditions before Carl took over was that he not just go in there and fire my people. I was concerned. I wanted to protect the jobs of good people who I considered to be honorable workers, who I considered honest and loyal to the corporation. And that condition was agreed to by both Spilotro and Dorfman. I even saw Dorfman about it. I knew Dorfman quite well. So I felt comfortable with Carl there.

"Now, it's about ten o'clock at night exactly one day after I have left the building, and I get a call from Bobby Stella. He calls me at home. He says, 'Frank, this guy's got twelve pink slips ready.' I said, 'So what?' It didn't dawn on me, and Bobby isn't all that articulate. I said, 'Come on, Bobby, speak up.'

"And he starts, 'Well, he wants to get rid of so-and-so and so-and-so and so-and-so . . .' I said, 'What?' and he just kept going down a list of top people, my key guys.

"Bobby's name wasn't on the list, naturally. Bobby Stella couldn't be touched. But he gave me the other names and I said 'Bobby, holy shit! Are you sure of what you are saying?' And he said he was sure.

"I said, 'Okay,' and I got a hold of you-know-who. Tony. And I raised some shit with him. That's all I can tell you. We met in a parking area with public phones near a delicatessen. I remember, it was about ten thirty when he showed up. I said, 'Tony, what the fuck is this? You know, you gave me your word. Here's a guy who's going to be firing Art Garelli, Gene Cimorelli, this guy, that guy. He's no goddamn good. I'm out of there one day and this shit takes place?'

"Tony was red faced and embarrassed. I said, 'Tony, get Carl Thomas.' He gets him on the phone right there. I'm listening in. By now it was about eleven P.M., because the delicatessen was closing.

"Tony said to Carl, 'I need to see you. I need to see you right away.' And Carl said, 'Yes sir.' And Tony gave him the location where we were at.

"In about ten minutes Carl pulls up and gets in our car. And that Tony was a real diplomat. I didn't say a word. Tony says, 'Listen, you cocksucker'—that's how diplomatic he was—he says, 'You cocksucker, are you crazy?'

"'Tony, what's the matter? What's wrong?' Carl is saying.

"'You ain't firing anybody, you sonofabitch,' Tony says. 'You hear me?'

"Carl says, 'Tony, wait a minute. You've got a beef with the wrong guy.'

"'What are you talking about?' Tony says.

"'Well, there's a misunderstanding here," Carl says. 'I was told to show Frank total respect no matter what he asked for, and whenever I saw him. Anything, anytime. I was also told to do what I wanted, and to bring my own people there.

"Tony asks, 'Says who?'

"Carl says, 'Says Dorfman.'

"I could see Tony was shocked. Tony says to Carl, 'I don't give a fuck what Dorfman told you. I'll straighten this out with him. Don't you touch any of those people, goddamn you. Now, get the fuck out of here.'

"We got a stay of execution, and my people stayed in their jobs."

♦ ♦ ♦

"During the months I was there," Thomas said, "Glick was gone most of the time, a couple of trips to Europe. He had a jet he was flying out maybe Sunday night and . . . back Tuesday morning. I can't remember a period where he may have been there two weeks in a row.

"When I was there Glick and I had discussions about Rosenthal. It was one of his pet topics when we had dinner together. He and Rosenthal did not get along. We did not discuss skimming. He didn't exercise any control as far as skimming went. He never discussed it with me, and I wouldn't discuss it with him if he asked me.

"After a while I tried to discuss hiring and firing with him because I couldn't get anything done, I couldn't move anybody. His reaction went from confusion to a shrug; he just didn't do anything about it. By that time I started to realize that Rosenthal was in the picture.

"After about a month or six weeks of banging on doors, I got a phone call one night, and it was from Frank Rosenthal. We met and I told him I was trying to clean up the Stardust. Put my own people to work.

"He told me to go back to who talked to me and straighten things out. Obviously (he said) I didn't know all the facts. He was obnoxious, to say the least. He was very upset I was trying to fire people he had in there and I was trying to run things. He was very angry and he acted like it was his place. . . . It was about a forty-minute meeting and I didn't have too much of a response. I was kind of shocked. Later, when Dorfman got to Vegas for three or four days and I asked him what was going on, he said, 'Don't worry about it. Everything is going to work out. There's things in the works. Keep going the way you are going, and as you take any money, give it to Rosenthal.' I expressed reservations about turning the money over to Rosenthal, but Dorfman never took anything too seriously. 'Don't worry about it,' he said. 'It will work out in time.'"

(Lefty has always denied having anything to do with the skim, and he has never been charged with skimming a casino.)

◆ ◆ ◆

There was never the time. On December 2, 1976, everything changed once again: one of Lefty Rosenthal's greatest long shots came in. Las Vegas District Court judge Joseph Pavlikowski ordered Argent to rehire Rosenthal.

After three days of hearings, Pavlikowski ruled that Lefty should be reinstated because he had not been granted his full rights at the Gaming Commission hearings. Lefty, the old handicapper, did not mention to the press that Judge Pavlikowski was the man who had married him and Geri at Caesar's Palace back in 1969 or that when Pavlikowski's daughter was married in one of the Stardust's main ballrooms a few years later, the wedding was partially comped. According to the *Las Vegas Sun*, Pavlikowski denied any inference of wrongdoing.

Pavlikowski's ruling shook the state's licensing laws and took the state gaming officials and their political allies by surprise. Peter Echeverria, the Gaming Commission chairman, promised to appeal; he said that if the ruling was upheld, it would weaken the state's ability to keep criminal elements out of the casinos.

◆ ◆ ◆

The morning after the court ruling, Lefty Rosenthal walked back into the Stardust Hotel and told Thomas to move his stuff out of the big office immediately or it would be thrown out onto the street in the morning.

The Carl Thomas skim at Argent ended the day Rosenthal returned. "I talked to Rosenthal," Harry McBride, one of Thomas's crew who served as Argent security chief, later testified. "We sat down in the lounge . . . and he said, 'You know, there's a lot of money to be made here, but . . . I don't think you're the one that is going to do it." After that there was very little conversation between myself and Mr. Rosenthal."

16.

"Let me ask you this question. Is it Minnesota or Fats?"

Lefty Rosenthal was back. He was back like a barnacle. On February 4, 1977, only two months after Rosenthal walked in and reclaimed his office from Carl Thomas, the Nevada Supreme Court reversed Pavlikowski's ruling—but Lefty stayed put. The court ruled that there were "no constitutionally protected rights" in cases involving gambling licenses and that "gambling does not carry the same rights as other occupations"; it went on to say that if Rosenthal wanted to remain in his gaming post, he would have to apply for licensing as a key employee. Rosenthal was prepared: he resigned as head of the casino and was immediately appointed by Glick as Argent's food and beverage director. The post paid $35,000 a year, $5,000 less than the $40,000 salary the Gaming Commission considered the minimum for key employees.

Rosenthal then embarked on an all-out campaign to get a license. What had started out over a year earlier as a simple suit over Rosenthal's right to a gaming permit escalated into a full-scale war between Lefty and the state's politically powerful licensing czars. If Rosenthal succeeded in challenging Nevada's gaming laws, he could call into doubt the state's right to license anyone in the gaming industry. He and Oscar Goodman went into federal court and claimed he had been denied his constitutional right of due process; he vowed to go all the way to the Supreme Court if necessary. He flew off to Florida to try and reverse his legal problems in Florida and North Carolina since both issues had come up at his hearing. He hired Erwin Griswold, formerly dean of Harvard Law School and U.S. solicitor general, to represent him in federal district court.

Eventually Rosenthal and lawyer Oscar Goodman accumulated over three thousand pages of hearings—as well as charts, visual aids, and two pamphlets, "Gaming Agencies' Efforts to Deprive Frank Rosenthal of Livelihood" and the biographical "Lifetime of Betting and Being an Oddsmaker and Handicapper."

One judge who was asked to read all six volumes of hearings before handing down a ruling refused absolutely to do so. "I can't read this any more than I can read three Sears catalogs and the Old and New Testaments," said Judge Carl Christensen.

Rosenthal was no longer just bothersome and litigious. He was dangerous. He was all over the place. Like many men who come noisily to public life—like Donald Trump and George Steinbrenner, to take two other examples—he began to crave the spotlight. He believed that his title change might circumvent his licensing difficulties. At the Tropicana, the entertainment director was a man named Joe Agosto, whose actual responsibilities had nothing whatsoever to do with entertainment: he was in charge of the skim at the casino. A known associate of Nick Civella, Agosto was an ex-con but his entertainment-director title effectively shielded him from the necessity of a key-man license.

But just in case charges arose that Rosenthal's title was just a cover for what he was really up to—running the casino as usual—Lefty threw himself into his new job description. He announced that he would be the host of a talk show that would promote the Stardust and, of course, its food and beverages. And he began to write a column for the *Las Vegas Sun*.

◆ ◆ ◆

From Frank Rosenthal's column:

> Women's Lib. . . . Thought I would take a run over to the Las Vegas Country Club for lunch with Argent Executive Vice President Bob Stella. Looking for the change of pace and possibly a story or two. My attention was immediately focused upon the ladies of Las Vegas. . . . Phyliss La Forte (very style conscious, formerly of New York, bionic eye for high lines and super curves . . . a very elegant young lady in or out of her tennis suit). . . . Sandy Tueller (the doctor's wife), a mighty fine woman, tennis accentuated, and very proper, stylish too. . . . Barbara Greenspun (the epitome of fashion par excellence). The publisher's wife is a genuine "knockout" (Taste of perfection). Slack ensemble, lavish dresses, blouses, and more, a genuine New York Fashion plate. An enormous wardrobe. Barbara Greenspun may very well be one of the finest dressed women from coast to coast. My professional eye (my wife Geri concurs) and you can take that to the bank. To the remaining ladies of the club, my apologies. The professional eye (Geri) advises that you're all out of sight, and I'm running out of space.

From *The Frank Rosenthal Show:*

PAM PEYTON: Mr. Rosenthal, I've got some more letters again this week, to ask you.

FRANK ROSENTHAL: Okay, we're ready. . . . I'm ready for whatever you've got.

PAM PEYTON: You don't have to. You don't have to do it.

FRANK ROSENTHAL: I'm ready, Pam.

PAM PEYTON: Okay. You handled last week's questions very well, I must say. You know.

FRANK ROSENTHAL: Whatever you've got, I'm ready for.

PAM PEYTON: Okay, this is another strong one.

FRANK ROSENTHAL: Okay.

PAM PEYTON: Here it goes. "Dear Mr. Rosenthal: It looks to me like you and the gamers have buried the hatchets and seem to be much more passive and content. Am I reading the situation accurately?" J.M., of Las Vegas, Nevada.

FRANK ROSENTHAL: Pam, you dasn't bury the hatchet with the gamers. To bury the hatchet would be to ask for an ambush. What you must do, you must stand up and be very conscious of their position. They are men that are dedicated to a proposition to chase me from here to Chicago. And I doubt very much if they're going to get it on.

PAM PEYTON: And Timbuktu?

FRANK ROSENTHAL: We're going to hang in there right with them, and when they bury the hatchet, so will I. But I don't see that coming.

PAM PEYTON: They've certainly been giving you a hard time.

FRANK ROSENTHAL: Yeah, they're tough. But so what? You know, we're here. Here we are.

PAM PEYTON: Life goes on, right.

FRANK ROSENTHAL: We're right here.

PAM PEYTON: This is a really good question here. I'm really

quite fond of this one. . . . "Dear Mr. Rosenthal: You might think this to be a foolish question." It's a long question too, I might add. "But I would wonder if a fellow who just recently moved to Las Vegas less than three months ago could possibly find a nice attractive female by frequenting Jubilation? You seem to know your way around, especially at Jubilation. And some people I have met tell me that you know all the good-looking girls in town. How about giving a lonesome newcomer to this area some advice, either by a written response or during your telecasting? It would be greatly appreciated. Certainly by a couple of other single friends of mine that are in the same boat as I am. I'm really not that fussy, and have a good appearance, and hope to make Las Vegas my permanent home. But, Frank, the women in this town, at least in my short experience, seem to be difficult to come by." This by R.L., of Las Vegas, Nevada.

FRANK ROSENTHAL: It sounds like an autobiography. . . . Well, on the serious side . . .

PAM PEYTON: Do you want me to repeat it?

FRANK ROSENTHAL: No. . . . I do know many of the very lovely dancers in Las Vegas. I've had the pleasure of being the entertainment director for the Stardust Hotel. And certainly, you get the pleasure to meet many beautiful young ladies like yourself. But Pam, I'm married, and the fellow who writes the letter . . . I mean, what can I tell him? If he wants to come down to Jubilation and take a look around here, they're all here tonight.

PAM PEYTON: There's a lot of nice girls here. This guy's crazy. He must not be bothering to talk to any of them. . . .

FRANK ROSENTHAL: If he's lonely, he won't be lonely around Jubilation. I've got to tell you.

PAM PEYTON: This is true. Here's another letter. "Dear Mr. Rosenthal: Will the departures of former Gaming Commissioners Claire Haycock and Walter Cox . . . have any effect on your licensing situation or your legal strategy?" By J.B., of Las Vegas, Nevada.

FRANK ROSENTHAL: No, I don't think so, Pam. I think the Gaming Commission is loaded up. . . . I think it's kind of stacked.

PAM PEYTON: It's kind of *As the World Turns*.

FRANK ROSENTHAL: *As the World Turns*, right. Before you ask another question, we're going to take a short commercial break. We'll be right back with the very, very fine adagio team of Sharon Tagano and David Wright.

The Frank Rosenthal Show began in April 1977 and appeared erratically thereafter at eleven P.M. on Saturday night for two years. At one point, the local television columnist Jim Seagrave of the *Valley Times*, writing about its unpredictable irregularity, referred to it as the *Where's Frank?* show, but Seagrave got hooked early: "There seems to be something about Frank Rosenthal that makes his guests want to tell the truth," he wrote after the show's debut. "Maybe it's those steely, narrow eyes, hypnotic and penetrating. Or perhaps it's his deliberate, carefully measured manner of speaking, like that of a judge handing down a sentence. Most likely, it's his overall demeanor, which radiates schoolmaster's sternness and impatience for frivolity."

Rosenthal's first guests were Allen Glick and the Doumani brothers, who owned an interest in four Las Vegas hotels. Fred Doumani announced to Rosenthal that Nevada was becoming a police state, an opinion that was dutifully covered in the Monday newspapers. As a rule, the show contained a series of plugs for various Argent hotels, nightclubs, and performers from the Lido Show; interviews with handicappers Joey Boston and Marty Kane on that week's upcoming games; drop-ins by near greats like Jill St. John and O. J. Simpson; and the occasional appearance of a genuine superstar, like Frank Sinatra. Rosenthal introduced everyone in the vernacular made famous by that equally unlikely host Ed Sullivan: the women were "very lovely," the bands were "very, very fine," the dancers were not just "very, very fine" but "highly trained" and "very flexible, very pretty, very long legged," the performers at the Stardust were "very, very talented." The show was amateurish and self-serving, but it had a strange addictive quality, and before long it was the top-rated local show, when it was on.

FRANK ROSENTHAL: Let me ask you this question.

MINNESOTA FATS: Yeah?

FRANK ROSENTHAL: Is it Minnesota or Fats?

MINNESOTA FATS: I was born and raised in New York, and I live in Illinois, but the director of *The Hustler*, Robert Rossen, wanted Minnesota Fats. He says it was a most illustrious name. And that's what he wanted on the marquee. And they wrote a big article in Illinois, where I live. I married a Miss America from Illinois. I've been around there for forty-some years. And so the state of Illinois wrote a big article about a most illustrious name. And that's what it was all about.

FRANK ROSENTHAL: If you had to do it all over again, how would you do it?

MINNESOTA FATS: If I had to do it all over again, there's be no way on earth I'd do it any other way. I hung in poolrooms and saloons ever since I was two years old. Never had a bad day in my life.

Laughter. Applause.

MINNESOTA FATS: I was with the most gorgeous creatures the world has ever known. Drove limousines when millionaires was jumping out of windows. You could catch millionaires with a net in 1930. With a net, on Broadway. . . .

FRANK ROSENTHAL: The part I like the best is the fact that your stardom in pool has brought you good romances.

MINNESOTA FATS: Romance? I had the finest romances on earth. Jane Russell was one of my sweethearts.

FRANK ROSENTHAL: No kidding?

MINNESOTA FATS: Long before she met Howard Hughes.

FRANK ROSENTHAL: Really?

MINNESOTA FATS: Mae West still sends me Christmas cards on Christmas. And Hope Hampton was a friend of mine. A girlfriend. She was a belly dancer in 1890. And Fatima. Fatima danced for me at the sultan's palace in Istanbul and then again in Cairo, Egypt, at Shepheard's Hotel. I've had a pretty good life, you know. I've been everywhere on earth. I was at the North Pole twice last year. For *Sports Illustrated*. I entertained a bunch of top scientists. Eighty-three below. I was there in my summer suit. All them suckers had bear rugs on. . . . I had a guy took me thirty miles in a dogsled. I couldn't lift the coat that he was wearing. And there I was in a silk mohair suit. I never was cold in my life.

FRANK ROSENTHAL: Where do we go from here? Oh boy oh boy.

Applause.

Lefty was now a star. And Geri felt increasingly ignored. "She'd get loaded and go off for a few days, and Lefty would stew about where she went," said ex–FBI agent Mike Simon. "She'd come back and he'd accuse her of seeing Lenny Marmor. She'd deny it. That was the basis of their relationship, accusation and denial."

"All Lenny had to do was snap his fingers and she'd run," Lefty said.

At one point, Rosenthal became so angry at Geri and Lenny that he got involved with a young woman who was a friend of Marmor's. Her name, believe it or not, was Pinky.

"The girl was about twenty or twenty-one, and I went after her to try and put Lenny Marmor down," Lefty confessed. "This girl was number one with Marmor. And I told Geri, 'I'll show you how I can bring this bitch here.' And I did. I got the girl to come to Las Vegas. And then I met her in California.

"I was trying to start up a little romance. I guess it was a little silly at the time. She was gorgeous. But when I called her from the hotel in Los Angeles, the first thing she said was, 'You need to send me a thousand.' Oh yeah. And I did. And then naturally, after a couple of dates, she's looking for twos and threes.

"I talked to the girl about Lenny. Initially, I thought I had her bullshitted. But I didn't. She had me conned. Every word I said was either recorded or memorized, and she took it right back to Marmor. Believe me, this guy had a way with certain types of girls. He honestly did. He had her locked up."

At one point Rosenthal became so frustrated at his wife's continuing attachment to Marmor that he told her Marmor had been killed.

"Geri went wild," Lefty said. "She panicked. She ran to the phone and called Robin.

"'Where's your father?' Geri's screaming at Robin. 'Get your father! Find him!.'

"Then she sat and waited about an hour for Robin to call back. I didn't say a word.

"When Robin called back she told Geri that he was all right. Geri turned to me. 'You sonofabitch,' she said, 'why did you do that?'

"I said, 'You'll never know.' But the reason I did it was so that I'd be able to see for myself how much she still cared for him and not for me. He was still in her heart."

In the later part of 1976, Geri also became reacquainted with her old beau Johnny Hicks. Hicks was working as a floor man at the Horseshoe Casino and was conveniently living in a condominium right across the street from the Rosenthal home. "She was always after him," said Beecher Avants, homicide chief of the Las Vegas police department.

One afternoon Hicks left his apartment and was shot five times in the head. Steven Rosenthal, Geri and Lefty's eight-year-old son, came upon the crime scene on his way home and told his mother and father that something had happened outside. Geri and Steven went out to see what the police cars were doing on their usually quiet block and found out that Hicks had been shot. "We tried to talk to Geri," Beecher Avants said, "but she told us, 'Go fuck yourself. I'm not talking to you.'"

"She came back to the house furious," Lefty said. "In her mind she thought I had something to do with the thing. That was crazy. But she always felt I had him killed."

◆ ◆ ◆

Lefty Rosenthal's mind was not on his domestic problems. He had four casinos to run, on top of which he had to pretend he wasn't running them at all. And he had a television show. After only a few months on the air, the show was so successful that Rosenthal decided to move it from the television studio he had been using to the Stardust Hotel itself. "For the first time in the history of Las Vegas," the press release said, "a regularly scheduled television show will emanate live from a casino." The show was not truly regularly scheduled—it had appeared only about five times in its first five months; but the announcement was fraught with promise: Frank Sinatra would make his talk show debut on the first show. Jill St. John and Robert Conrad would also appear. A special studio was built at the Stardust, and a thousand people turned up to watch the show taped at 7:30 P.M. on August 27, 1977. They cheered as Sinatra gave his opinion on a subject of more than routine interest, blasting the NCAA for placing the University of Las Vegas basketball team on a two-year probation.

At 11 P.M., the public tuned their televisions to KSHO, Channel 13, to watch the show and instead saw a little cartoon character holding a card that read ONE MOMENT PLEASE. The moments stretched into minutes and more than an hour. The videotaping equipment at the station had broken down. Hours later, the station resumed broadcasting with *The Decline and Fall of the Roman Empire.* "We don't know exactly what happened," said Channel 13 general manager Red Gilson. "This was a one-in-a-million occurrence. It's almost an impossibility to have two tape machines break down at the same time."

Once again Frank Rosenthal was on the front pages of the Las Vegas papers; and the following day he was there again suing the television station for damages in excess of $10,000 and charging that the breakdown had disastrously injured the reputation of *The Frank Rosenthal Show.* Rosenthal and his staff made noises for several days about taking the show to another television station; one of the local columnists even suggested sabotage. But when no other station took the bait, the show resumed on Channel 13 and became a strange and amazing local curiosity, one that made Rosenthal seem permanently entrenched.

Meanwhile, Lefty's seemingly endless legal battles with the Gaming Commission continued. The U.S. Supreme Court decided not to review Lefty's case, and gaming officials once again demanded that Glick fire Lefty from his food and beverage job and stop him from using the Stardust lounge to broadcast his TV show. Lefty and Oscar Goodman immediately sought a restraining order in federal court, and on January 3, 1978, Lefty got a belated Christmas present. Federal District Judge Carl Christensen said that while the Gaming Commission could bar Lefty from getting a gaming license, it could not bar him from working in the Stardust in a nongaming capacity.

Glick, therefore, quickly appointed Lefty the Stardust's entertainment director, a post traditionally considered far enough removed from the casino operation that it had often been used as a safe haven for those with licensing problems—like Joe Agosto at the Tropicana.

"Nobody in the state believed that one," Murray Ehrenberg, who remained Rosenthal's casino manager, said, "so we had agents hanging around watching Frank, me, and everyone else all night long, trying to catch him being the boss. But Frank didn't have to do whatever he did for everyone to see. We'd talk to him later about this or that. We could be having a sandwich and ask about a guy's credit. We could be watching his show and he could say he wanted somebody hired or fired. What did it take for him to be the boss? He was the boss."

◆ ◆ ◆

Rosenthal's acquaintances in the mob were as irritated by his celebrity as were his enemies in law enforcement. Joe Agosto, the entertainment director at the Tropicana, who actually supervised the skim there, began to call his boss, Nick Civella, to complain about Lefty Rosenthal; Agosto was concerned that Rosenthal's mania for publicity would eventually affect Agosto, and both of them would be thrown out of the casino business. At one point, Agosto telephoned Carl DeLuna, the underboss of the Civella crime family; the FBI was listening.

AGOSTO: Nobody can handle any more. He [Rosenthal] is a killer, he's got a killer instinct, he's gonna pull everybody into the mud. Now I'm concerned about that. I don't want any shit to spill over, to make it impossible to live in this fucking town. He's starting out on the wrong foot now, and somebody . . . should tell this fucking guy where the stop sign is. I mean if he committed suicide, he should accept the fucking deal, that's all, don't put another half-dozen fucking people in the firing line.

DELUNA: Uh huh.

AGOSTO: You know what I mean?

DELUNA: Uh huh.

AGOSTO: Now I mean the thing is getting out of hand. If I was a stranger, if I didn't know this guy's friends and I was only here to protect my own little nest—you know what I mean?

DELUNA: Uh huh.

AGOSTO: I would take action myself, without asking anybody permission, you follow me? If I didn't know better.

DELUNA: What are your fears, Joe? . . .

AGOSTO: I am afeared of this motherfucker when he cannot take the consequences of his actions. He's already made threats. . . . What I'm saying, I feel very strongly about it—there are certain stop signs, certain limitations, where the muddy water splashes on other people's laps. . . . I'm afraid now of the oversplash. There is no question that at the least that will happen. The best that will happen is that he will not get indicted, but there is no question that he's gonna get thrown out of the fucking place, and if he cannot see the sign, he's gotta be the dumbest son of a bitch I've ever come upon in my life.

17.

"Look at that fuck. He doesn't even say hello."

Tony Spilotro was finding Lefty's celebrity harder and harder to take. He had to watch him on television. He had to watch him walk into the Jubilation nightclub trailing a chorus line of showgirls, lawyers, and bookmakers, all kissing his ass. "People were falling all over themselves to get me tables," Rosenthal said, "and I think Tony grew to resent the fact that I was able to move about more freely than he was."

Says Frank Cullotta: "Tony resented Lefty because Tony felt he was the real boss in Las Vegas, and there was Lefty walking all over the place taking bows as though he was the big man in town. I was sitting with Tony in the Jubilation one night when Lefty walked in. When Tony and I went there the boss always gave us a table by ourselves. He never sat anyone nearby because we didn't want anyone on the eary. Around our table there was nothing but white tablecloths, even if the joint was crowded.

"And this night in comes Lefty and he's got his whole entourage from after the TV show. He's got a couple of the dancers he's got his eye on, and there's Oscar and Joey Boston and all of Lefty's ass kissers.

"Tony sees Lefty walk in the joint, and everybody jumps up to shake his hand. And Lefty's loving it. Tony's just watching. He's getting pissed, especially when Lefty doesn't even nod over in Tony's direction for respect. It's like Lefty's saying, I'm the big man in town and fuck you.

"I don't know if that's what Lefty's thinking. I'm saying that's the way Tony starts to take it. One night he says to me, 'Look at that fuck. He doesn't even say hello.'

"I tell Tony, 'How the fuck's he gonna say hello? He's not even supposed to be in the same joint as you.' And Tony says he knows that, but there are ways to say hello and ways not to say hello.

"Tony was beginning to feel that Lefty was getting way out of control. That the TV show and everything was going to his head. That he had a gigantic ego to start with and this was all getting out of hand. He said Lefty was getting so nuts that the other night when he was having some drinks, Tony's friend Joey Cusumano was at Lefty's table and Lefty said, 'I'm the biggest Jew in America,' meaning the biggest Jew in the mob.

"Joey answered him, 'Oh yeah, Frank, I didn't know Lansky was dead.' Tony loved that story. He told it to everybody. That Joey slapped Lefty right back in his place."

♦ ♦ ♦

"Whenever the papers mentioned Tony," Rosenthal lamented, "they always used my name in the next paragraph. No matter how many times I told them that even though I had a long personal relationship with Spilotro, I had no business dealings with him, the media always linked us together. It was no help. In fact, I'm certain I would not have had the kinds of licensing problems I had except for being linked all the time with Tony.

"The truth is—and I know this for sure—Tony was as light as a feather in the outfit. The public perception was the opposite of the facts. All Nevada—Moe Dalitz, my own wife, for God's sake—all thought Tony was the boss of Las Vegas. But the truth was, he wasn't. But he began to believe his own PR.

"But not everyone went along. People would come up with all kinds of propositions saying they were coming from Tony. Most of them didn't even know Tony. Lots of times the propositions were just not good business, and they'd get turned down.

"Lots of time, members of his family were turned down for things just because of his reputation, and that really frustrated him. One time, his own brother went to get a job at a casino. I've got to say his brother was more than qualified. Legitimate. But in forty-eight hours the poor guy got fired—because of his last name. The casino owner didn't want to put up with the heat he knew he'd get from the Control Board. Tony went nuts. He's ready to go to war with the casino owner. I told him to take a Valium and go home."

"It was a very tough time for Tony," Cullotta said. "He'd get so mad he wanted to whack everybody. One time some newspaper reporter was writing stories on him and he hated them. 'I want to kill that SOB,' he says to me. I told him it would be the end for everybody; they'd bring out the army. He kept saying, 'You're wrong. We'll put guys in line. It'll help us. One night I met him on a desert road way out. He had a plan. He wanted to take over the Midwest. He starts talking about the guys he can count on. Then he talks about who are the guys we have to kill.

"I'm thinking, 'Who am I dealing with here.' He's talking to me about taking on the world. I knew all the players and all the while he's giving me the names of who has to be whacked.

"I slowed him down. I said, 'Tony, let's say you're successful—and I don't think the chances are fifty–fifty. What do you think will happen in Kansas City, Milwaukee, Detroit, New York?'

"He jumps right in and says that I'm talking about places east of the Mississippi. We're not part of that. Let's stick to the Midwest. He's arguing geography. The truth is the east of the Mississippi crews don't have anything to do with the Midwest and the West, but murdering several family bosses might change a little of that for a while.

"No, no, Tony only wants to discuss it in terms of Midwest crews.

"Okay, I say, do you think the other groups are not going to be aware that there's a mad crew in Chicago who took over without permission? You'll be considered the most dangerous crew in the world. Also, if you knock out the top bosses of Chicago, what makes you think their underlings are going to fall into line?

"But he had dreams. He would become the pope of the mob and Lefty would become Lansky. That's the crazy way he was talking, standing out there in the desert. I went along because otherwise I would have never come home.

"You think if I turned him down on this he could afford to have me walking around knowing what he had planned? He'd have blown me away before I got in the car.

"I think he wanted Lefty to endorse his plans, too, but I think Lefty turned him down or something, because later he got very pissed whenever Lefty's name came up. He used to say that everytime he had any ideas about doing anything and he needed Lefty's help, Lefty used to 'X' him out. I could see he was coming to hate Lefty. He thought Lefty was pissing on his parade. Lefty had turned him down one-too-many times."

♦ ♦ ♦

The Las Vegas FBI had been on Spilotro's case for years and had built up a considerable dossier on him and his crew. The information was assembled in order to prove that Spilotro was what the newspapers always said he was—the mob's main man in Las Vegas and the true power behind the Stardust Hotel. But almost none of the information picked up on the FBI bug seemed to confirm Spilotro's reputation.

Spilotro and his crew of bookmakers, shakedown artists, loan sharks, and burglars were exactly that—bookmakers, shakedown artists, loan sharks, and burglars. They did not seem to operate anywhere near the top of the casino business. In fact, they were lucky to get the minor assignments handed them by the bosses back home accomplished. "We got Spilotro running errands more than running casinos," retired agent Bud Hall admits.

Typical activities picked up on telephone taps and room bugs between April 13 and May 13, 1978, dealt with the mundane and tedious details of getting people jobs and comps. The FBI heard Spilotro's brother Michael call their brother John to discuss getting a friend of his a job at the Hacienda. They overheard Culinary Union official Stephen Bluestein call to ask Spilotro about getting someone's daughter a job at the Stardust. They heard Spilotro call Marty Kane, the manager of the Stardust's sports book, and tell him to fire a woman he had just hired and put a young woman friend of Spilotro's to work instead. They taped Spilotro's go-fer Herbie Blitzstein calling Joey Cusumano at the

Stardust and asking Cusumano to get him some Stardust pay envelopes so he could make up some for himself. They even caught the local police calling Spilotro to tip him that an IRS agent had been allowed to review Spilotro's police record.

♦ ♦ ♦

The series of phone calls that perhaps most perfectly typify the scut work that Spilotro was asked to do for the bosses in Chicago took place on May 1, 1978. It began with a call from Joseph "Joey the Clown" Lombardo, one of the outfit's top street bosses and Spilotro's capo. Herbie Blitzstein, who hung around the Gold Rush along with his girlfriend, Dena Harte, answered the phone. Lombardo wanted to know why his request for free room, food, and drinks at the Stardust for Barbara Russel, Gregory Peck's secretary, had been ignored. Spilotro got right on the phone with his Chicago capo and promised he would immediately look into the problem.

"I tell ya," Spilotro said, "I'm awful sorry. I don't have any idea what took place."

"When I call you," Lombardo said, "you're supposed to take care of it."

Spilotro said he had even left a message at the hotel that the request was from Lombardo.

"In other words," Lombardo said, "you didn't do a damn thing."

Spilotro assured Lombardo he would look into the lapse immediately and for the next several hours the FBI listened in as Spilotro tried to disentangle the botched comp. After determining from Blitzstein that the request had been made, he called Leonard Garmisa, an acquaintance of Lombardo's and of Teamster pension fund chief, Allen Dorfman. Garmisa had originally asked Lombardo for the favor.

Gold Rush, May 1, 1978, 3:12 P.M. Outgoing call secretly recorded by the FBI between Spilotro, Leonard Garmisa, and Dena Harte, Blitzstein's girlfriend:

SPILOTRO: (off the phone) . . . this guy's Dorfman's friend. What can I tell ya?

GARMISA: Hello.

SPILOTRO: Yeah, Irv.

GARMISA: Who?

SPILOTRO: Irv.

GARMISA: Irv who?

SPILOTRO: Is this Irv Garmisa? That's who.

GARMISA: Who is this?

SPILOTRO: Tony Spilotro.

GARMISA: Tony, it's Lenny Garmisa.

SPILOTRO: Oh, Lenny, how ya doing Lenny?

GARMISA: All right.

SPILOTRO: Well, I'm close anyway.

GARMISA: Huh?

SPILOTRO: I'm close, aren't I?

GARMISA: Yeah, you're very close, but I didn't know it was you. How ya feeling, Ton?

SPILOTRO: I feel fine, excepting that I called, that's very ag-gravating, that's all.

GARMISA: Well, I told him not to call ya. But I wanted him to know, that's all.

SPILOTRO: All right, let me hear what happened, Irv.

GARMISA: Lenny.

SPILOTRO: Lenny, let me hear what happened.

Garmisa then tells Tony that while they had missed talking directly he had given his request to one of the men answering the phone at the Gold Rush.

SPILOTRO: Right. That's fine, he got the messsage, and . . .

GARMISA: So, I said, listen, call up this lady, Barbara Russel, she's staying at the Stardust, she's already checked in. Whatever the hell you can do, do for her. You want to charge it to me, you're more than welcome, but give her the royal treatment. I said, that's it. That's the last I heard. Now today, Gregory Peck called me up to invite me to his daughter's birthday party, so I talked to his secretary. I says, Barbara, did you have a good time. She says I had a marvelous time. Did anybody call ya? She says what do you mean? I says, well, I told you I'd have somebody call you. She says, nah, nobody called.

SPILOTRO: Okay. All right. Let me ask you something.

GARMISA: Yeah?

SPILOTRO: Was she charged?

GARMISA: I think that she, well, I don't know.

SPILOTRO: Do you think? All right, let me tell you something, Lenny. You get on the fucking phone, and you find out if she was. Okay? And, I'll get the money back, how's that?

GARMISA: Do me a favor.

SPILOTRO: But, if she . . . hold it, you listen. If she was charged you get on the phone and you call Joey back. This girl was supposed to be in red. Do you understand what red is? Lenny?

GARMISA: Yeah.

SPILOTRO: That's a comp.

GARMISA: Yeah. I know.

SPILOTRO: All right, now you don't know if she was comped or not?

GARMISA: I have no idea, but I don't think so.

SPILOTRO: You don't think so?

GARMISA: I don't think so, but I'll call her, if you want me to call her on the other phone while you're waiting.

Garmisa then called Peck's office and when he got back on the phone it was clear from his tone, according to the FBI monitors, that he was sorry he had ever gotten involved in the mess.

GARMISA: She told me she checked in under Mrs. Barbara Russel, but some way they put it under her husband's name. Your people probably tried to reach her and probably couldn't reach her under Barbara Russel, it was under Dale Russel.

SPILOTRO: Under Dale Russel?

GARMISA: And it was under her name, it was for three stinking nights, it don't mean, I'll send her something. I swear to God, Tony, I love ya, it's kind of you to call, but don't worry about it. I told that to JP [Joey "the Clown" Lombardo], but . . .

SPILOTRO: Yeah, but that's not the idea, Lenny. When Joey says he'd like something done, it's done.

GARMISA: I know.

SPILOTRO: Now, if they go there under Dale Russel, then we can't find her.

GARMISA: I didn't know it either. So you know I just found out two seconds ago. So don't worry about it, all right?

SPILOTRO: . . . I want you to call Joey, and I want you to . . .

GARMISA: I'll call Joey.

SPILOTRO: He's home right now.

GARMISA: I'll explain to him right this second.

SPILOTRO: In the meantime, I'm gonna double check it. But I could sure see what happened here.

GARMISA: Just not, just found it out . . .

SPILOTRO: Okay, Lenny.

GARMISA: . . . on the other phone. I got to go. Thanks, Tony.

SPILOTRO: Good enough.

GARMISA: Okay.
SPILOTRO: Bye, bye.

The FBI recorded over eight thousand conversations on 278 reels of tape in seventy-nine days in the spring of 1978, and most of it was as mundane as the conversation over Gregory Peck's secretary. Nonetheless, in June, the bureau launched a massive raid in which over fifty agents served everyone from Spilotro to Allen Glick with search warrants. The warrants, which were served in Chicago and Las Vegas, allowed agents to seize cash, filing cabinets, weapons, tape recordings, and financial records, and all of this was itemized on the front pages of the Las Vegas papers, along with the customary sentences linking Spilotro to Rosenthal and the Stardust. But within months almost all of the seized materials were returned to their owners; the widely publicized raid turned out to be a bust. Spilotro was free to continue operating.

18.

"The truth is that Allen R. Glick has never, nor will he ever, associate with anything other than what is lawful."

Sometimes they called him Genius and sometimes they called him Baldy; whatever he was called, Allen Glick was a mistake, and the mob wanted him out. In the beginning, Glick had looked like the perfect mark, but he was turning out to be much more trouble than he was worth. For one thing, he was too attractive a target: the press loved to kick him, to poke fun at his inexperience, to mock his seriousness, to imply that there was something suspicious about his stewardship. For another thing, he was considerably more clever than anyone at the Teamsters' pension fund had expected.

In 1976, as part of a routine investigation of Glick's petition to raise additional funds to repay his debenture holders, the American Stock Exchange discovered that Glick had lent $10 million in Argent money to some of his private corporate subsidiaries—with no schedule to pay the money back. Then, in 1977, the Securities and Exchange Commission disclosed that within a week of receiving the Teamster loan back in 1974, Glick had taken $317,500 from it and used it to remodel his home and pay off personal debts. The SEC charged Glick with using Argent "as his private source of funds in flagrant disregard of his fiduciary duty to Argent's debenture holders." According to the *Wall Street Journal*, Glick had paid himself more than $1 million for his management services and charged the amount against his debt to Argent, thus unilaterally reducing the amount he owed. The SEC also accused Glick of dissipating Argent funds on several unprofitable ventures, including a government building project in Austin, Texas.

"Wunderkind Las Vegas casino owner Allen Glick" had become "beleaguered Las Vegas casino owner Allen Glick." The SEC was suing Argent; the slot machine skimming scam was still under investigation; the Tamara Rand murder was unsolved. Three hundred thousand dollars had been advanced to an advertising agency for ads in a local newspaper called the *Valley Times*—and some of the ads had never appeared. Contributions had been given to political candidates—and they had publicly given them back.

Glick's problems were heightened by the fact that the Teamster empire was collapsing; he was a footnote in that collapse, but a highly entertaining one. Glick's ongoing hubris was just begging for comeuppance. "The truth is that Allen R. Glick has never, nor will he ever, associate with anything other than what is lawful," Allen R. Glick announced to the *Wall Street Journal*.

One of the people who read the *Wall Street Journal* article on Glick's loans to himself was Nick Civella, the Kansas City crime chief whom Glick had flown to meet four years earlier in the room with the lone lightbulb. Civella was furious that Glick had his hand in the till. It was hard enough stealing from a casino, without having the casino owner ahead of you in line. Civella would have called Glick himself to say so, but for one inconvenience: he was in jail, serving a short stint for making illegal bets on an interstate phone (his phone calls were monitored). But during a family prison visit with his brother Carl "Corky" Civella, Civella passed the word that something had to be done about Glick. So Carl Civella and his top lieutenant, Carl "Toughy" DeLuna, began a series of trips to Chicago to meet with the other mobsters who were partners in Argent with the Kansas City group. The plan was either to force Glick out or to force him to buy out the mob for millions of dollars in cash.

The point man on this plan was Toughy DeLuna. DeLuna was an armed robber and hit man, but he had the soul of a bookkeeper: he kept meticulous notes of his travels and itemized all his expenses on three-by-five index cards and in notebooks. The names of the people were in code, but they were easily decipherable. Allen Glick was called Genius. Lefty Rosenthal was called Crazy—which DeLuna misspelled as "Craze." Joe Agosto of the Tropicana was Caesar—misspelled "Ceasar."

In late 1977, DeLuna and Carl Civella flew to Chicago to meet with the boss, Joe Aiuppa, and the underboss, Turk Torello. "Talk was of Genius taking the place for himself," DeLuna wrote on his index card, thus documenting the mob's first attempt to get rid of Allen Glick by having him buy them out. The proposal was actually made to Glick by Lefty Rosenthal, as Glick testified years later.

Q: Let me ask you this, Mr. Glick, did you and Frank Rosenthal ever have any discussions concerning Frank Rosenthal by the Argent Corporation?
A: Yes, we did.
Q: And approximately when did those discussions take place, if you recall?

A: Sometime I believe in 1977.

Q: And what was the nature of those discussions?

A: Mr. Rosenthal came to my office one afternoon and informed me that he had the consent of the partners to propose a buyout, a buyout of the partners. And he outlined what he had in mind that he thought would be acceptable to the partners.

Q: And what were those terms?

A: He told me that he felt approximately $10 million in cash payments should be offered to the partners in order to regain their 50 percent ownership.

Q: . . . Who, if anyone had been identified, was acting in a representative capacity of these alleged partners?

A: Mr. DeLuna, Carl DeLuna. As we stated, Mr. Rosenthal. Mr. Thomas. . . . I would say, Mr. Dorfman. . . .

Q: Did you give serious consideration to that proposal, Mr. Glick, to purchase the Argent Corporation from the partners, the alleged partners, for $10 million.

A: . . . I gave serious intentions as far as Mr. Rosenthal was concerned. As far as the concept in what he proposed to me, I didn't give it serious consideration.

Q: Did Frank Rosenthal take those suggestions seriously?

A: I would just like to add to what I said. I took it serious because it came from Mr. Rosenthal. I didn't take it serious as it was either a feasible or plausible thing to do. But yes, he did take it very serious.

Q: How did you become aware that Frank Rosenthal took those discussions seriously with you?

A: Sometime after that particular discussion, he came back to me and he said that on behalf of the people he represented—and he used the word "partners"—that was an acceptable proposal.

Q: And what did you say to Mr. Rosenthal?

A: I told him that there was no possible way that something like that could be transacted. I was not interested nor would I allow myself to be involved in anything of that nature, because what he was talking about is $10 million in cash, nonreportable income. I said that it was not something that I would want to be involved in. He said that he represented to the partners that I okayed and sanctioned his representation of an affirmed act in regards to this buyout as he termed it. I didn't know what to think, because as far as I was concerned Mr. Rosenthal was a pathological liar, psychotic, and I just dealt with him on a daily basis keeping those definitions in mind as to what type of person he was.

Q: And how did Mr. Rosenthal react to your refusal then to go along with this $10 million buyout?

A: He was very upset, and he said that the partners would certainly be hostile to his negative response for me. Once again, the threats surrounded all of the sentences, as far as his descriptions to me of what actions the partners would take. That I did consider serious even though he was a pathological liar in other areas. . . .

Q: In the original concept, as you and Mr. Rosenthal discussed it, what role, if any, did Frank Rosenthal envision for himself?

A: . . . That he would be the chief executive officer, and that he would want to run the company as, in fact, president of the new company.

Q: And would he have any other ownership?

A: Yes. He would have a fifty percent ownership interest. . . .

Allen Glick went on behaving as if he believed he had some power in his own corporation. Rosenthal tried to force him to sell the Lido Show to Joe Agosto at the Tropicana, but

Glick refused. As a result, Carl Civella and Carl DeLuna continued to fly to Chicago to plot against Glick, and DeLuna continued to write down everything that happened—unwittingly creating an incredible paper trail for the law enforcement agents who eventually uncovered it.

In January 1978 they met with Frank Balistrieri, Joe Aiuppa, Jackie Cerone, and Turk Torello, who was being treated for stomach cancer. According to DeLuna's notes: "Talk was entirely of replacing Genius. Craze [code for Frank Rosenthal] was supposed to be there but couldn't come." On April 10, he met again with Aiuppa, Cerone, Torello, and Tony Spilotro, who was apparently in the neighborhood and dropped by. According to those notes: "Talk was of who should see Genius. It was decided to be me." On April 19, DeLuna returned to Chicago with Carl Civella to meet with Aiuppa, Cerone, and Frank Rosenthal: "The talk again was of me going to see Genius. (We had talked of it ten days ago. Note card of 4-10.) Craze gave me his home number. He and I agreed that our first meet would be at the avocatto's [lawyer Oscar Goodman's office] and we made a tentative appointment for next week. 22 [Joe Aiuppa] suggested waiting since ON's [Nick Civella's] almost here [released from prison] but MM [Carl Civella] said he'd like for us to get it done before ON [Civella's return]. So that's why for Craze and I with Genius next week." DeLuna meticulously noted his expenses for the trip: $180 out, $180 in, and $7 in parking fees, for a total of $387, leaving a cash-on-hand balance of $8,702.

◆ ◆ ◆

In late April, Carl DeLuna flew to Las Vegas and had a meeting that was the final chapter in the education of Allen Glick, as Glick later testified.

Q: Mr. Glick, I want to direct your attention to on or about April 25, 1978 and ask you if you had an occasion to meet with Carl DeLuna?

A: Yes I did.

Q: Where did you meet Carl DeLuna?

A: I met Mr. DeLuna in Mr. Oscar Goodman's law office.

Q: And who is Oscar Goodman?

A: Oscar Goodman is a Las Vegas attorney.

Q: Did you know Mr. Goodman prior to that?

A: Yes. At one time he represented Argent Corporation.

Q; And who was present on that date?

A: It was myself, Mr. DeLuna and Mr. Rosenthal. . . .

Q: Did you see Mr. Goodman present that day?

A: No I did not.

Q: You entered that office, what did you observe?

A: I entered the office and there was an entree room where Mr. Goodman's secretary sat, and I went past Mr. Goodman's secretary into Mr. Goodman's personal office.

Q: And when you entered that personal office, what did you observe?

A: I entered Mr. Goodman's office and behind Mr. Goodman's desk with his feet up on the desk was Mr. DeLuna.

Q: Tell the ladies and gentlemen of the jury what occurred in that office on April 25, 1978.

A: I entered Mr. Goodman's office. Mr. DeLuna, in a gruff voice, using graphic terms, told me to sit down. With that he pulled out a piece of paper from his pocket—he was wearing a three-piece suit, I believe—out of his vest pocket . . . and he looked down at the paper for a few seconds. Then he looked up at me and he informed me he was sent there to deliver one last final message to me from his partners. And he began reading the paper. Do you just want me to—

Q: Describe as best you can recall what was said and done other than profanities.

A: He said that he and his partners were finally sick of having to deal with me and having me around and that I could no longer be tolerated. He wanted me to know that everything he said would be the last time I would hear it from him or anyone else because there would be no other opportunity for me to hear it unless I abided by what he said. He informed me that it was their desire to have me sell Argent Corporation immediately and I was to announce that sale as soon as I left Mr. Goodman's office that day after the meeting with Mr. DeLuna. He said that he realized that the threats that I received perhaps may not have been taken by me to be as serious as they were given to me. And he says that since I perhaps find my life expendable, he was certain I wouldn't find my children's life expendable. With that he looked down on his piece of paper and he gave me the names and ages of each one of my sons. And he said that if he did not hear within a short period of time that I announced the sale, that one by one he would have each of my sons murdered. With that he continued on with his general demeanor, which was vulgar and animalistic. And the meeting ended with me saying that I was willing to sell—which I was before that meeting—and that I would do it.

Q: Did Mr. DeLuna indicate anything about his own personal expendability?

A: Yes he did.

Q: What did he say?

A: He said that if I thought that for some reason I didn't take him serious or for some reason he wouldn't be around there would always be someone to replace him and there would always be someone to take the place of the partners when they left.

Within days of his meeting with Carl DeLuna, Allen Glick went to the Nevada Gaming Commission and told them he was going to sell his interest in his casinos. But he made no public announcement; he wanted to wait until he could get a deal in place. He began a series of unsuccessful negotiations: at first he tried to sell his partners on an arrangement under which the casinos would be leased from him; then he negotiated with several groups of would-be purchasers, many of them, he said, put together by Rosenthal. They included Allen Dorfman, Bobby Stella, and Gene Cimorelli, Argent executives loyal to Rosenthal, and the Doumani brothers.

◆ ◆ ◆

Meanwhile, in May, a murder occurred in Kansas City that had no connection whatsoever with the casino business. For several years the Civella family had been at war with another local crime family over control of some topless bars in a new Kansas City development. In November 1973, Nick Spero, a member of the other crime family, had been found shot to death and stuffed in the trunk of his car; now, in May 1978, his brothers Carl, Mike, and Joe had been shot in a bar, and Mike had been killed. As a result, the Kansas City FBI had stepped up its telephone surveillance of the Civella family and had planted a bug in the back of Villa Capri, a local pizzeria.

"We put the bug in there because we were looking for information on the murder," retired FBI agent Bill Ouseley said. "Instead, at about ten thirty on the night of June 2, 1978, Carl DeLuna and Nick Civella's brother Corky sat down in the back of this two-tabled sliced-pizza restaurant and they start talking about buying and selling Las Vegas casinos, and about ordering Allen Glick to sell his casinos.

They talked about the various groups lined up to buy Glick's casinos and how they wanted the group backed by their man—Joe Agosto at the Tropicana—to take over, and not a Chicago-mob-backed group that included Lefty Rosenthal, Bobby Stella, and Gene Cimorelli."

The conversation—which was about fifteen minutes in length—detailed for the first time in the mob's own voice the influence and power organized crime exerted in Las Vegas. Bill Ouseley was fascinated; he had been keeping up his mob charts and files for years, and when DeLuna and Civella started talking, none of their half sentences or code names got past him. In addition, his mother was Italian, so he even understood their Sicilian phrases.

"It was like the Rosetta stone for all of our suspicions," Ouseley said. "No one had ever recorded mob guys talking about buying and selling casinos and who should and should not be permitted to take them over. Still, it was hard for us to believe that Toughy DeLuna, in his windbreaker and pizza apron, was negotiating the sale of multimillion-dollar Las Vegas casinos. We didn't know for sure until eight days later, on June tenth, when Allen Glick called a press conference in Las Vegas and announced he was planning to step away from the Argent Corporation."

The Kansas City FBI went into court for permission to extend its wiretap authorization on the Civella crew; it put a spotter plane on DeLuna in order to present to the court the elaborate antisurveillance steps he went through on a typical day. Says Ouseley: "All the evasiveness, the fact that DeLuna and Civella were going from place to place to make phone calls, that DeLuna even carried a pouch filled with quarters and routinely made evasive driving maneuvers like spinning U-turns on highways and zipping through private driveways, indicated to the court that these guys were up to no good. Our surveillance of DeLuna took us to the Breckinridge Hotel. DeLuna would go there just about every day because there were dozens of public phones. In order to get wiretap orders on a public phone, we had to be able to prove to a federal court judge—in private, of course—that DeLuna was using these phones for illegal purposes and that the phones themselves were being used as part of the conspiracy. We brought everyone from the office out to the hotel. We had secretaries and clerks standing at phones so when DeLuna arrived and started his conversations they would be able to overhear anything he said that might be suspicious enough to get us the probable cause we needed to legally bug the hotel phones." FBI agents heard DeLuna talking about Caesar (Joe Agosto) and Singer (the code word for Carl Caruso, the man who it later turned out brought the Tropicana skim from Las Vegas to Kansas City). He talked about C.T. (Carl Thomas) and investigations. In the end, the bureau was given permission to tap just about every phone the Civella crew regularly used—including the phone at Civella's attorney's office.

◆ ◆ ◆

"Until the late 1970s, there had been a hiatus in law enforcement in Las Vegas," said Mike "Iron Mike" DeFeo, who was the deputy director of the Justice Department's Organized Crime Strike Force in 1978. "There was corruption. There were judges who made things difficult. Paul Laxalt, as both a senator and governor, complained that there were too many FBI and IRS agents in the state. Our wiretaps were leaked. One judge used to unseal grand jury minutes we asked to be sealed. At one point, one of the corrupt cops who worked for Tony Spilotro had his sister-in-law working as the chief clerk of the court. All this meant for law enforcement was years and years of frustration. We were beating our heads against the wall.

"And then finally, when a break did come, it didn't come out of Vegas but out of the back room of a Kansas City pizzeria. It was fortuitous. It was luck. But mostly it was the fact that the Kansas City supervisor, Gary Hart, and his squad knew there was something to be pursued on that wire and they pursued it. If you listen to that wire, even today, it's not all that obvious. These guys didn't talk with footnotes. You hear DeLuna telling Carl Civella about how he was going to get Genius to get out of the Stardust. None of it is all that clear or all that direct. Lots of it is impenetrable. Lazy listeners could have easily missed it."

◆ ◆ ◆

From the tap at the Villa Capri Pizzeria: "Well you see this guy wants to make a public announcement," said Carl DeLuna. "Genius, Genius wants to make a public announcement. He is the last thing Caesar told me, if he can give Jay Brown [Oscar Goodman's law partner]—oh, yeah, Carl, I told you about the public announcement. Remember the point I told you, that Genius was there the night that Joe went to cash the check and Jay Brown was there at the Stardust. Genius was looking at Jay Brown . . . the way Joe was. He said Genius is all for this deal. He wants it to go through. He wants to make a public announcement, right. Which, those were my words to him, do what you got to do, boy. Make your public announcement that you are getting out of this for whatever fuckin' reason you want to pick and get out. I put that in his head. Make a news conference."

♦ ♦ ♦

"Correctly interpreting this conversation was the key," said Mike DeFeo, "but it was Carl DeLuna who made the case for us in the end. He was an inverted, compulsive note taker. He kept notes on everything. Every twenty-dollar roll of quarters. Every trip. Every gas tank filled. He did it so that he could never be questioned about his expenses, because he would be able to show where the money went. DeLuna's notes and the telephone tap at Spilotro's Gold Rush and later at Allen Dorfman's insurance company in Chicago all confirmed what we knew all along—that there was a strong link between the mob, the Teamsters' Central States pension fund, and Las Vegas—only now we were in a position to maybe do something about it.

"We broke ground in some areas. We began the largest and most complicated wiretap and bugging investigation ever to uncover the mob's influence in Las Vegas. The standards for electronic surveillance, for instance, were expanded from fifteen to thirty days, and we managed to get coverage on that bank of phones at the Breckinridge, even though there was only probable cause on, say, four out of ten of them.

"We got permission to vandalize DeLuna's car if there was any possibility of our bug being discovered. We got permission to burglarize the home of Civella's relative Josephine Marlo to get the car door opener from her car so we could get the garage door open to plant the bug that would turn out to be the most important bug in the case.

"We also had to deal with the traditional privacy and respect aspects of the law. The rules had always been that there would be no bugs in bedrooms or bathrooms, but during our investigation we found that Allen Dorfman would immediately go into the bedroom or bathroom to talk. We had to ask permission to get around that. And of course we got into the Quinn & Peebles law firm."

The man the FBI was tapping at Quinn & Peebles was Nick Civella, who had been released from federal prison on June 14, 1978, and had established his offices at his lawyer's firm. There he was known as Mr. Nichols. Civella and his partners were facing a crisis, no question of that: the Tropicana Hotel, which was the source of thousands of dollars in skim money for the Civella crew, was in financial difficulty; in the course of licensing a new owner, the Gaming Commission had discovered that Tropicana skimmeister Joe Agosto was also a man named Vincenzo Pianetti, and the U. S. Immigration and Naturalization Service had been trying to deport him for ten years. Agosto himself did not help matters: he promptly called a press conference and went berserk, screaming and yelling in Sicilian dialect. Agosto's fears—that Lefty Rosenthal's problems would eventually splash over onto him—turned out to be well founded: in July, when the Gaming Control Board ordered Rosenthal to apply for a key license in spite of his title as entertainment director, it ordered Joe Agosto to apply as well.

Though he was a famously guarded man, Civella was probably as open as he would ever be using the phones in his lawyer's office to solve these problems. He was convinced that even the FBI wouldn't tap the privileged conversations of a lawyer and client.

19.

"Gentlemen, these are the hazards of doing business. Sometimes people are going to steal even from you."

On November 28, 1978, Carl Thomas and Joe Agosto arrived in Kansas City for a meeting with Nick Civella. Thomas had recently been put in charge of the skim at the Tropicana Hotel, and now there was a problem: Civella believed that he was being skimmed by the very people Carl Thomas had put in charge. Casino manager Don Shepard—who was known by the code name "Baa Baa" and was one of Thomas's most reliable count room skimmers—had lost $40,000 in cash in a card game; when Civella heard about it, he immediately concluded that Shepard could never have accumulated that kind of money unless he was stealing it. Civella declared a secret moratorium on the skim; the idea was to expose the leakage: if the house's win did not increase by the amount that was usually skimmed, Civella and Agosto would know the skimmers were skimming the skim. But after six weeks, the moratorium had proved inconclusive, and Civella wanted to call it off. The problem was how to control the skim when it began again. Had they explored all the possible methods of skimming? Was there a way to do it to keep people like Shepard from stealing?

This, of course, was a problem as old as the skim itself. "In the beginning," Murray Ehrenberg, Lefty's former casino manager at the Stardust, said, "the casinos' owners did the count. But soon the state realized the owners weren't giving them a fair count on the tax revenue, so they passed a law that outlawed the owners from even entering their own count rooms. Even today, a casino owner can't go into the count room.

"That law meant the owners had to pick front men to do their count for them, and after a while, the front men began to wonder, 'Why am I counting the way I'm counting?' Pretty soon, the real count never hit the door.

"Front men like Charlie 'Cuby' Rich, who was a close friend of Cary Grant's, had a lockbox that was so tightly packed with ten-thousand-dollar stacks of banded hundred-dollar bills that one time when I saw him open it up, the lid literally sprang open. There must have been three or four million dollars in that box.

"In the early days, precredit, the fifties, the sixties, even the early seventies, people came to Las Vegas with cash. Everybody played with cash. You couldn't get the paddle into the slot at the craps table, there were so many hundred-dollar bills crammed into the drop boxes.

"That's why the front men, who were the big shots in town, got the law passed that kept the wiseguys, who were the real owners back then, out of town. The front men set it up with the politicians and the cops so that the real owners, the racket guys, couldn't set foot in town."

Front men like Meyer Lansky's brother Jake had the first count for the New York people. "Moe Dalitz had the first count for the Midwest and Cleveland. And the bosses back home, the guys who were in the Nevada Black Book, had to stay home and take the word of their front men on the count.

"That was the game. The first count meant twenty for Big Tony, and thirty went south, right into their pockets. After a while, why tell Big Tony it's twenty?

"The wiseguys might have been tough at home, but they were easy pickings out here. You can go as far back as Bugsy Siegel. Del Webb charged Bugsy fifty dollars for a five-dollar doorknob and sold him the same palm trees six and seven times. He also had a crew of Greek blackjack dealers from Cuba who had a lot of relatives, and they took enough out of the Flamingo in one year to open casinos all through the islands. The wiseguys never woke up to this.

"Even when you know what can happen, it's almost impossible to keep a casino from leaking cash. At the Stardust, for instance, you've got a dealer on the floor making fifty dollars a day. You've got the Eye in the Sky man making a hundred dollars a day. And there's millions of dollars sitting on the floor. You don't think people go to work scheming over that? The outfit had a thousand eyes and they still came up empty.

"At the Fremont, the count room was on the second floor, and the security guards would take the drop boxes out from under the tables, put them in carts, and take them upstairs for the count. But on the way up, in the elevator, with the door closed, they had a copy of the key that opened the boxes, and they'd open them up and grab out a fistful of bills. They never took too many out of any one box, and they evened out the take.

"They were smart. If they had a chance, they'd walk around the room and see which of the tables was hot and which weren't, and then they would take the cash out of the active boxes.

"No one would have ever caught them, except one day

they accidentally grabbed a fill slip (the record of chips requisitioned by tables from the cashier), and when the auditors saw that a fill slip was missing from the drop box, they realized someone was getting into the boxes, and that was that.

"We had engineers at the Stardust who made a fortune. They could go all around the casino without raising suspicions. Who'd ask them questions? They're checking pipes. Checking electric circuits. Air conditioners. You wanna be hot? Who knows? Who cares?

"Well, one of the places the engineers had to check a lot was the Eye, and they'd go up there, and if there was no one in the Eye—the bosses were so cheap they didn't man the Eye around the clock—the engineer would come down with a blue card in his pocket. If the Sky was being manned, he'd come down with a red card. The blue card was the signal to steal. The engineer got a piece of everything the dealers in on the signal stole.

"Today, cheating a casino is a felony, and a five-to-twenty-year bit. But in those days, if you got caught, they'd just slap the guys around and chase them out."

◆ ◆ ◆

Agosto and Thomas met to discuss the Tropicana skim with Civella, his brother Carl, and Carl DeLuna at the home of Carl Civella's sister-in-law Josephine Marlo. Marlo's house was around the corner from Civella's in an Italian neighborhood, and it had one big advantage: it was possible to drive into the garage, close the garage door, and enter the house from the garage, thus evading the eyes of neighbors and whoever else might be watching. But the FBI knew that Civella used Marlo's home for meetings, and had managed to get authorization to put a tap into the basement dining room.

No one had a clue. The meeting began at 10 A.M. and ended at 6 P.M., and when it was over, there were eight reels of tape that became a landmark in law enforcement: the Civella brothers, DeLuna, Agosto, and Thomas ate spaghetti, drank wine, and laid out a primer on how to skim a casino. The Marlo tape was an extraordinary document, illuminating, hilarious, breathtakingly candid; it was ultimately responsible for the end of the role of the mob in Las Vegas. On it Carl Thomas described how the skim operated at the Tropicana and how it had worked at Argent. He took the Kansas City crew through the advantages and disadvantages of various forms of skimming, from Thomas's favorite method, just stealing the cash, to his least favorite, filling out fill slips in triplicate and then removing the money. He talked about short-weighing coins and auxiliary banks. He described the method he used at Slots O'Fun, the small casino he operated on the Strip, and explained why it wouldn't work in a larger casino. He spoke philosophically about how the men you trust to steal for you are bound to steal something for themselves. "Gentlemen, these are the hazards of doing business," Carl Thomas said at one point in the meeting. "Sometimes people are going to steal even from you. . . . Every day [at Slots O'Fun] two guys count my money. And we only take a hundred dollars a day. But it's still a hundred dollars—thirty thousand dollars a year; that's a lot of money for us. A little joint. I know these guys are taking a hundred a day. They might be taking a hundred and thirty. But you'll drive yourself crazy over whether the guys are collecting another forty-dollar skim. You gotta realize, what if they get nailed, Nick? You know what these guys are giving up? They'll never work again. . . . We're asking these guys to jeopardize their livelihood. But Nick, as much as I love you, as close as we are, you know better than anybody every time I come here to see you, I jeopardize everything I have. . . . Same way with these guys. They're taking this money because they're our guys. You gotta give them some leeway." Carl Thomas talked and talked and talked. As he said years later—after being sentenced to a fifteen-year prison term as a direct result of that afternoon—"I must have been out of my mind."

♦ ♦ ♦

Less than three months after the Marlo meeting, FBI agent Shea Airey and Gary Jenkins of the Kansas City police intelligence unit knocked on Carl DeLuna's door and presented him with a search warrant allowing them to look for records and papers. For months, the bureau had been watching DeLuna use the pay phones at the Breckinridge Hotel; they had been listening to him speak about the delivery of "packages" and "sandwiches"; they had seen him take notes on the wrappers from his rolls of quarters.

Now they began to search his house. They found packages of cash—$4,000 in Sandra DeLuna's lingerie drawer; $8,000 hidden under DeLuna's underwear; $15,000 in an armoire. There were four pistols, a handbook on poisoning, a police scanner radio, a black wig, a key-making tool, 130 blank keys, a book on how to make silencers. All sorts of things, but no records or papers. And then they got to the basement.

"You know how you go to a relative's house and they haven't thrown anything away for years?" said one Kansas City police officer. "That's what the basement was like. He was probably one of those guys who said, 'You'll probably never know when you'll need it." In a locked room in the basement, agents found notebooks, steno pads, hotel note pads, index cards, all of them covered with neatly written notes in red or black ink, dated, and neatly itemizing all of

DeLuna's expenses. The messages are in code, but the code was easily deciphered once it was matched to surveillance and wiretapped conversations. The notes showed the breakdown and distribution of the skim—to 22, or Joe Aiuppa of Chicago; to Deerhunter, or Maishe Rockman of Cleveland; to Berman, or Frank Balistrieri of Milwaukee; to ON, or Nick Civella of Kansas City.

"As far as the search was concerned, DeLuna was the ultimate gentleman," said FBI agent William Ouseley. "His wife made coffee and brought out cookies."

As Airey and Jenkins began to pore over the notes, FBI agents arrested Carl Caruso—aka the Singer—as he got off a plane from Las Vegas at the Kansas City Airport. Caruso's legitimate business was running junkets to Las Vegas; at the same time, he carried the skim money from Joe Agosto at the Tropicana to the Civella mob. That night he was carrying $80,000 in his jacket pockets—money he had been given by Joe Agosto, who had been given it by Don Shepard.

Warrants were also served in Las Vegas on Joe Agosto, Tropicana stockholder Deil Gustafson, and Don Shepard, and in Kansas City on Nick Civella and Carl Civella. "Nick Civella knew we had a warrant and he stood back," said one agent. "I don't think he'd ever had his house searched before. We came up with absolutely nothing pertinent. The only thing we found were diamonds. Bags full of cut diamonds. Maybe that's where he put his money. And we found a clipping from an unknown publication that I've never forgotten. Civella had apparently cut it out—it was unsigned and undated—and kept it because of its sentiment. When we read it we were chilled. We understood how seriously he took this Old World code and business of his. The clipping said, 'This monster—this monster they've engendered in me—will return to torment its maker, from the grave, the pit, the predestined pit. Hurl me into the next existence. The descent into hell won't turn me. I'll crawl back to dog his trail forever. They won't defeat my revenge. Never. Never."

Two days after the search, DeLuna met with three of his gang at Wimpy's, a restaurant in Kansas City. The FBI bug in the restaurant picked up the entire conversation, which included an admission by DeLuna that he expected to be sent to jail for a few years. "But I think, in a course of time, it might take a year, year and a half, and, and we're all gonna wind up with three, four. I know I almost have to. I already started brainwashing Sandy." He urges the others to prepare their wives as well.

DeLuna was eventually sentenced to thirty years in prison. His arrest and the recovery of his notes provided the FBI with a blueprint of the skim conspiracy; in fact, it would probably not be an exaggeration to say that the Marlo meeting and Carl DeLuna's notes are responsible for knocking the mob out of Las Vegas casinos.

20.

"I know the voice. I've known it all my life. It was Tony's."

"She was drinking and taking pills," Lefty said. "She didn't seem to care that I was under a lot of pressure. One night my ulcer had been acting up and I was upstairs in bed. I had called her on the intercom and asked her to get my dinner ready. My pain was beginning to show.

"After a while, I said over the intercom, 'Geri, is it ready?' She said, 'Any second, dear.' What she didn't tell me was that she was so fucking drunk she never started dinner. Then, in a panic, she put the soft-boiled eggs on, burnt the fucking toast, and brings it up half-assed.

"When I look at it, I'm literally in pain. I gave her some shit. And I'm leaning back in the bed. She's facing me, and she leaps toward the cabinet.

"I'm in a prone position. I did my best to leap with her in a kind of roll, but she got her hand on the cabinet before I did. I was probably a half second behind her, but she already had her hand on the pistol.

"We bumped heads and I was bleeding from the forehead, but she started bleeding from the nose. I had hit the bridge of her nose.

"The two kids came from their bedrooms in the rear. They saw we were struggling. I said, 'Geri! Geri! The kids. Stop it!' And I finally got the gun away, but she still wouldn't stop struggling because she was so fucking drunk.

"I called Bobby Stella to come over right away to help me with the kids and the blood and everything. I told him to call my doctor, who rushed over right away. He took us to his office, where he patched me up pretty easily, but he had to give her a couple of stitches.

"She started mumbling about how I had broken her nose. I asked her, 'Geri, what did you intend to do with the gun?'

"'Nothing,' she said. 'I was just drinking. I was wrong. I shouldn't be drinking.'

"And by the time we got home, everything was calm.

"The next morning I'm going to work and she walks me out to the car and you'd think she was the perfect suburban housewife.

"'Take care of yourself,' she says, and gives me a kiss.

"I'm at work about an hour and I call the house. I ask her how she's feeling and she says, 'I feel great. How are you, my love?' I detected her drunk voice.

"I got in the car and went back to the house. I parked the car down the block and snuck into the house. I wanted to see what was going on. Geri was on the phone. I think she was talking to her daughter Robin.

"I hear her say, 'You've got to help me kill this motherfucker. Please help me.'

"'Hey, she can't help you Geri,' I said, walking into the room. 'Here I am.' She almost died.

"'You told me less than two hours ago you loved me and

now you're trying to get me killed.' She hangs up the phone.

"'Look what you did to my nose,' she says, right back to my face. There was no winning with her. This is the way our lives had been going for a couple of years.

"After a while, when I'd get home, I'd come home very cautiously. Not just because of her pistol, but I was concerned that she would really hire someone."

◆ ◆ ◆

"Both Geri and Frank had terrible tempers," Geri's sister, Barbara Stokich, recalls. "They had tantrums. There was ketchup and mustard on the ceiling. Geri was spoiled. Even as a child when she got mad she would scream and fall to the floor and beat her hands and feet into the ground.

"Geri was too strong willed. To her, life was not a two-way street. She needed to dictate the terms. And Frank was exactly the same way.

"Once, in my house, after they had another fight, she admitted that it wasn't always Frank's fault. She admitted that she wasn't always fair to him. But she said he wanted her to give up drinking, and she said she'd rather die than give up alcohol.

"I think Geri's original plan was to divorce Frank right away if it didn't work out, but nine months after the wedding she had Steven and he was everything to her. She adored Steven. She hadn't understood how things would change when she had a kid. Now she could never leave Steven.

"She felt alone. I'd get calls at three in the morning. Why wasn't he home with her and the kids? Lefty was living the big life. She heard that he was going out with showgirls. She knew it. She found receipts for jewelry in his pockets when she took his clothes to the cleaners.

"She'd come over to my place and let off steam and say if he could fool around, she could fool around. And she did."

◆ ◆ ◆

"Geri took the kids on a vacation to La Costa," Lefty said. "When she left we weren't getting along too well. On the second day she was drunk and couldn't get on the phone. I didn't talk to her for the next two days.

"Then, just before they were supposed to come home, I still hadn't heard from them. I checked the hotel and was told they had moved out two days ago. I really began to panic. I couldn't even find them on any of the airline manifests.

"I called Robin's boyfriend. He was a decent kid. I told him I was looking for my wife and kids. At first he said that he didn't know anything. Then he told me that Geri and the kids were with Lenny Marmor and Robin. He gave me a phone number.

"Lenny Marmor answers the phone. He sounded sharp. Slick. A smooth way of talking. He had a fake slight Southern accent.

"I said, 'Lenny, this is Frank Rosenthal. I want to talk to Geri.' He said she was not there.

"'Lenny,' I said, 'I want to talk to Geri. It's very important. I want my kids. I want her to put them on a plane, quick.'

"He said, very sincerely, 'Frank, believe me, I don't know where she is. But can I call you back in a few minutes?'

"'Fine,' I say, and I hang up.

"That was it. They all hit the road. Geri, Robin, my kids, and Marmor.

"That night Geri calls Spilotro. He calls me right away and says she's worried that I was going to have them traced and killed.

"He told her: 'I can't help you. Just send the kids back now. Frank's in a panic.'

"She calls. 'Hi.' 'Hi.'

"I told her I wasn't going to ask where she was; just put Steven and Stephanie on a plane as quickly as she could. Then call me back and give me their arrival time. Then you can do what you want to do."

"Geri then asks, 'If I were to come back, would you forgive me?'

"I told her I didn't know. I said I'd try. I know I still cared for her, but I said, 'Right now you've got to send me the kids.'

"She hung up and talked to Lenny and Robin. And what does Lenny say?" Geri later told Rosenthal. "He tells her to get the money out of a safe deposit box I had in Los Angeles, dye her hair, and take off with him and the kids for Europe. Geri told Lenny no because she knew me and said that I'd hunt them down until I found them. She called me back and said she was sending the kids. She called later with their flight number. The housekeeper and I went to the airport and we got the two kids.

"A little while later Geri calls. She's feeling me out. I said to her, 'You didn't go to the box, did you?' She didn't answer me. I said, 'Geri, what happened to the money?' She said she made a mistake.

" 'How serious a mistake?'

" 'Serious,' she says.

"Remember there's over two million cash in that box.

" 'What's it under?' I ask.

" 'Twenty-five,' she says.

"Twenty-five thousand?

"'Yes,' she says. She bought him some clothes. A new watch. Junk. Real pimp stuff.

"I said: 'Don't worry about it. It's no big deal. I'll have a Lear out there in a couple of hours to pick you up. Just hold that key. Don't let Lenny near the key. If he gets the key, he'll be able to open the box.

"'You've lost twenty-five thousand dollars to that pimp,' I said. 'I can handle that. I can't handle any more.'

"Geri said when she told Robin she was coming back to me, Robin said she felt like she had no mother. Robin's loyalty had always been to Lenny Marmor, her natural father.

"Len had never married Geri. He had gotten married three times, but he never married Geri, the mother of his daughter. Still, Geri was as loyal to him as she could be to anyone. It was unreal.

"In a few hours I get a call from the pilot, who gives me the time he expects to land, and I get out to the airport and she wobbles off the plane. She's got a big smile. Like nothing happened.

"On the drive home we're talking about the box. She said she couldn't get the safe deposit key from Robin. But there was no danger since the banks had been closed.

"We started arguing, again. When we got home the phone was ringing. It was Spilotro.

"'How are things?' he wants to know. I tell him things are okay. Geri says: 'Is that Tony? Can I talk to him?' I said no.

"Tony says: 'I want to talk to her.'

"I say no again.

"Tony now says, 'I want to talk to her. Do you hear me?' He's sounding a little strong.

"I said no again, and I thank him for his help, and he interrupts.

"'But I said I want to talk to her,' he says.

"I hung up on him.

" 'Was that Tony?' Geri asked. 'I wanted to talk to him.'

"I told her I wanted to talk about the money in the box. The next morning we waited for a call from Robin. I didn't answer it because I didn't want to spook anything.

"Robin said that Lenny had been trying to get Robin to give him her key to the box.

"Geri says, 'I am begging you with my life, don't do it. Don't listen to your father.'

"Geri is crying on the phone and begging Robin. A terrific performance. Robin surrenders . . . She promises she won't raid the box."

♦ ♦ ♦

"As the marriage began to fall apart," Geri's sister, Barbara Stokich, said, "Frank would beat her up and she'd come to my place. She'd have a black eye. A black-and-blue face. Ribs. One night it was so bad we took pictures. Right in my house.

"Then Geri and Robin got mad at me because I wouldn't give them the pictures. They wanted to take him to court. I didn't give them the pictures, because the pictures didn't prove it was Frank who beat her. They just showed she had been beaten. I remember I destroyed them. She thought she was going to be able to use the pictures to prove that he beat her when she took the case to court. Robin used to tell me everything that went on, until she turned on me for not turning over the pictures."

♦ ♦ ♦

"Lefty made her life miserable," said a retired FBI agent familiar with the case. "He cheated on her all the time, and he

didn't care if she found out. He started to keep tabs on her like she was a Vegas version of a Stepford wife.

"He used to tape her schedule for the day onto the refrigerator in the morning, and he wanted to know where she was going to be every minute of the day. He also made her check in with him during the day.

"He even bought her a beeper so he could always get ahold of her, but she kept 'losing' it, and that drove him even more nuts. One time she was about a half hour late coming home with the kids. She said she got caught behind a long freight train that used to come through late in the afternoon. He made her stand there in front of him as he called the railroad freight yard and got the dispatcher just to double-check the time the freight went through.

"But no matter what he did to her, she'd never leave him, because there were always presents. Geri was an old hooker. He bought her when they got married, and she stayed bought."

♦ ♦ ♦

"Looking back," Lefty said, "I realize we probably had three or four months of peace in our whole marriage. That was it. I was a fool. I was naive. I had really wanted a family. I never understood I couldn't control her.

"One night I was in the Jubilation doing my TV show and Geri was in the audience. I see that Tony was also there. I see her go to the ladies' room. I see Tony tried to stop her, but she fluffed him off. I didn't know why, but the whole little thing didn't sit right with me. I didn't say anything."

♦ ♦ ♦

"Geri was a disaster," Tony Spilotro's pal Frank Cullotta said. "She was drinking a lot. She was doing a lot of coke, uppers, downers, everything.

"She caused Lefty a lot of embarrassment right at a time when he was having problems of his own with the Gaming Commission.

"Nobody liked Lefty. He was egotistical and he'd walk through a joint without acknowledging one person. He was arrogant. Lefty paid his dues to Chicago, but he acted like he didn't have to acknowledge Tony any longer."

♦ ♦ ♦

"It was about two in morning, and Tony comes into the Stardust with another guy, and they're loaded," Murray Ehrenberg, the Stardust casino manager, says. "He's not even supposed to be in the place, but everybody pretended like we didn't know who he was.

"He goes over to a hundred-dollar blackjack table and starts playing five blacks [$500] a hand. He's playing all alone and he's losing. I see him go for ten thousand dollars out of his own kick in about twenty minutes.

"He starts to abuse the dealer. When he gets a card he doesn't like he skips it back at the guy and asks for another. The pit boss nods for the dealer to do it. If that card's no good, Tony throws it back and tells the dealer to shove it up his ass. We're praying he gets good cards, but one after another are bad, and he's getting very pissed. We're just trying to get out of the night alive.

"Then Tony asks the pit boss for fifty thousand dollars credit. He knows the pit boss can't extend that kind of line, and pretty soon I'm dragged in.

"'Call you-know-who and get me my money,' Tony says.

"I called Lefty on a special phone line we had set up at home. I tell him the Little Guy was in the place and wanted fifty credit. I told Lefty the guy had already lost ten of his own.

"Lefty was mad. Tony wasn't even supposed to walk in the Stardust, forget about play and ask for credit. Lefty told me to put Tony on the phone and told Tony he'd make him even. Give him back the money he lost. But he ordered Tony to get out of the casino that instant, before some rat who worked in the Stardust tipped off the control board and he got everybody in trouble.

"Tony wasn't that drunk. He didn't want to create a war. Because of the skim and Lefty's license and everything else, the control board was already coming down very hard on the Stardust.

"I okayed Tony's ten thousand, which, of course, he never paid back, but Lefty didn't care about that. Lefty just wanted to make sure that I didn't put Tony's name down on any credit slip or anything in the place.

"When Tony left he was really angry, but there wasn't much he could do about it. Deep down he might have known Lefty was right, but he didn't have to like it."

◆ ◆ ◆

"It was a Friday or Saturday night," Lefty said. "It was after the TV show, and I was at the Jubilation. Joey Cusumano was standing next to me. I called the house. No answer. It's two o'clock in the morning and there was no answer.

"I told Cusumano I was going home. It was only a five-minute drive.

"When I got there I found Geri and Steven missing. My daughter's ankle was tied to the bed with a clothesline rope.

"I can't believe this. I'm untying the kid and the phone rings.

"'How ya doing?' It's Tony.

"'Not good. What's on your mind?'

"'Relax. Relax. Everything's okay. She's okay. You two have been fighting. She wanted to discuss your problems.'

"He said Geri had dropped Steven off with a neighbor. He said I should relax and come over to the Village Pub.

"I drove over there raging. It was kind of crowded. Tony was waiting inside the front door. He tried to quiet me down.

"'Don't make a scene,' he says. Tony is standing between me and the door, but I know Tony. I'm not going to brush past him disrespectfully. I tell him I'm okay and walk all the way around him.

"Inside, she's in a booth with her back to me. I have to go past her and turn around to confront her. I sat down.

"I called her a few names. She was being careful. She was loaded. She just kept saying I should let her alone. After a while, I took her home. On the way out, Tony told me not to be too rough on her. 'She's only trying to save your marriage,' he said."

◆ ◆ ◆

"She was a beautiful person, but he drove her to drink," Geri's friend Suzanne Kloud, a makeup artist on Lefty's TV show, recalls. "He'd drive anybody to drink. He'd come home after his show at three or four in the morning, kick her out of bed, and talk to one of his girlfriends on the phone for two hours.

"He didn't care about her feelings. He was always screwing around with the dancers, and he flaunted it. She told me that one time he flew into Los Angeles and he spent fourteen thousand dollars at Gucci for some dancers and he bought another one a seventeen-thousand-dollar necklace.

"She said she found the receipts in his pockets when she'd take his clothes to the cleaners. I mean, here's a guy who's not exactly looking for a quiet evening at home.

"He was always abusive to her, almost like he hated her. One night after the show she thought she was having dinner with him. He was surrounded by all his flunkies and she went up and interrupted him.

"She grabbed his arm. She wanted to know, in front of all those people, when they were leaving. It was stupid. He pulled his arm away.

"He says, 'Don't you fucking touch me,' to his own wife in front of a whole crowd.

"I grabbed her and we went off to eat. I asked her why she did such a thing—it was only going to create a scene. But Geri seemed to always cause scenes with him. She knew what drove him nuts, but she'd do it anyway. She told me she didn't know why. She just had to do it.

"But as miserable as he was, he'd also bring her stuff. He gave her the most incredible jewelry. He gave her a pink coral-and-diamond necklace and she had a cat's-eye necklace surrounded by diamonds. The necklaces were worth two hundred thousand and three hundred thousand dollars. And she lived for that. If you were a hustler, that's your God."

◆ ◆ ◆

"I remember I was watching football," Lefty said. "She knew I was preoccupied. She said, 'I'm going to my sister's.' She said she was dropping Steven off at some neighbors and taking Stephanie to Barbara's with her.

"She wanted to know if I might want some McDonald's on her way home. I said maybe. She knew I liked McDonald's. She gave me Barbara's number. I didn't have her sister's number. I didn't give a fuck about her sister. She left the number near the phone and left.

"About halftime I decided to call her sister. I was going to tell her to bring me back some McDonald's.

"I called and Barbara said she was at McDonald's getting lunch for Stephanie.

"I said okay, have her call me when she gets back.

"I go back to the game, but after a half hour I still haven't heard from Geri, and the mental computer starts clicking time.

"I called Barbara back and asked if Geri got back.

"'No,' she says.

"Now I'm a little annoyed. She was supposed to be getting a McDonald's for Stephanie and she hasn't done it. What about Stephanie's lunch?

"I tell Barbara, 'Make sure she calls me when she gets back.'

"Fifteen minutes. No Geri.

"I call back. 'Okay Barbara,' I say, 'get in your car and bring my daughter home.'

"I then go and get Steven, and Barbara brings Stephanie back, and now that I've got the kids home, I can try and find Geri.

"On that day Geri had taken my car. It was bigger than hers. I had a mobile phone in my car. So I rang my mobile number just in case. The phone gets picked up, but it's a man's voice. Muffled. Covered up. But I know the voice. I've known it all my life. It was Tony's. I knew Tony's voice no matter what.

"I hung right up. Uh oh. What the hell do I have here? Just to make sure, I called the number right back, but this time I get the operator saying that the mobile number is not in service at this time.

"Now I'm not able to watch the football game. I've got a real problem coming up. It gets to be about seven or eight o'clock at night. No Geri. Finally I get a call from her manicurist.

"'Frank,' he says. 'Geri is hysterical,' he says. 'She ran out of gas and she had to get towed, and she feels she's in trouble with you.'

"I stayed calm. 'It's okay,' I said. 'Put her on.'

"She's crying. 'I love you. I'm sorry.'

"She didn't sound right, and I didn't think she knew it was me who got Tony on the car phone, but I didn't want to say anything right then.

"I had to go to Los Angeles for a few hours the next day. I asked her if she wanted to come. Do some shopping. She said she didn't feel like it. She wanted to get a manicure. So off I went while she stayed home.

"When I got back late in the afternoon she was home, and I noticed her hands.

"'Gee,' I said, 'you didn't get your manicure?'

"'No,' she said. 'I didn't feel like it. It was raining.'

"'What did you do?'

"'Oh, nothing. I had lunch with my sister.'

"'That's nice,' I said, but I'm ninety percent sure she's on the bullshit. 'Where'd you go?' I'm being casual, but I sense she's catching on.

"'The country club.'

"'What'd you have?'

"And she told me some salad or something.

"'And what did Barbara have?'

"She told me what her sister had.

"'Okay,' I said, 'get your sister on the phone. I want you to ask your sister what she had for lunch.'

"Geri gets a piece of paper and writes down her sister's phone number and starts to go down the stairs to give the paper to our housekeeper to call Barbara.

"I grabbed the paper.

"'You didn't have lunch with Barbara, did you?'

"'Yes I did,' she says.

"'Okay,' I said, 'then I'm calling her.'

"I pick up the phone.

"'All right, all right,' she says, kind of annoyed. 'I didn't have lunch with Barbara.'

"'Then what were you doing?'

"'I was just fooling around with some of my old pals. I know you don't like them, and I didn't want to say. That's all.'

"I said, 'Look Geri, the best thing is for me to tell it the way it is. I feel you've been with somebody. I know it. We both know it. I just hope it wasn't with one of two guys.'

"'What two?' she asks, looking me in the eye. Almost a smile.

"'Tony or Joey,' I say. She just looks at me with a little smile. 'Geri,' I say, 'this is no fucking game. I'm not going to listen to any more games. You go down the line with me right now, or you're out of here.' I'm telling her if she bull-shits me the marriage is over.

"She was full of Tuinal. She told me it was Tony. She told it straight. No big deal. She said they had been half boozed when it began. I'm listening to her and I'm getting sick inside.

"Then she says, 'Oh, by the way, he's gonna be calling up at six o'clock.'

"Now I want to die. I'll have to talk to him like I don't know what she's just told me. I tried to explain that we were all in danger. I told her not to tell Tony she'd told me about it. If Tony suspected I knew, he might think I'd make a beef back home, and she and I would both be killed. I knew him. We'd both just disappear. She said she understood. It had been a crazy thing. She'd get us all out of this. But she needed a little time to back him off. She couldn't just stop seeing him in the morning. He'd get suspicious I'd found out. The plan was to let it die out nice and smoothly.

"At six o'clock the call came in. It was the loudest ring I ever heard. She told Tony that I just got back and wasn't feeling well and that she'd talk to him in the morning.

"She filled me in on the background. She said that they had been seeing each other for six months to a year. I remembered when Geri and I were dating. I remembered taking her with me to Chicago. One of my first stops was to see Tony and Nancy and his brothers. I walked into Tony's house with Geri. She was in a classy miniskirt. I remembered he said, 'Holy shit! Where did you find her?'

"I took her to see my friends back home. We went to the country ranch and saw Fiore. I could see he was pleased and approved.

"But now it was over and I had a choice. I could go to Chicago and take a position against Tony, but I was trying to prevent a war. I felt there would be no winners. I told her that. She said she understood and that it was over and that she would break it off.

"I asked what if Tony didn't want to break it off, and she said that would be no problem. She'd just back him off. If you listened to her she was really convincing.

"Instead, I later found out, they went right on meeting—in motels, or his apartment in the Towers across from the club, or wherever.

"Plus, he starts asking me all the time: 'Is anything wrong? Is everything okay?' He's poking. I know him. One night I'm at the Stardust. One of the guys says to me, 'Our buddy's gonna call.'

"I knew he would be calling on one of the six booths in the back of the casino. I went back and waited for the call.

" 'How are you?' he asks me.

" 'Fine,' I say.

" 'I just wanted to ask you something,' he says, and he starts talking to me about some horseshit thing he would never pay attention to. Then he gets around to why he called.

"He asks: 'How are you and Geri getting along?'

" 'Why do you ask?'

" 'I just wanted to ask you something.'

" 'What?'

" 'Do you still love her?' he asks me.

" 'Yeah,' I say. 'Sure I do. Shouldn't I?'

" 'No, no,' Tony says. 'I was just asking.'

"She had obviously told him we had been to see Oscar. I told her I was thinking about a formal separation. A divorce. Even without the Tony situation—which no one knew about—I had told her this thing wasn't working."

♦ ♦ ♦

"In late 1979 and the early 1980s we were on Spilotro all the time," retired FBI agent Emmett Michaels said. "It was routine. He'd think he slipped us, but we always had him from the surveillance plane. This time the plane tracked him to a mobile trailer he had way out on Tropicana Avenue.

"It was a hot day, and when we got there we just sat on him for a couple of hours. This was a place he used to go with his girlfriends. I knew his home life wasn't the best because one time when I was bringing him in on some periodic questioning, he asked Nancy for some cigarette money. 'Fuck you,' she said, 'get your own cigarette money.'

"On this day, Tony had no idea that the plane had taken

him to the trailer and that we would be waiting there when he left. There wasn't even a wire in the place. We were sitting in a van a couple of blocks away using glasses. I'll never forget it. The door to the trailer opens and out comes Tony, and right behind him, out comes Geri Rosenthal. They had been in there over an hour.

"Geri was Nancy Spilotro's best friend. We couldn't believe it. We kept passing the glasses back and forth just to make sure. It was her, all right. She was about a foot and half taller than him. No mistake. We knew that it was only a matter of time before the word got out that Tony was having an affair with Lefty's wife. I mean, who could keep a secret like that?"

♦ ♦ ♦

"Even though Spilotro tried to be discreet, she didn't," retired FBI agent Mike Simon said. "It was the worst-kept secret in town. In no time, everybody knew. Geri began showing up at the beauty parlor and gym with presents that she said came from her new sponsor, which is hooker talk for a boyfriend or protector.

"She also began telling her friends that her new sponsor was Tony Spilotro. Geri did not keep up any pretenses."

♦ ♦ ♦

"Spilotro openly flaunted his relationship with Geri as a show of power," Kent Clifford, the chief of Las Vegas Metro intelligence, said. "He could have had dozens of women younger and prettier than Geri Rosenthal, but power is an aphrodisiac.

"But Spilotro's ego got in the way. I'm sure Spilotro felt, 'I can do it and nobody can do anything about it. She's my girlfriend, my moll.' It was a stupid thing for him to do."

♦ ♦ ♦

"I go to Chicago," Cullotta said, "and they heard about something. 'What the fuck's going on out there?' Joey Lombardo says. 'What's he doing? Fucking the guy's wife?'

"I lied. I said no. I played dumb. I said I didn't know anything about that. What could I say—that Tony was fucking Lefty's wife and that the FBI and Metro were all over everybody?

"'We hope he's not,' they said, but I can see that they are perturbed.

"Next, Joe Nick, that's Joe Ferriola, sees me. 'What's going on with that fucking Jew?' he says. 'He's acting crazy. The Little Guy wouldn't be fucking his old lady, would he? Because, if he is, that's a problem.'

"I lied again. I said no. There's nothing going on. The fucking guy is just crazy. Tony could have been called in and killed for jeopardizing everything, but by now they're sure Lefty was a psycho. Only the bosses, like Joey Aiuppa, backed Lefty, but only because they had known him for so many years.

"Later that night, I was in Rocky's Lounge, North Avenue and Melrose Park—that was Jackie Cerone's joint—and I was at the bar with Larry Neumann and Wayne Matecki, two stone dead killers, scary looking guys, and Cerone comes at me at the bar.

"'Is there a problem with the Jew guy and his old lady?' Jackie Cerone asks me. Shit, I think, this is all over town. Somebody brought this story back, and the only person I knew who could bring the story back was Lefty.

"I told Cerone that Lefty and his old lady argued all the

time, and that's all. Then he looked at me and asked: 'Is the little guy fucking her?'

"I said no. What could I say? Jackie Cerone was a boss and he hated both Tony and Lefty.

"'Well,' Cerone says, 'we wouldn't want to jeopardize anything with our friends.'

"When I got back to Las Vegas I told Tony about these questions and he got hot. We were walking back and forth in front of the Gold Rush on West Sahara, and he's got his mouth covered because the Gee was using lip readers with binoculars.

"'That fucking Jew motherfucker,' he says. 'He ran back there and cried. The Jew fuck is gonna start a war. I gotta think about it.'"

♦ ♦ ♦

"I assumed she had backed Tony off," Lefty said, "but when I suspected she was still talking to Lenny Marmor, I had my home phone bugged. I put the tapes in because when I'd get home and she'd be on the phone, she'd quickly hang up or say, 'I'll call you back.' And I wanted to make sure she didn't try and kidnap my children again.

"The tape reels had a one-hour limit. I had the unit set up in the garage. First couple of days I found out that she talked to Nancy Spilotro a lot. And I'd hear things like, 'Guess what Mr. Know-It-All just said to me?'

"One day she called her father and said, 'I wish you'd kill the sonofabitch.' I could hear her glass tinkling in the background. Her father asked if she was drinking.

"'Daddy,' she says, 'I haven't had a drink in months.'

"As I listened to the tape, I had to eat a lot of shit. It was very hard. I couldn't tip my hand that I knew what she was saying behind my back.

"And then, after a couple of days, I heard her talking to Tony on the tapes. He talked very quickly. She'd tell him when I was coming home. This was after she told me she was going to back him off. After I warned her of the danger and everything. And now I'm listening to her talk to Tony with my own ears, planning where they could meet. 'I'll meet you at the baseball field.' 'Vincent is playing tomorrow afternoon.' 'I'll see you at the ball game; he'll be working.' 'Frank'll never call.' That kind of stuff.

"I couldn't even look at her, I was so angry with what I heard. She was going to get us killed.

"The kids had a swim meet the next day and went to bed early, and that night, I said, 'Geri, level with me. If you've never leveled with me before, tell me the truth. Are you still seeing our friend?'

"I told her, 'You're just as much at risk as I am. They'll kill you before they kill me or him.'

" 'Don't worry,' she says. 'It's over.'

"Meanwhile, I know I've got her on tape and she's still meeting the guy.

"I asked, 'Do you have any contact at all with him?'

" 'No dear,' she says.

" 'Are you sure?' I say.

" 'After all we've been through, I'm surprised you could even ask,' she says.

" 'Okay, Geri,' I say. 'Swear.'

" 'I swear,' Geri says. 'I would never. Can't you ever let it go?'

" 'Swear to me,' I say. 'Swear to me on your son's life and then I'll let it go.'

"She looks right at me. She's angry. 'I swear on our son's life,' she says. 'Now will you stop?'

" 'You bitch!' I said. 'I've got you recorded.'

"And I took out the small recorder with the cassette and I

pressed the play button, and she heard herself talking to Tony.

"'Turn that off!' she screamed at me. 'I don't want to hear any more!'

"'You bitch,' I say. Now I'm really hot. 'I'm gonna throw you out this fucking window!'

"She starts screaming. 'Steven! Help! Steven!'

"The poor kid comes out half asleep. He's about nine. Now Geri had me backed off.

"'If you don't get off me,' she said, 'I'm calling the police.'

"I walked out and went to the casino. I had some dinner and later went back home and fell asleep. I made my priority Steven and Stephanie's swim meet."

♦ ♦ ♦

Lefty had already begun to divide things up shortly after Geri returned from her trip to Beverly Hills with Lenny Marmor. He'd filed a quit claim agreement in court separating the properties in preparation for the dissolution of the marriage. According to the terms of the agreement, Lefty got almost everything: the house at 972 Vegas Valley Drive; lots 144 and 145 at Las Vegas Country Club Estates on Augusta Drive; and the couple's four Thoroughbred race horses—Island Moon, Last Reason, Est Mi Amigo, and Mister Commonwealth.

But three safety deposit boxes at the First National Bank of Nevada, Strip branch, remained in both their names. According to Rosenthal, he needed someone to have access to the cash if he was under arrest or otherwise unable to get to his own money.

Lefty had also gotten Geri to agree that she would lose her right "to care, custody and control of their minor children if she engaged in alcohol and or barbiturates."

♦ ♦ ♦

Geri's letter to Robin:

4-5-79
3:12 AM
My Dearest Robin . . .
Honey I don't want to worry you but I don't know how much more I can take here. As I sit here tonight I have a cracked rib, 2 black eyes, bruises all over my body & I don't have to tell you how I got all of it. All in the last two weeks. Last night he came home drunk & choked me until I lost consciousness. I really can't tell this to anyone but you because *no* one cares. Believe it or not I can handle all the shit but I also might take the gun & fuckin kill him one night. He almost killed me last night. When I regained consciousness he was standing over me so drunk & ready to kick me. He doesn't even care or know what he's doing anymore when he drinks. Tonight he came home and started again so I screamed at him to go back out & leave me alone & he started to get mean again so I just sat there & let him rant & rave & prayed he wouldn't hit me again. I'm deathly afraid of him. . . .
Please write me. I love you & don't talk on my phone—he listens—Mom.

♦ ♦ ♦

"We were in the Jubilation and Tony got the idea of whacking Lefty," Frank Cullotta said. "He didn't say Lefty's name. He said 'the Jew.' He said, 'The Jew, I'm not sure yet. But if I'm right, I need you to get a guy. You got somebody?'

"I says, 'Yeah, the big guy.'

"He says, 'Well I don't want you hitting him on the street.'

"I says, 'Who?'

"He says, 'The Jew.'

"He says, 'I'll set him up, so when he pulls up, you scoop him. You'll know where the hole's at.'

"We'd just have to move the plywood, drop him in the hole and cover it up.

"And then Tony says, 'But I'll let you know when.'

"I says, 'Okay.'

"He says, 'I'll let you know, but for now I'm not sure.'

♦ ♦ ♦

"She started staying out all night," Murray Ehrenberg said. "Who knew what she was doing? She was either loaded or high most of the time. But Frank wasn't much better. He was getting drunk and bouncing around every night with his dancers. He's throwing money away. Buying them this. Buying them that. He lost a bundle playing blackjack. He was probably the worst blackjack player I ever saw, or else he was punishing himself for something."

♦ ♦ ♦

"I owned the Upper Crust Pizzeria," Frank Cullotta said. "We had food, but it was also a hangout. One morning, really early, we were still preparing the food—it must have been seven, eight, eight thirty—Geri pulls up. She comes out of the car and leaves the car door open. She looks haggard. She was the kind of woman you didn't want to challenge in public because she could make a real scene. She'd flail around and scream and swing her arms, and she was tall and striking looking and she was a nightmare to handle.

"She comes storming into the restaurant yelling, 'Where the fuck is he?'

"'Please, Geri,' I say, 'calm down; don't make a commotion.'

"'I want to see him now,' she says. 'Where is he? I'm gonna kill that motherfucker. Now.'

"I tell my old lady to watch her—she's hysterical. We put her in a booth in the lounge and I lock the front door. She wanted to talk to Tony immediately.

"I call Tony and she's screaming in the background that she's gonna kill the Jew. Meanwhile, I know if Nancy finds out about all of this with Geri, there's gonna be hell to pay.

"Tony never drove in Las Vegas. He always sat in the passenger's seat. This morning he's there in two minutes. He had Sammy Siegel drive him. Sammy would be at his house from early till late playing gin rummy with Tony and taking Tony anywhere he wanted to go. That was Sammy's job.

"Tony walks in the door and he tells me to move her car around back so nobody sees it. I told Ernie to put her car in back.

"I walked away, but I can see that he's talking to her and he's moving his hands up and down in a chopping motion like he always did, and she's got tears come down her face and she's nodding a little bit, and finally he tells her to leave.

"Her car was round back and we're standing there when she drove off. Tony turns and looks at me. 'I fucked up,' he said."

21.

"I just fucked Tony Spilotro."

"**F**rank was scared to death," Murray Ehrenberg said. "Frank was a pretty private guy. He never wanted to show his emotions. He never did. He was always in himself, except the night he called and asked me to come over. That's the first time I ever heard panic in his voice. 'Come on over,' he said, 'and bring a gun.' He said he needed some protection. He said he didn't want to be alone for some reason. He wanted somebody there. I thought maybe he needs protection and a witness or something. I said, 'Don't worry. I'll be right there. And I'll bring my kid's hunting rifle. When I saw him he was really in shock. It's the first time I'd ever seen him that way, and I'd worked for him for years.

"After I got there he calmed down and we were sitting there half asleep when we hear this noise. We jumped up and went outside and here comes Geri. She was pie-eyed. Her eyes were wild. She was out of it. Absolutely wild. She went right through the garage door. She dented up the car. I was standing there. She just missed my feet. She didn't even wait for the garage door to lift. She hit the door on the bottom.

"She'd been out all night."

♦ ♦ ♦

"I could hear her through the closed windows," Lefty said. "I could hear her say, 'Where are my kids, you motherfucker?'

"Geri didn't usually talk that way. That's another reason why I thought there was something the matter with her. Booze? Pills? Drugs? What, I didn't know.

"I asked her to roll down the window, which she did by about one inch, and I got as close as I could and asked her to cool it. 'Can we talk this over? Be careful.'

"'Fuck you,' she screams again, and puts the car in gear and crashes into the lowered garage door.

"Now the neighbors are all up and they're standing in the street, and now a couple of cop cars show up at the house. There are two cops there. I know them.

"Geri says she wants to get into the house. The hell with her, I say. But I know I don't stand a chance. She's got me dead. Here's the nice wife of the notorious casino guy and gambler with connections to the mob. The whole nine yards. I'd be chopped meat to her in court.

"Still, in response to Geri's request, I ask her, 'Where's your asshole boyfriend?'

"'What boyfriend?' she says, straight faced.

"'You know who,' I tell her.

"Geri turns to the cops and demands that they get me to let her in the house. It's half my house, she says.

"The two cops are anti–Frank Rosenthal. No question about it. I'm Mr. Notorious.

"'Hey Frank,' one of them says, 'why don't you let her in the house? Let her in so we can all go home.'

"I say I'll give her the key if she only stays in there five minutes. Why not? The money, the jewelry, the kids are all gone. There's nothing for her to steal.

"In about three minutes she's out of the house. I'm in the driveway with Murray Ehrenberg and the cops. She has her hands behind her back.

"She gets to about ten feet of me and she twirls around and she has a pistol aimed at my head. The cops took off. You've never seen anybody run like they did. They ran back to behind their cars and hid.

"Geri looks at me and she says: 'I want my money and jewelry or I'll kill you.'

"She's waving the gun all around the place.

"And who pulls up around now but Nancy Spilotro.

"Nancy starts talking to Geri and she starts taking Geri's side. I said, 'Nancy, this is not your problem. You've got your own problems.'

"And out of the corner of my eye I see Tony Spilotro drive by real quick. He's in a car and he's wearing a cap and beard.

"The cops are telling Geri to put the gun down. Nancy tells Geri to put the gun down. I said, 'Geri, don't shoot. You don't want to go to the electric chair.'

"It's almost humorous, it's so mad.

"Suddenly, Nancy grabs Geri's arm and the cops come from behind the cars and quickly cuff her. Then I get dumb in the head. I see Geri there with her hands cuffed and she starts crying. 'Dear,' she says, 'they're hurting me! Don't let them hurt me. Don't let them do it.'

"I tell the cops to let her alone. I told them I'm not pressing any charges and we've got a license for the gun.

"I'm worn out. I guess I was still trying to save something here. I don't know. Looking back it doesn't make sense. None of it made any sense.

"Anyway, after the cops left, we all went into the house. Geri and me and Murray Ehrenberg."

◆ ◆ ◆

LAS VEGAS METROPOLITAN POLICE DEPARTMENT
OFFICER'S REPORT
D.R. 80-72481
09-08-80   0900 HRS
Location of Occurrence . . . 972 Vegas Valley Drive, Las Vegas, Nevada. Country Club Estates.
DETAILS:

On 09-08-80 at approximately 0900 hours, this date, I, Officer Archer and Officer Brady Frank were dispatched to the Country Club Estates, 972 Vegas Valley Drive, Las Vegas, NV in regards to a family disturbance which was getting out of hand and reported by Security of the Country Club Estates.

Upon arrival we were at the East Security Gate, we were contacted by Mrs. Frank Rosenthal, who was extremely upset and wanted to return to her residence, at 972 Vegas Valley Drive, and retrieve her personal belongings.

At this time she was also talking about the Security officers not accompanying her to her house, that she would contact the FBI.

While trying to obtain information from Mrs. Frank Rosenthal, a Nancy Spilotro arrived in an Oldsmobile, bearing Ut, (Utah) NLE697, blue in color. Mrs. Rosenthal was driving a tan Mercedes coupe, CWN014, NV.

Mrs. Spilotro advised these Officers that she was here to pick up Mrs. Frank Rosenthal and that Mrs. Rosenthal was extremely upset and hysterical, however, Mrs. Rosenthal refused to get in the vehicle with her and sped off down the street with her Mercedes.

Mrs. Spilotro advised these Officers that there was a shouting match and that she would assist in attempting to remedy the disturbance between the husband and wife.

We all went to 972 Vegas Valley Drive and Mr. Frank

Rosenthal was in the driveway with his wife, his wife rammed the rear of his Cadillac that was in the garage with her personal vehicle, being a Mercedes, causing minor damage.

We managed to get the vehicle shut off and Mrs. Frank Rosenthal started an argument with her husband, however, he did not wish the Officers' assistance and stated it was only a family disturbance and that he would take care of it and resolve the situation.

Nancy Spilotro also was assisting Frank Rosenthal in trying to calm his wife and keep the disturbance from annoying the neighbors in the area. At this time they asked these officers if everything was in order and the officers could leave.

These officers started to leave at which time Mrs. Frank Rosenthal ran into the residence at 972 Vegas Valley locking her husband, Frank, outside.

She then came out a side entrance of the residence and came around the front holding her stomach. She was screaming about jewelry and that Frank had hers and she wanted it. Along with money.

These Officers were not aware of the fact that she had a weapon until she started across the street in front of 972 Vegas Valley Drive at which time, a chrome-plated .38 special was seen by these officers after she had pulled it from her blouse.

She was waving the gun about, these officers requested assistance. At which time, Nancy Spilotro approached Mrs. Frank Rosenthal, managing to calm her down some and then as she had her back up against the building, Mrs. Spilotro grabbed Mrs. Rosenthal about the arms, wrestling her to the ground, at which time, these Officers closed in and assisted Nancy Spilotro in taking the weapon from Mrs. Frank Rosenthal.

The weapon being a .38 caliber snubnose Smith & Wesson chrome plate, air weight, "Ladies Special," Serial #37J508. "Geri Rosenthal" was engraved on the pearl handle. It had a capacity of 5 rounds of .38 caliber cartridges. The one cartridge out of the hammer of this weapon had been spent and fired, however, it is not known by these officers if it was fired inside the house or at another time. The weapon was impounded for safekeeping by this Officer A. Archer.

During all this family disturbance, Mrs. Frank Rosenthal kept telling her husband that she was going to the FBI. He told her, "go ahead, you fink." He stated, if she did, she would be in trouble herself. Mr. Frank Rosenthal took his wife into custody, after the officer had retrieved the weapon along with Nancy Spilotro and took her off into the garage area of the residence again. And had closed the garage automatic locking doors excluding these officers from the building area.

♦ ♦ ♦

"We were in the kitchen," Ehrenberg said. "Nancy went home. Geri started washing dishes. Like nothing was wrong. She was just standing there. She'd settled down. You know. Frank and I were talking and he looks up at her. She had just turned around, as if she's looking for cigarettes, and he says, 'What?'

"And out of the clear blue sky, she said, 'I just fucked Tony Spilotro.' That's exactly what she said. I was there. In the house. I heard it. She said, 'I just fucked Tony Spilotro.'

"Frank said, 'What did you say?'

"She said: 'I just fucked Tony Spilotro.'

"He said: 'Shut your mouth.' He didn't get excited, like, you know, a husband would. Like, 'I'll kick your ass, you tramp,' or anything. He said, 'Keep your mouth shut.'

"I mean it must have hit him like a hammer. With his ego and everything. She could have picked anybody in the world but this guy. Then she said she had to make a phone call and didn't want to use any of the phones in the house. She drove away so fast we could hear her bouncing over the speed bumps.

"After she left, we sat around for a few minutes when he jumped up. That's when he realized that she was going to the bank.

"He said get in the car. And me, like a schmuck, I got in the car. He drove. He was going lickety split because the bank was on the Strip."

♦ ♦ ♦

LAS VEGAS METROPOLITAN POLICE DEPARTMENT
80-72481   9-08-80

This is a continuation of the Officer's report dictated by Officer A. Archer PN489 on 9-08-80 of a Family Disturbance occurring at the Rosenthal residence at 972 Vegas Valley Drive.

DETAILS:

At approximately 1030 hours I, Officer B. Frank, and Officer A. Archer, were dispatched to a recall to a family disturbance at the Las Vegas Country Club Estates. The person calling, being Mrs. Rosenthal, asked that the Officers meet her at the Karen Avenue entrance of the Las Vegas Country Club at the guard station.

I was the first Unit arriving there, being Unit 2-J-2, and contacted Mrs. Rosenthal, who was on the telephone at the guard station.

After approximately one minute, she turned to this Officer while still on the phone and asked me to talk to the subject she was conversing with, being a Mr. Bob Ballou, who she stated was president of the First National Bank, Strip office.

I then talked to the subject, Mr. Ballou, who stated that he had been contacted by Mr. Rosenthal and also Mrs. Rosenthal separately during the previous night and early morning hours in regards to items owned by the Rosenthals which were in safety deposit boxes at his bank office.

He further stated that he advised each of them that the items in the safety deposit boxes were held in joint ownership and if either of them wished to pick the items up, they could do so at the bank opening at 1000 hours on Monday morning, being 9-08-80.

Apparently there had been a request to remove items from the safety deposit boxes either by one or both of the Rosenthals prior to the ten o'clock opening. Mr. Ballou related to me that Mrs. Rosenthal stated she was going to be enroute to the bank mentioned above and it possibly would be a good idea to have an Officer present at the arrival because of the family disturbance which was involved here earlier. I advised him that if so requested by Mrs. Rosenthal, I would follow her to the bank to keep the peace at that location. At this time I hung up and immediately Mrs. Rosenthal asked me to accompany her, following her vehicle to the bank that she was going to remove items from the safety deposit boxes at the FNB at 2780 Las Vegas Boulevard South.

I then advised control that I would be following Mrs. Rosenthal who was driving a tan Mercedes coupe bearing Nevada license CWN014 from the Country Club entrance to the FNB on the Strip. She advised on arriving that she was going to remove her belongings from the safety deposit boxes. I advised her I was there to keep the peace and what she did with the bank was her own personal business.

Inside the bank there was some yelling by Mrs. Rosenthal directed at Mr. Ballou who apparently is the bank vice president at that branch. Mrs. Rosenthal presented, I believe, it was two or three keys for boxes which were then carried out by Mrs. Rosenthal and bank employees and set on a counter and Mrs. Rosenthal then removed what appeared to me to be a large quantity of cash. She stated also there was jewelry she was taking from the boxes and also appeared to be some documents removed. Mrs. Rosenthal had stated to this Officer at the Karen entrance and also when we arrived at the bank, that this Officer could have the cash which was in the safety deposit boxes, however, this Officer advised her that he would not be taking any cash from her under any circumstances. Mrs. Rosenthal then exited the bank and was walking toward her car.

As Mrs. Rosenthal and myself exited the bank, Sgt. Greenwood arrived at the scene in the front parking lot. These Officers were talking to Mrs. Rosenthal as she put the above mentioned items, being cash, jewelry and documents, in the trunk of her Mercedes vehicle and approximately a couple of minutes later Mrs. Rosenthal was looking toward Las Vegas Boulevard and she stated, "There is Frank."

She jumped in her car and took off at a fairly high rate of speed going southbound on Las Vegas Boulevard. At this time Mr. Frank Rosenthal and another WMA (White Male) who was also at the family disturbance scene earlier in the morning, arrived with Mrs. Rosenthal driving a yellow Cadillac which had been in the driveway at the original disturbance.

At this time Sgt. Greenwood was conversing with Mr. Rosenthal for a couple of minutes while this officer was standing back a few feet. Mr. Rosenthal and the white male subject with him entered the bank and came out a couple of minutes later. They then got into their yellow Cadillac and also left the location. At this time, Sgt. Greenwood and also myself resumed normal patrol.

♦ ♦ ♦

"We pulled in and there were police all around there," Murray Ehrenberg said. "They wouldn't let Frank out of the car. They said, 'We're trying to stop any trouble.'

"Frank got very hot. He tried to push through, but they stopped him. They leaned against the car doors and we couldn't get out. He was trying to muscle his way out. I said, 'Frank, be quiet.' But he looks right at the cops and says: 'Take your fucking hands off my car!' He says that to the cop!

"He's yelling: 'She's stealing my money!' but the cops still wouldn't let him out of the car. They held him back until after Geri took off and then they said, 'Okay, go ahead.' The whole thing was an act the cops had concocted with her."

♦ ♦ ♦

"That night she called from Beverly Hills," Lefty said. "It was after midnight. I said, 'Geri, this is no good. You can keep your jewelry, but I want my money and my jewelry.' All I hear is a click. She hung up.

"Then I get a call from Tony.

"He says: 'I heard what happened. Is there anything I can do to help?'

"I sense here that he isn't sure that I know about his situation with Geri, so I still don't say anything. I still play dumb.

"I say there isn't anything. Things had been bad between us for a while.

"Tony then says he wants to meet me. Famous last words. I don't want to meet him. I know what can happen here.

"I say that I'll meet him, but I don't want anyone to see us, so I give him the name of another lawyer—not Oscar—and we meet there.

"Again he asks: 'Anything I can do?'

"I said that in the event he heard from Geri he should tell her to get my stuff back.

"Tony knows things don't look right. He has got to be thinking, 'Oh boy, what a mistake.'

"I'm smiling. My lifelong buddy. I didn't understand it. There was nothing of his I wanted. I couldn't conceive of his wanting my wife. I couldn't shake it.

"My attitude at the attorney's office was calm. I know I'm safe. And he knows that if my friends in Chicago know what he's done, he loses. If there's a trial back there, he's gone. He knows all that. That's why I have to be so careful.

"'Thanks for meeting,' I say.

"'I hope it works,' he says.

"Then Geri calls Tony.

"'Hey, you better listen to him,' Tony tells Geri, 'or we're both getting killed.' I only know this because Geri tells me later.

"'What do you want me to do, you fucking midget?' Geri says.

"'You return half the money, two hundred and fifty thousand dollars, and his jewels,' Tony says. 'This is a direct order from me to you.'

"Now that's about as close to a mob order as you can get, and when Geri told me about it later she was pissed.

"At the time, Geri says, she told him, 'Fuck you!'

"Geri then calls me.

"'Your little fucking friend called and gave me an order,' she says.

"I said, 'Geri, you're in very deep.'

"'You got somebody to pick up the money and jewels?' she asks. 'If I give them back, will you promise to leave us alone?'

"I told her yes, and I sent a friend to L.A. to get them. But when he met her she only gave him two hundred thousand dollars and the jewels. Later she said Tony had stolen fifty thousand dollars out of her car when she went to rest at his house after she left the bank."

♦ ♦ ♦

Rosenthal filed for a divorce on September 11, 1980, three days after Geri drove away from the bank. Three days later, he got a call from the Psychiatric Ward of Harbor General Hospital in Torrance, California. He was told that his wife, Geraldine McGee Rosenthal, had been arrested by LAPD attempting to undress on Sunset Boulevard. She was under the influence of alcohol and drugs.

Lefty flew to Torrance: "When I got to the hospital, I went into her room and she was in a straitjacket. She wanted me to loosen it, but I said I couldn't do that. She started scream-ing at me. She was hysterical.

"The psychiatrist suggested that Geri stay at Torrance for two weeks. From what I saw, I agreed. I flew back to Las Vegas that night, and then, a couple of days later, I found out that she had been released from the hospital and that her father and her daughter would try to get her to go for psychiatric care.

"I filed for a divorce. It was uncontested."

Lefty got what he wanted: custody of the children. In re-turn, he agreed to $5,000 a month alimony and visitation rights. Geri kept her million dollars in jewelry and the Mer-cedes she drove off in.

◆ ◆ ◆

"Almost anyone else would have let it go," Murray Ehren-berg said. "I mean, the woman is sick and she's gone. He's getting a divorce. He's got custody. He's already got half of the money and all of his own jewelry back. Geri only kept about a hundred thousand dollars and her own jewelry. Anybody else would have thought of themselves lucky just to be rid of her, but not Frank.

"With everything else he's got all fucked up out there, he decides to sue the Las Vegas Metro Police Department for false arrest, and then he sues the cops who kept us from get-ting out of the car at the bank, for six million dollars. They're cops. They don't have six cents. It's crazy. And, of course, he didn't win. All he managed to do was get the whole damn soap opera rehashed in the papers over and over again."

22 ♦

"We're either going to make a lot of money today or we're going to be very famous."

There were stories in the newspapers about Lefty and Geri, and Tony and Geri, and Lefty and Tony, and stories from anonymous law enforcement officials who "feared a Rosenthal-Spilotro mob war." The FBI purposely exploited the publicity. William K. Lambie Jr., a director of the Chicago Crime Commission, received copies of the Rosenthal-Spilotro news clippings from a Las Vegas law enforcement source, who asked if Lambie could spread the story around Chicago with the "express purpose of upsetting Joe Aiuppa."

A Lambie memo on file at the commission said his Vegas source had "furnished copies of news clippings regarding the Spilotro-Rosenthal affair. . . . He asked that I contact a local member of the working press so that the story would appear in the local print media together with a paragraph indicating that federal authorities had long been aware of the Spilotro-Rosenthal affair because of their surveillance of SPILOTRO. This information is designed to further upset AIUPPA."

There were stories about Rosenthal and Spilotro in the Chicago newspapers, including one in Art Petacque and Hugh Hough's Sunday column in the *Chicago Sun-Times*. But by that time, Joe Aiuppa had more to be upset about with Tony Spilotro than philandering.

♦ ♦ ♦

"Nobody knew that we were doing the burglaries until we got too notorious," Cullotta said. "But as soon as I opened up that fucking pizza joint, Tony started coming around too much. It was better when I used to sneak off and meet him in different parks. Tony was a restaurant guy all his life, and my joint to him was like a pleasure. He loved the business and he wanted to be a part of any restaurant business, especially with his buddy, you know.

"And there was nothing that he couldn't do. He'd say, 'Look, you need any money, you tell me. I'll put whatever we need in this joint.'

"It's my joint, but he loved to be there with the recipes, and he was there all the time. He just loved it. And meanwhile, he was just fucking destroying the business. You know, we used to have all the movie stars come in there. And the cops used to stop them on the street.

"Like Wayne Newton. He's coming into my place to eat, and he's pulling up, and he's got an entourage of people with him. The cops jump out of their cars and they tell Wayne, 'You know where you're going?' 'Yeah,' he says. 'I'm going to the Upper Crust.'

"They says, 'Well, syndicate men own that place.' He says, 'I'm going in there to eat food, not talk to them.'

"And it's all because the cops saw Tony was there all the time. That's when everything went downhill. I used to be able to move around. They were thinking I was nothing.

Just a nobody guy out there. Until they put me in the joint with him. They put me there with him. 'Hey, who is this guy?' And then they checked me out and they see that we're going back to when we were kids.

"That's when it was all over. It was too late. Then I said, 'Fuck it.' Until then I played real low. I lived high, but I was low profile. I was under investigation for different things, but not for being affiliated with Tony or OC. Until we were together too often.

"I was a stubborn guy. I don't believe that I have to register when I come to town because I've got a sheet or did time. So I never registered as a felon with the sheriff. And nobody bothered me until they spotted Tony with me all the time.

"To me that was bullshit. Fuck it. Fuck this privileged town. I used to tell them to go fuck themselves. I wouldn't tell them where I lived. And then they'd arrest me. And I'd get a rap. And I'd fight them. I didn't give a fuck. The judge'd throw the cases out, but the cops arrested me all the time. And I'd still fight them. I would never tell them where I lived. I mean, they knew where I lived. I just refused to tell them.

"I was busting their balls all the time.

"Now Tony's in my place all the time and he sends his kid and the baseball team in, and everybody's there all the time. And to tell the truth, I don't mind it. I love it. But so did everybody else, including the police.

"They used to park in the lot and watch. And that's where they got all their pictures. You see all those surveillance pictures of Tony coming out of a restaurant? They're all coming out of my restaurant.

"We did good up there until the night the cops killed Frankie Blue. Tony and I were sitting at the patio outside in front of the restaurant. Frankie Blue pulled up. He was a maitre d' at the Hacienda. His father, Stevie Blue, Stevie

Bluestein, was a business agent with the Culinary Workers Union.

"He was a good kid. I told him, 'Frankie, take them fucking Illinois plates off that car.'

"Tony told him, 'It's not a good idea to have them plates on there, Frankie.'

"The kid says, 'I'll change them.'

"Then he says, 'I got a couple of fucking guys following me around.'

"We say, 'It's probably the heat.' We told him about the Illinois plates. That only means Chicago to the Vegas cops.

"He says, 'I don't know. They've been following me around too much.'

"He says, 'I had a Bonneville just follow me around the corner to here.'

"So he gives Tony and me a kiss and he leaves. He's a good respectful kid.

"I think now that he thought that some guys were trying to rob him. It turns out there were a couple of heist guys specializing in maitre d's because their pockets are filled with twenty-dollar bills. He didn't know the guys were cops, because he never would have done what he did. He's not stupid. That kid's been around wiseguys all his life. And the cops killed him. They were in an unmarked car.

"A half hour later, we get a phone call from Herbie Blitzstein. Herbie lived right over there where it happened. Herbie said, 'They just killed Frankie.' I said, 'He just left.' He said, 'They fucking emptied two guns on him by my house.'

"I said, 'We've gotta reach these motherfuckers.' He said, 'They just declared war.' 'Well whenever they're ready,' I told him. I said I knew it had to be Gene Smith. Because I knew Gene Smith's going for him. Smith was a fucking gung ho cop.

"What happened was Frankie left here and they followed him. He had a gun in the car. He didn't tell us that. He said that he didn't know who was following him. They claim that when they tried to curb him he pulled the gun out. They jumped out of their car and they fired one nine-millimeter and a thirty-eight into the door of the car. Well, they killed him. Immediately. Then they said they found the gun in the car. 'In his hand.' This is what they said.

"He might have made a rash move when he got near his security gates. He was in a guarded community, where there are gates that open and you drive in. And they killed him right out in front there.

"So Tony and them go over. He tells me to stay at the place. 'Listen for the phone,' he says; 'I'll be right back.' And they jumped in some cars and they went over there. It was horrible. The cops panicked. Everything was getting very tense. And the police out here are real fast on the draw. They're scared. They're always shaking. They're shaky guys.

"Then they all came back. Tony. Herbie. The father, Stevie Blue. Ronnie Blue, the brother. And they all came back over and they're all crying and we're talking, you know. Trying to talk out of sight. You know. And we didn't see a fucking cop around. They just like pulled everybody off the street because they knew something was going to go down because Tony was fucking smoking.

"I mean he was smoking. He was planning stuff. He had an idea to start a race riot. He figured he'd use the blacks to start it up and then we can, you know, wipe a few of them out—and he didn't mean blacks.

"Use it as an excuse. Make it like a few blacks were killed by some cops and it'd just snowball, because in that town the cops really mess around with the blacks. They had them contained in certain areas, and we were going to go in and uncontain it.

"That's what Tony really wanted to do, but it never came about. Too many other things started happening. First, they tried to blame us for driving by and shotgunning a cop's house. We didn't do that. Somebody else did it and threw it on us.

"At the time Tony said, 'These motherfuckers are trying to frame me for shooting this cocksucker's house up. They're using a reverse on us.' They did it on purpose to take the heat off them for the Bluestein killing.

"So the cops killed the kid. I never saw Tony so upset. He was kicking chairs. Walls. Everything. He really loved that kid. At the funeral everybody showed. Tony commanded the kid got shown respect. Even Lefty went to the wake, but he was not standing next to Tony."

♦ ♦ ♦

The questions raised by the killing even further strained the relationship between Spilotro and the Metro cops. Metro would do anything to get Tony, and he would do anything to embarrass them. In November, when a security guard at the Sahara casino tipped Metro intelligence that Spilotro was having lunch with Oscar Goodman in the coffee shop, chief of Metro intelligence Kent Clifford was delighted. Police officer Rich Murray, who was on patrol nearby, was rushed to the location. Spilotro was in the state's Black Book and officially banned from entering any casino in Nevada. A violation could subject him to arrest and the casino to a fine of up to $100,000.

The Sahara security guards had kept an eye on the Spilotro table ever since they got the tip from special agent Mark Kaspar of the FBI. Before calling Metro, the security guards had even called the FBI to make certain there was an agent Kaspar.

When Metro's Rich Murray got to the coffee shop, the Spilotro table was pointed out to him by the security guards who greeted him. The security guards said that Spilotro's lawyer, Oscar Goodman, had just gotten up and gone to the men's room.

When Murray approached Spilotro and asked for identification, Spilotro said he did not have any. When Murray said he suspected the man was Anthony Spilotro, the man denied that he was Anthony Spilotro. As Murray was about to take Spilotro into custody and downtown for booking, Oscar Goodman returned and started insisting that the man was not Tony Spilotro. Murray arrested him anyway.

Ten minutes later, as Murray was in the process of booking Spilotro, Detective Gene Smith arrived and realized Murray had arrested Tony's dentist brother, Pasquale Spilotro. Of course, Pasquale Spilotro was immediately released, but not until the press had all been alerted to the fiasco.

Metro intelligence chief Kent Clifford always believed the department had been set up. For one thing, Mark Kaspar denied, in a sworn affidavit, that he had ever made a call to the Sahara about Spilotro. For another, Goodman apparently had not told Murray that the man in question was Spilotro's brother.

The anger between Clifford and his Metro cops and Spilotro and his men escalated, and at one point they accused one another of shooting up one another's houses and cars. It got so bad that one day, when Clifford received information that two of his detectives were on a hit list, he strapped on a gun, brought along an armed sidekick, and the two of them flew to Chicago.

He went straight to the homes of Joe Aiuppa and Joey

Lombardo—Spilotro's two immediate bosses—in order to confront them. But when Clifford and his sidekick arrived at Aiuppa's house, the only person at home was the boss's seventy-two-year-old wife. They then went over to Joey Lombardo's house, but his wife, too, was the only Lombardo at home.

In later explaining his journey to Chicago to the *Los Angeles Times*, Clifford said he then "tracked down" Lombardo's attorney and went over to see him, warning the lawyer: "If any of my men are harmed I will return to the homes I just visited and kill everything that moves, walks or crawls."

Clifford said he then went to a hotel and waited until 2:30 A.M., at which time he got a call wishing him a "safe trip." This, he said, was the prearranged code with Lombardo's lawyer that the alleged hit on the two detectives had been called off. Clifford, who is now a real estate salesman in Nevada, has refused repeated requests for interviews.

◆ ◆ ◆

"It was all going bad," Cullotta says. "You've got that nut job Kent Clifford knocking at Lomby and Aiuppa's door. I don't want to know what Aiuppa heard from his old lady when he got home that night. Some Metro cops got loaded one night and pegged a couple of shots at John Spilotro's house and just missed hitting his kid. They out-and-out murdered Frankie Blue and everybody knew that, no matter what they said. And on top of everything, Tony's under a lot of pressure for money and he puts the pressure on us to earn.

"Joey Lombardo had just been indicted along with Allen Dorfman and Roy Williams for trying to bribe the senator from Nevada on some Teamster pension stuff, and Lomby needed cash. Tony had me driving my guys nuts. We were knocking over jewelry stores every other week. We ran out of places in Las Vegas. We were flying out to San Jose, San Francisco, Los Angeles, and Phoenix. Usually I brought all the swag to his brother Michael, in Chicago, but now even Michael got eighteen months on a bookmaking case, so we were fencing the stuff all over the place.

"I first heard that there was over a million in cash and jewelry in the vault at Bertha's Jewelers on West Sahara Avenue from Joey DiFranzo, about a year before. We knew it was a family business and there was a safe with at least five hundred thousand dollars in cash. You could see the jewelry in the place just by looking in the windows every day.

"The place was fully alarmed, but I went inside pretending to buy something just to case the place. As I talked to the woman waiting on me, I kept maneuvering her so I could see inside the vault. I saw that inside the vault they had no alarm.

"I told Tony about the score and he said for me to 'fill in' Joe Blasko. Blasko had been a cop, but he got kicked off when they found he was working more for Tony than the Sheriff, so Tony always made sure he was earning.

"Tony said maybe Blasko could make a quick fifty thousand dollars on the Bertha score so he could get the guy off his back for a while.

"Unfortunately, one of the guys in on the deal was working for the Gee. It was that asshole Sal Romano. We didn't know it at the time, but the feds had Sal on a drug case and he was trying to skate by giving up Tony and us.

"I always knew there was something wrong with him, but everybody thought he was fine, and Ernie Davino said he was a great pick man and a lock expert.

"There was Ernie Davino, Leo Guardino, and Wayne Matecki, who were going to go in through the roof.

"Sal Romano, Larry Neumann, and I were going to be driving up and down the street keeping our eyes out, plus we all had police scanners and walkie-talkies to the guys inside and each other in the cars.

"Across the street from the place we had Blasko, the cop, in a truck he used for cleaning cement, with a great big Superman painted on it. Blasko was sitting in there with a police scanner and a walkie-talkie, too.

"We picked the Fourth of July weekend because we expected no one would be around, and if we had to make a blast or something, people would think they were fireworks. Plus, since Monday was a holiday, nobody would probably get into the place until Tuesday, giving us even more time to get rid of the merch.

"We started during the early evening. I remember when we got there it was still almost light.

"In Bertha's we went in through the roof to circumvent the alarms. I had already cased the place for motion detectors. They're the little boxes with little red lights on the wall or door. They look like home fire alarms.

"Bertha's didn't have motion detectors, but there were other regular alarms. I could see the tape. All the doors had tape.

"Normally, you could pull your truck up to the side of the building and make a hole. At Bertha's, though, we figured if the vault wall was steel, not just cement, we needed torches, and that could take forty-five minutes. And that's why we decided to go in through the roof.

"But right when we got started, I get signaled by Sal Romano. He says his car is stuck in the parking lot in the rear of a shopping center a little down the block from Bertha's. He says he can't start the damn thing.

"I drive over and pick him up, and I don't understand it, because I had just checked the car out before the robbery.

It's wrong. I'm pissed. I use my Riviera to push his car out of the way. Far away. We don't want it anywhere nearby the score.

"Also, I radio Larry Neumann and I tell Larry to pick up Sal on Sahara Avenue on the other side of the street from Bertha's so they can go up and down the street watching out together. I mean, four eyes are still better than two.

"Meanwhile, I hear from the guys that they have broken through the roof and they're going inside.

"Then I get a call from Larry saying he's driving up and down Sahara and he can't find Sal. Sal was supposed to be standing out there at the curb waiting for Larry to pick him up.

"Now Larry's cursing Sal and saying he should have killed him long ago.

"'Uh oh,' I think. Then I see radio cars coming down the street, and I say over the walkie-talkie, everybody get out of there.

"We had rendezvous spots for the guys inside and I told them to get out of there, that the cops are on the way. From inside I hear them say it's too late; the cops are coming through the roof.

"I get stopped right away, but they don't get Larry until Paradise Road.

"Finally, they bring us all in, and there ain't no Sal Romano. That's when I was certain he was the rat. The feds had set us up. They were on us from the first.

"Sal walked the streets of Chicago for a week after that. I resented that Tony didn't kill the guy for me. I told Tony that Sal was the rat, but he just put it off.

"Anyway, the Gee had been waiting for us in a building right across the street. They had been watching us out of some windows with binoculars. We didn't stand a chance.

They were going to use the Bertha's case to bring us all down, and they did.

"The Bertha's arrest was the beginning of the end of Tony's crew at the Gold Rush. They got us all that day, and that left Tony pretty exposed.

"On the morning of the score, I remember I saw the Gee go by. I knew most of their cars and faces. I said to Tony, 'The Gee doesn't work on weekends; why are they here?'

"He said, 'They might not be with you, they might just be on me.'

"They were watching us constantly.

"When I took off I said to him, 'We're either going to make a lot of money today or we're going to be very famous.'"

♦ ♦ ♦

The arrests of Spilotro, Cullotta, the ex-cop Blasko, and the Hole in the Wall Gang were the culmination of a three-year investigation into Spilotro's Vegas operation, according to Organized Crime Strike Force prosecutor Charles Wehner. And while the Justice Department did not exactly come up with the kinds of evidence that could support its original premise—that Spilotro ran casinos for the mob—there were thousands of bugged conversations and miles of audio and visual surveillance tapes that showed Spilotro ordered murders, armed robberies, burglaries, and shakedown plots as the town's mob boss.

Oscar Goodman, who accompanied Spilotro to his arraignment, at which he was freed on $600,000 bond—later reduced to $180,000—said the arrests were little more than a vendetta by law enforcement against his client. He said not one of his clients had ever been as harassed as Spilotro.

"And these latest wiretaps too," Goodman said, "are the result of a continuous fishing expedition by the government in an attempt to find some vague, misrepresented excuse to continue their campaign to come up with something that will incriminate Anthony Spilotro."

But according to retired FBI agent Joe Gersky, who spent years on Spilotro's case, "This was different. This time we had a live witness, somebody who had been a part of the Hole in the Wall Gang, somebody who had been in on the planning of Bertha's—we had Sal Romano.

"We had never had a real witness against Spilotro before. Romano had told us about the robbery, who would be in on it, and when and where it would be carried out, and he had been right a hundred percent. Plus we had him in custody, protected and alive."

23.

"I don't really consider him a friend of mine anymore."

This was the most dangerous time. Years of surveillance and phone taps had begun to bring in the indictments. In addition to the Hole in the Wall Gang indictments, Allen Dorfman, Roy Williams, and Joey Lombardo had been indicted for trying to bribe Nevada senator Howard Cannon. Nick Civella, Carl Civella, Joe Agosto, Carl DeLuna, Carl Thomas, and others had been indicted as part of the Tropicana skim, and Joe Aiuppa, Jackie Cerone, and Frank Balistrieri and his sons were expected to be among others indicted in the Stardust skim. Allen Glick had already been granted immunity by several grand juries in return for his testimony, but so far his lawyers had kept the prosecutors at bay.

It was a time when the defendants and their lawyers would spend months poring over hours of wiretaps and bound volumes of typed transcriptions. The lawyers were looking for loopholes. The defendants were looking for potential witnesses to murder.

It was a time when just being suspected of cooperating with the government was enough to get you killed. And even if you didn't cooperate and got a long stretch in prison, you could still be in danger, because now you could be perceived as far more vulnerable to the government's sweet deals.

"I've heard them go around a room," Cullotta said. "'Joe, whadda you think of Mike?' 'Mike's great. Balls like iron.' 'Larry, whadda you think of Mike?' 'Mike? A fuckin' marine. To the end.' 'Frankie, whadda do you think of Mike?' 'Mike? You kidding? Mike'd put his arm in fire for ya.' 'Charlie, whadda you think of Mike?' 'Why take a chance?' And that's the end of Mike. That's the way it happens."

It is a dangerous time because the mob bosses know that in addition to the wiretaps—which can be argued over by attorneys—the prosecutors need witnesses or coconspirators who can explain what actually happened, who can point the finger, who can translate the impenetrable shorthand verbiage of most wiretaps.

◆ ◆ ◆

"Charlie Parsons, the FBI guy, came to see me," Frank Cullotta says. "It was about eight months after we all got arrested in Bertha.

"'We've got some information,' he says, 'that your friend Tony Spilotro has a murder contract out on you.'

"That was a Friday. I just nodded to the guy. I'm thinking about what happened a few weeks before. I was asleep. *Boom! Bing! Boom! Boom!* 'What the fuck?' I said. 'What the hell's all those shots?' I got up real quick. I go look out the window. These guys in a van are going past. They shot the guy in the apartment next door.

"He was walking to his apartment. Next door to me. This

guy's a square John. What is this shit? And I go back to sleep. I had to take it at face value at the time, but I started thinking about it.

"Then Parsons plays me a tape. You can hardly hear it. But I could hear it. I could hear Tony asking for an okay.

"Now mind you, when they ask for an okay, it's not, 'Hey, I'll hit Frank Cullotta tonight?' It's more like, 'I need to take care of some dirty laundry. The guy didn't wash what he was supposed to the right way, which caused that problem I talked to you about . . .'

"That's me. I'm the problem because I was the only one who could tie Tony to everything. Sal Romano, that rat bastard, he never talked to Tony. Sal talked to me, and I talked to Tony. That's how we had it set up from the start. None of my guys ever talked to Tony about anything. They didn't even know I had to cut Tony in for a quarter; they just suspected it because we operated without any interference.

"But now I've got to think Tony knows I'm facing a long stretch. I'm a predicate felon. I'm looking at thirty years. Tony's got to think why wouldn't I give him up for a deal? The man's not dumb. I would have figured it the same way.

"And the guy Tony's talking to about laundry is aware of what Tony was talking about.

"I hear the guy say, 'Okay, then just take care of it. Clean your laundry then. No problem.'

"But the guys Tony got to do the job missed. If he had me on the case, it would have been done right, but who knows where he was going for the work, now that my whole crew was buried?

"He farms the job out, and they shoot the wrong guy. They shoot the guy next door to me.

"I'm thinking to myself, 'Hey, this guy tried to hit me in the head.' If I beef on him now to the G, the most that he could do, tops, is a ten-year-sentence bit—do six, and he's out.

"That ain't gonna hurt him. He's a young guy; he'll get out. How could it hurt him? They ain't gonna give him RICO [federal racketeering charges that carry long prison sentences]. They'll never be able to lay the RICO on him and give him life. Tony's been too sharp for that."

Three days later, Monday morning at 8:15 A.M., FBI agent Parsons got a phone call.

"Do you recognize my voice?" Cullotta asked.

"Yes," Parsons said.

Within twenty minutes Cullotta was in a safe house guarded by a half dozen agents. They began to debrief him and took him to Chicago for a hearing.

"I don't know how I wound up with that transactional immunity, but I did. That's the best kind of immunity you can get. In other words, when you've got transactional immunity, you can't be tried for anything you talk about. No matter whatever it is. But the Chicago judge gave me that kind of immunity, and I didn't even know what the fuck he was doing when he gave it to me. What do I know about immunity? I walk out of court and the FBI guy says, 'I think the judge made a mistake.'

"They were shocked."

♦ ♦ ♦

After Rosenthal was forced out of the Stardust, you could set your watch by his schedule. So could a car bomber.

He got up early in the morning to take the kids to school. He then spent almost all of the day at home working on his handicapping picks for the weekend and doping out some stocks he had become interested in. Two or three days a week he would go to Tony Roma's restaurant on East Sa-

hara Avenue at about six o'clock at night and meet his old bookmaking pals Marty Kane, Ruby Goldstein, and Stanley Green. They would usually stand at the bar and have a couple of drinks while discussing the week's sports picks, and shortly after 8 P.M. Lefty would order some ribs to go. He and the group usually broke up about 8:30, or whenever Lefty's takeout order was ready. Lefty would then leave the restaurant, get into his car, and go home before the children went to bed.

On October 4, 1982, Lefty followed his usual pattern. But when he got into his car with the takeout order, it exploded. He remembers seeing tiny flames shoot out from the car's defroster vents, and he also remembers that the inside of the car began filling with sheets of flame as he struggled to get out the door.

He grabbed the door latch and rolled to the sidewalk, rolling around on the ground for a while because his clothes were on fire. Then he stood up and saw that his car was entirely on fire. Suddenly two men raced up to him and forced him to the ground, urging him to stay calm and to cover his head.

Just as the three of them hit the ground, the flames reached the gas tank and the four-thousand-pound Cadillac Eldorado rose about four feet off the ground. A fireball of shredded pieces of metal and plastic shot about fifty feet into the sky and then began to rain blackened shards and soot over hundreds of square feet on the busy parking lot. (The two men who had forced Lefty to the ground turned out to be two secret service agents who had just finished dinner.)

The explosion was so intense and loud, according to Barbara Lawry, who lived across the street, that it "sounded like a train fell through my roof." Lori Wardle, the cashier at Marie Callender's Restaurant, across from Tony Roma's,

said, "I ran outside, and the parking lot was mobbed with cars. Rosenthal's car shot right up in the air, and flames went about two stories into the air. It was a huge explosion. It blew the windows out of the back of the restaurant."

A local TV news crew was having coffee nearby when the explosion occurred, and they took pictures of Rosenthal, minutes after the explosion, wandering dazedly around the parking lot and holding a handkerchief to his bleeding head. He was also bleeding from cuts on his left arm and leg. He can be seen asking Marty Kane and his other pals to call his doctor and make sure his children were assured that he was okay and that they be brought to the hospital.

Alcohol, Tobacco agent in charge John Rice, investigating the case with Metro, said Lefty was "very fortunate" to have survived the blast.

"Ninety-nine times out of a hundred, a bomb like that should have killed him," Rice said. "Except, in the model of an Eldorado Cadillac, the manufacturer installed a steel floor plate beneath the driver's seat for added stability. It was that steel plate under the driver's seat that saved Lefty's life.

"The steel plate deflected the bomb upwards and toward the rear of the car instead of up and forward. He should change his name from Lefty to Lucky."

♦ ♦ ♦

The press and police arrived at the emergency room while Lefty was being treated for his cuts and burns. As Lefty's head cleared, he looked up from a hospital bed to see a circle of concerned faces looking down.

"It was all the hotshots from the FBI and local cops,"

Rosenthal said. "And they were not there out of friendship.

"I was still being treated when the first two guys from the FBI came in," Lefty said. "They were polite. They said, 'Jesus, we're sorry about this. Can we be of any help?'

"I said, 'No you can't. Will you please leave me alone?' They said, 'Are you sure?' I said I was sure. They left.

"Then came the Metro guys. At that time John McCarthy was the sheriff. Anyway, they walk in. They said, 'You ready to talk now?' I said, 'Get the fuck out of here.' That's a quote. 'Get the fuck out of here.'

"After they treated me at the hospital, I told my doctor I needed more help. I needed more painkiller. I was really in terrible pain. So he gave me a second shot, and then he helped get me out through a back way he knew about so I could avoid the newspaper people who were piled up in the lobby and front of the building. When I got home my housekeeper was there and I was grateful that the kids were already sleeping.

"I was home about thirty minutes when the phone rang. It was Joey Cusumano.

"'Are you all right?' he asks.

"'Yeah, are you?' I said right back.

"'Thank God. Thank God,' he says. 'Is there anything you need, Frank?'

"'Not a thing, Joe,' I said, 'but if I do, you'll be the first one I call.'

"And I'm on the bullshit with him, because I knew Tony Spilotro was right there with him. Cusumano's on the phone, but it's Tony asking the questions. But by then my nerves had calmed down. I'm trying to go over things. You know. The pain wasn't so strong at this time. The morphine was still there. I was trying to replay what happened and tried to figure out who did it."

♦ ♦ ♦

The explosion was big news. The newspapers and TV news shows led with it for days. There was immediately speculation as to whether Spilotro had had anything to do with the bombing and whether the bad blood between the two old friends over Spilotro's affair with Lefty's estranged wife might have ignited the bomb.

FBI agent Charlie Parsons told the press that Spilotro and the Chicago mob probably were behind the murder attempt. He suggested the lingering bitterness and hard feelings between Spilotro and Rosenthal over Geri were probably responsible for the bombing.

Parsons said he even made Rosenthal an offer to become a government witness: "Lefty, the mob can't take a chance you won't talk. Now they must kill you. Can you take the chance they won't? Come with us. We'll protect you and your children."

Joseph Yablonsky, the FBI Las Vegas chief, said Rosenthal's escape was a "miracle" and that "the hit man probably came from out of town—although there are persons in Las Vegas capable of constructing such a device."

The day after the explosion, Lefty recalls that local cops and federal agents kept knocking at his door with questions. Lefty was concerned about what the police were doing to protect him and his family, but the cops only wanted to know about his relationship to Spilotro and whether the two men were feuding. Lefty said Parsons even offered him carte blanche in the federal witness program.

"After what organized crime has done to you," Parsons insisted, "you owe them no loyalty."

Metro intelligence chief Kent Clifford put it even more bluntly: "Lefty," he said, "you're a walking dead man and you will receive no police protection unless you provide us with intelligence information."

Rosenthal responded to Clifford by calling the sheriff and newspapers to complain about Clifford's threat—pointing out that as taxpayers accused of no crimes, he and his family were entitled to police protection no matter what the intelligence chief felt about him personally.

The next day, Clifford's threat to Lefty was blasted in the Vegas editorials, and Sheriff John McCarthy publicly apologized for Clifford's remarks. He said Rosenthal was entitled to police protection regardless of his personality or his lack of cooperation in assisting law enforcement officers. Editorials, both in the newspapers and on TV, took up Lefty's battle, pointing out that Lefty's young children and housekeeper could very well have been in the car at the time and that all citizens are entitled to protection under the law.

Kent Clifford had performed a feat Lefty Rosenthal had been unable to do in years—get him some favorable press.

◆ ◆ ◆

Media and police attention to the incident was so intense that Lefty decided to hold a news conference in his own home and lay to rest some of the more provocative and dangerous innuendos and stories that were getting into the papers. He received about a half dozen reporters in his silk pajamas. He still had some bandages visible on his forehead and left arm.

During the forty-five-minute interview session, Lefty said that the feds and local cops had "strongly suggested" the car bombing was engineered by Spilotro. While he knew that the bombing "didn't come from the Boy Scouts of America," Lefty said, he refused to accuse anyone he knew of such an act.

He said he would be "very, very unhappy and very, very angry" if it turned out that his longtime friend Tony Spilotro was responsible. Lefty said he did not believe it and that it "would be a very unhealthy situation for all of us. I don't even want to entertain that thought.

"I don't really consider him a friend of mine anymore," Lefty continued, "but I am not prepared at this time to believe Spilotro was responsible. I am not willing to believe that he would have the ability to do such a thing. I had no reason to feel that either myself or any member of my family was in danger, and I conducted my life no differently than anyone else. Obviously, I was wrong. I am not going to turn on Spilotro. I don't feel the need to do this. It is not my way of doing things."

Lefty said he wanted to find out "who did it and make sure it doesn't happen again . . . but I have no thought of revenge. If I say I'm looking for revenge, then I'm as low as they are." He did not feel the bombing was a message or a warning. "I don't know the motive for this first attempt. I'm going to do everything I can to stop them. I'll do what I have to do to protect myself and my kids."

◆ ◆ ◆

There are two serious theories about who tried to bomb Frank Rosenthal. The first—which the FBI believes—is that it was Frank Balistrieri. Balistrieri was actually known as the Mad Bomber owing to his habit of blowing up his adversaries. And an FBI wiretap in Balistrieri's office a few weeks before the bombing had recorded Balistrieri telling his sons that he believed that Frank Rosenthal caused their problems. He promised his sons that he would "get full satisfaction."

The second theory, popular with the Metro cops, is that Spilotro did it.

♦ ♦ ♦

"Geri flew into town after the bombing," Lefty said. "She said she wanted to take care of me. Protect me. But the flame was out in me. She said, 'You know I can change.'

"She tried to give me her phone number that day, but I said I didn't need it. She could always reach me."

24.

"Foul play is not ruled out."

Geri Rosenthal moved to an apartment in Beverly Hills. "She was running with a bad crowd," Lefty said. "Lowlifes. Pimps. Druggies. Bikers. She had a boyfriend who was a musician and he was beating her up a lot.

"She was living a tough life. She came to Las Vegas for the holidays. She'd come into town if the kids had swim meets. She'd come in for parties. The kid stuff. That sort of thing. I never looked forward to it, because I never knew what she would do. One time, I was taking her back to the airport, and she started screaming that she wanted more money. I could see she was already loaded. She was bringing back messages from her sicko pals. 'Get more money out of the creep.' Oh yeah. I know what they wanted her for. I threatened to dump her luggage right out on Paradise Road if she didn't shut up. She looked at me real hard and didn't say another word.

"Another time my son was looking out the window when she arrived and he commented on how thin she looked. When she came in the door I could see what he meant. She was like a rail. She had lost so much weight. She was all speed and pills.

"Malnutrition. She was living on pills.

"I said, 'Look what you're doing to yourself.'

"She went right past me and upstairs and got into the bathtub as though she still lived in the house. Her attitude was that she was still Geri Rosenthal.

"After we were divorced I offered her a hundred thousand dollars to change her name, and she said, 'You must be kidding me.' She used the name for whatever she could get. 'Don't you know who I am? Who my husband is?' That sort of thing. She used the fantasy for protection.

"I'd get calls from bars at one in the morning and she'd say things like, 'Tell this sonofabitch to leave me alone.'

"One night I got a hysterical call from a public phone. She's crying. 'Would you believe this sonofabitch beat the shit out of me?' she says.

"At this time Geri was going with a younger kid. He addressed me as 'Mr. Rosenthal' whenever we had spoken over the phone.

"I had already told him to behave himself. 'You understand you're dating my children's mother,' I said.

"'Yes sir, Mr. Rosenthal,' he said at the time.

"Now Geri is calling from a booth. She says she's bleeding and that this kid had beaten the shit out of her. I asked what I could do and she says call him. Make him stop. He will be at this number in about an hour.

"I take the number and now I'm up. I sit around looking at the clock for an hour. It takes a long time for the hour to pass, and then I dial the number, and who answers? Geri.

"'Hi!'

"What the fuck? 'Are you nuts?' I asked her. 'I thought

this guy was beating you up? What are you doing there? Why did you go back?'

"'Oh,' she says, 'I'm okay.'

"'Let me talk to the punk,' I tell her.

"'It's okay,' she says. 'I can handle it.'

"It later turned out she had this apartment and they were living there, and he threatened to break up with her and she got hysterical and decided in her drunkenness to get me to threaten the kid into not leaving her."

◆ ◆ ◆

At 4:35 A.M. on November 6, 1982—about one month after Lefty's car was bombed—Geri Rosenthal began screaming on the sidewalk in front of the Beverly Sunset Motel, at 8775 Sunset Boulevard, and stumbled into the motel lobby, where she collapsed.

A motel clerk called police, but when they arrived with an ambulance, she was in a coma. She never recovered. She died three days later at Cedar Sinai Hospital. She was forty-six. The hospital said doctors found evidence of tranquilizers, liquor, and other drugs in her system. There was a large bruise on her thigh and smaller bruises on her legs.

The story made the Los Angeles and Las Vegas papers, which reported that she had died of an apparent drug overdose and rehashed the recent events of her stormy marriage, her affair with Spilotro, her looting three safe deposit boxes of over a million dollars, and Lefty's car bombing. It was a story made for the tabloids and the cops. Captain Ronald Maus of the Los Angeles District Attorney's Office told the *Los Angeles Times*, "We're interested because of her past connections and the possibility of any organized-crime intrusions." Dr. Lawrence Maldonado, who pronounced her dead, said, "Foul play is not ruled out."

♦ ♦ ♦

"The way I found out was I got a call from Bob Martin's wife, Charlotte," Lefty said. "She said, 'Frank, I've got bad news. My furrier just called and said Robin was in the store picking up Geri's furs. Robin said that Geri had passed away.'

"I called the furrier immediately. I said my name is Frank Rosenthal. He knew who I was and he started thanking me for all the business I had given over the years. I said, 'Listen, is Robin Marmor there?' 'Yes, she's here to pick up Geri's furs. She says her mother is dead.'

"The furrier was named Fred something. I said, 'Fred, you don't give her a fucking thing. Do you understand me?'

"'Yes sir,' he says. And I hung up.

"I called the morgue. Yes, there was a body. She was dead.

"I got the M.D.

"I finally got a call two days later from Robin.

"Robin says, 'Mom's dead.' Like that. 'Mom's dead.'

"I pretend I don't already know. I get some details from her. She's making some arrangements for the funeral. I said let me get back to you. When I did we had a dispute over where Geri would be buried. I wanted it to be in Las Vegas, next to her mother, who had died. Robin and Len Marmor wanted her buried in Los Angeles. Finally Robin made the arrangements for the burial and chapel.

"I talked to the kids and told them both what had happened. They were able to comprehend. I asked if they wanted to attend the funeral and Steve said, 'Please, I don't want to.' Stephanie said: 'We're not going.'

"The speculation around was fifty percent that I had her killed and the other fifty percent that the mob had her killed," said Lefty. "They're all wrong. I spent about fifteen thousand dollars on an investigation. I got the details.

"I believe she was overdosed.

"They killed her. They did it to her—the people around her. They knew she was a wealthy woman. She was getting five thousand dollars a month from me in alimony. She had all her jewels. But when police checked her apartment, everything was gone."

◆ ◆ ◆

"At first they thought Geri might have been murdered because she knew too much about the outfit," Frank Cullotta said. "But that was all bullshit.

"What probably happened was that some of her druggie biker friends got the idea that Geri would inherit a fortune from the insurance if she suddenly became a widow. So first they tried to blow up Lefty, and when they missed, they knew they were in trouble, especially if Geri pieced their move together.

"That's why they killed her. Just four weeks after Lefty's car explosion. What a coincidence. And what was she doing wandering around that miserable area on Hollywood at four thirty in the morning? She wasn't. She was in a car with her killers, her pals, the guys who tried to blow up Lefty, who were now pumping her fill of pills and booze.

"All they had to do was stop the car, let her out on the street, and drive off."

◆ ◆ ◆

"They murdered my sister," Barbara Stokich says. "Somebody gave her an injection of something.

"Geri took a million in jewels when she left Frank. He had to talk to her to get back his money, but she kept the jewels, and they were all missing.

"She wanted to go back to Frank after she started living in Los Angeles. She missed the luxury. The protection. Safety. She liked calling him 'Mr. R.'

"After Geri died, my dad visited the places she had shopped. One of Geri's friends said she had been going to a psychologist for two months and was almost okay.

"Geri got five thousand dollars a month from Lefty, plus the credit cards and the Mercedes. But she didn't like to be alone. She went out to bars and drank all night. Meanwhile Lenny was married when Geri got back, and a black guy who she knew beat her unmercifully. To get her money and jewels.

"We found out she died because my husband, Mel, and I were visiting Dad and the landlord called. Some friends of his had seen an obit on Geraldine McGee Rosenthal and they wondered if it was my sister. We called Robin and she kept saying she didn't have time to talk to us. Finally Robin said the funeral was in two days. My sister had been in the hospital and in the morgue for a week, and nobody had told us."

◆ ◆ ◆

Geri was buried in Mount Sinai Memorial Park, 5950 Forest Lawn, in a private ceremony. Lefty and the two children did not attend.

"I didn't want to put the kids through that," he said.

In January of 1983, the L.A. County coroner said that death was accidental, an apparent lethal combination of cocaine, Valium, and Jack Daniel's whiskey.

◆ ◆ ◆

Papers on file in Los Angeles Probate Court said:

> The deceased died leaving no real property but left personal property consisting of numerous coins located in safety box #107, First Interstate Bank, Maryland Square Office, 3681 South Maryland Parkway, Las Vegas. The coins were ordered appraised by the court and valued at $15,486.
>
> The 125 coins included, among others, $4000 in silver dollars; $1200 in 1887 silver dollars; $133 in Stardust Casino gaming tokens; $6000 in 1887 silver dollars; $100 in 22 Indian Head pennies; Liberty Quarters, Shield nickels, and a 1797 large cent.

Half the coins in the box went to Lefty, under the terms of the divorce agreement; the other half was divided evenly among her three children: Robin, Steven, and Stephanie. According to court papers, Geri's heirs received $2,581 each.

◆ ◆ ◆

It was close to the end for everyone. Lefty's explosion and Geri's death were followed by indictments, convictions, and more death.

The hundreds of Justice Department wiretaps resulted in the indictments—and eventual conviction—of the major mob bosses who were involved in skimming the Stardust and Tropicana Hotels.

Weak links were cut. On January 20, 1983, Allen Dorfman, sixty, was shot and killed as he walked out of a suburban Chicago restaurant. Dorfman had just been convicted along with Joey Lombardo, Joe Aiuppa, Jackie Cerone, Maishe Rockman, and Teamster president Roy Williams for using the Teamster pension fund to try to bribe Nevada senator Howard Cannon to get favorable trucking legislation. This was Dorfman's second felony conviction in connection with the pension fund, and the judge had guaranteed him a long prison sentence.

Dorfman had just left the restaurant with Irwin Weiner, the sixty-five-year-old insurance broker and ex–bail bondsman who had originally hired Tony Spilotro as a bondsman in Chicago years ago. Dorfman had stopped off at a video store and gotten a copy of the film *Inadmissible Evidence* to watch that night at home. The film tells the story of a man wrongly accused of mob connections by the press.

Weiner told police he heard two men come up behind them and say, "This is a holdup!" and that when he ducked he heard shots being fired and didn't really see what happened. The gunmen escaped. The murder was never solved.

◆ ◆ ◆

On March 13, 1983, Nick Civella died of lung cancer. He had been released from the Springfield, Missouri, Federal Detention Medical Center two weeks earlier so he could "die in dignity."

◆ ◆ ◆

Joe Agosto was convicted in a check floating scheme that had allowed him to pour money into the Tropicana's meager coffers to enhance the skim. On April 12, 1983, Agosto decided to become a government witness. His testimony—along with DeLuna's notebooks—resulted in convictions and stiff sentences: Carl Civella and Carl DeLuna got thirty years each; and Carl Thomas got fifteen years. Frank Balistrieri got thirteen years.

♦ ♦ ♦

Joe Agosto died of a heart attack a few months later. The second phase of the Argent case—which charged some of the same defendants with diverting nearly $2 million in Argent money to the skim—needed a good witness. The government gave Allen Glick immunity, and he took the stand.

On trial in this case were the Chicago bosses Joe Aiuppa, seventy-seven, and Jackie Cerone, seventy-one; the Cleveland acting boss, Milton Maishe Rockman, seventy-three; and the Milwaukee boss, Frank Balistrieri, sixty-seven, and his lawyer sons John and Joseph. A conviction would almost certainly mean the elderly bosses would die in prison.

Glick took the stand and testified for four days, laying out in great detail how he had encountered Frank Balistrieri and how he had gotten his loan. He also spoke about being forced to sign over a 50 percent option on the corporation to Balistrieri's sons in return for $25,000. He testified about being forced to promote Frank Rosenthal and about being threatened by Nick Civella in a darkened Kansas City hotel room and by Carl DeLuna in Oscar Goodman's office in downtown Las Vegas.

Glick was a devastating witness. He was precise and incapable of being ruffled. He projected total honesty. Carl Thomas had become a government witness as well, in the hope of obtaining leniency on his fifteen-year sentence in the Tropicana case. He testified about the skim and about the mob's influence over the Teamsters. The feds also got Joe Lonardo, the seventy-seven-year-old Cleveland ex-underboss, who testified that he had served as a courier with Rockman and explained how Glick's loan had been arranged and who had profited from it.

Even Roy Williams, after having been handed down a fifty-five-year sentence in the Cannon bribery case, decided to cooperate with the Argent prosecution. He was wheeled into the courtroom clinging to an oxygen tank and testified that he had received $1,500 a month in cash from Nick Civella for seven years in return for his vote to give Glick the pension fund loan.

During the trial, Carl DeLuna had enough. He pleaded guilty before a verdict was even returned. He was already facing thirty years in the Tropicana case. What else could they do to him? Give him another thirty years? And why remain in court and watch the prosecutors showing blowups of his note cards to the jury while 21, 22, Stmp, and Fancy Pants watched incredulously at the wealth of damning detail DeLuna had managed to cram onto those tiny cards.

Frank Balistrieri was already facing a thirteen-year sentence for an unrelated case. He, too, pleaded guilty.

Tony Spilotro, who had been indicted in the Argent case along with everyone else, mostly on the basis of the phone calls he made to Stardust executives pleading for jobs and comps, was severed from the case because of his heart condition. Government doctors determined that Spilotro was not using his health as a ruse, and he was given time to have the necessary bypass surgery. He would be tried later.

When the guilty verdicts were handed down, it was no surprise, and neither were the stiff sentences: Joe Aiuppa, the seventy-seven-year-old Chicago boss, and his seventy-one-year-old underboss, Jackie Cerone, got twenty-eight years each. The seventy-three-year-old Maishe Rockman got twenty-four years. Carl DeLuna and Carl Civella received sixteen years, to run concurrently. John and Joseph Balistrieri were acquitted of all charges.

♦ ♦ ♦

Nineteen eighty-three was a turning point in the history of Las Vegas. The Tropicana and Argent cases were wending their way through pretrial hearings and on to trials and eventually to convictions. The last Teamster pension fund loan was paid off. The mortgage on the Golden Nugget was bought by Steve Wynn and paid off with junk bonds. The mob's main muscle—as far as controlling the financing of casinos—was over.

In 1983, slot machines became the largest casino revenue producer, surpassing all other forms of gaming. Las Vegas, which had begun as a town for high rollers, became a mecca for Americans looking for low stakes and ALL YOU CAN EAT FOR $2.95 buffets.

In 1983, the Nevada Gaming Commission suspended the Stardust's license because of yet another skim investigation and installed one of their own Gaming Control Board supervisors in Lefty's old office to run the Stardust. State officials were able to fire or force into early retirement many of the employees who had been a part of the various skims that had been going on for years.

And in 1983 Lefty Rosenthal and his family moved to California.

♦ ♦ ♦

"I was playing with the stock market a little bit and handicapping a little, strictly as a player," Lefty said. "But the kids, especially Stephanie, had become a world-class swimmer. She had been pretty good in Las Vegas, and she had entered and won dozens of competitions.

"In an effort to help her pursue that goal—and she was already prepared for Olympic qualifying meets—I moved to Laguna Niguel so they could train and compete with the Mission Viejo Nadadores, one of the top swim teams in the country."

The Rosenthal house was in Laguna Woods, in Laguna Niguel, a wealthy community about midway between Los Angeles and San Diego. It was one of nineteen houses cut into the lush coastal hillsides, with panoramic views of the ocean, the Crown Valley, and El Niguel County Club. Security for the Rosenthal house included several closed-circuit television monitors controlled by a wall-sized panel in the garage.

For most of 1983, Lefty's life revolved around the extraordinary feats his children performed as competitive swimmers.

"You see a headline about your child that says ROSENTHAL WINS TWO MORE GOLDS, and there can't be a moment of greater pride," Rosenthal said. He still has the clippings.

"Stephanie was really in a class of her own. She was just a marvelous athlete. With a level of tolerance for pain that was . . . I can't describe how . . . I can't tell you how much pain she took. I used to watch her train. I took her to both the morning and afternoon practice sessions. That was at four thirty in the morning and three thirty in the afternoon. You know, I just loved it. And I would watch my daughter train. And I saw the veins popping, and I saw her eyes were red, and she practiced in sleet and rain and cold. I was just in tremendous awe of what she was willing to sacrifice to get where she was at. You know, I really had great respect for her.

"Because no matter how talented you are, you need to have that endurance, that strength, that stamina. You know, to win. And Stephanie wanted to fucking win. You know, you're not going to beat that girl. She would not let you beat her.

"And this is not some proud poppa talking. This is the handicapper talking. She was the best. I mean, she kicked ass wherever she went. Oh yeah.

"I mean ribbons, medals, trophies. And Steven, unfortunately, had to be a part of that. And I didn't understand how deep the resentment became. They were just kids. He's only thirteen and she's ten. He was hurt a lot because I had to give Stephanie a hug. I had to put my hand on her head. I had to give her a kiss. I had to shake her hand. I had to cheer her on.

"And her brother would be in the same meet and would finish up the street. And what can you do? You know, sometimes I would say, 'Hey, Steve, okay. You need to train harder.' But Steven resented all of us. Us meaning me and Stephanie.

"Steve was a talented swimmer. More so than Stephanie, technically. That's the truth. Coaches around the country, his own coach, used to say, 'Frank, if you get that kid off his ass and we can get him to train, ain't nobody going to touch the guy. This guy's better than Stephanie.'

"But he lacked the willingness to get out there and take the pain. To train. To go fifteen thousand meters per day. To run. To do dry land exercises. To lift weights. He wasn't willing to pay the price. Consequently, when Steven went into competition, he wasn't prepared. And he'd get his ass kicked.

"But, you know, everybody's not meant to do that. I didn't disrespect him for that. I think he should have quit. Become a social swimmer.

"But Stephanie wanted the gold. These were the finest years of my life. I told Stephanie and some close friends, if Stephanie qualified for the nineteen eighty-four Olympics and gets a medal, my fucking life is complete.

"And I don't give a shit if I get a stroke one minute after. I won't want to come back. And I meant it. In other words, let me have that one thing. And I said, 'Stephanie, that's all want. I want to see it.'

"I told her, 'I caught a miracle getting out of that car with the bomb. Let me see you win a gold, Stef, and after that, I'm willing to say good-bye.'

"And she understood me. But she was young. She was just, you know, a kid. She had been training since she was six years old. Well, we went to Austin, Texas, where they started the Olympic trials. She was qualified in three events, but during her training period coming up to the time in Austin, I watched her. You know, I'm a handicapper. I use a watch.

"And I figure she's got two chances, slim and none, and slim was out of town. I was told by coaches, 'Frank, don't discourage her. You're going to kill it. Frank be careful. Frank. Frank.'

"But I would say driving home from a workout, 'Stef, you've got to train harder.' And she'd say, 'Dad, you don't know what you're talking about.'

"Anyway, I knew before we went to Austin. The main event. The hundred-meter backstroke. My nephew Mark Mendelson wanted to come down from Chicago, but I said wait until she makes the finals before flying down. He went to O'Hare waiting to see if Stef would qualify in the morning to make the finals in the evening. She had to finish in the first eight. There were a hundred and some people that would be swimming in that event. The top eight swim in the finals; the top two go to the Olympics.

"So it worked out that he'd wait at the airport and I'd get a message to him whether to fly down or not. I knew in my heart she didn't have a prayer. She came to me forty-five minutes before race time. She says her coach said she'd never looked better. I said to myself, 'Fuck your coach for bullshitting you.'

"He was playing a game with her. He was taking a shot. Maybe she could pull off a miracle. Well, there are no miracles in sports. It's one on one.

"I remember her time. It was two and a half seconds slower than she'd done six months earlier, when she qualified. She put her head down. I put my head down. Then I ran to the phone and got a message to my nephew, who was waiting at the airport.

"I said, 'Mark Mendelson, go on home.'"

♦ ♦ ♦

Lefty went home, too. His $375,000 house in Laguna Niguel had a rock fountain in the entrance, a spa, a gazebo, and a console made of African zebrawood in the bedroom. But when Rosenthal decided to hang wallpaper, he discovered it was impossible because the walls weren't straight—a defect that also made it impossible to install upgraded doors, new windows and shutters. "The house is falling and creaking and sinking," Lefty said at the time. "There is a big crack in the back wall, and even the mirror man had trouble because the place is not square. I have asked my general contractor to see whether the place even meets code standards."

Lefty sued.

He had to, he explained. The builders "were not even accepting my phone calls anymore."

♦ ♦ ♦

If Mike Kinz hadn't been seated high on his tractor, he would never have noticed the bare patch of earth. Kinz had leased a five-acre cornfield in Enos, Indiana, about sixty miles southeast of Chicago; the corn was about four inches high and in a couple of weeks would have grown tall enough to cover the field and obscure the marks on the ground that made it look as though something had been dragged about a hundred feet from the road to the bare patch.

Kinz suspected that a poacher had probably buried the remains of a deer carcass in the cornfield after removing the edible meat. It had happened before. So he called Dave Hudson, the wildlife preserve's biologist and game warden.

It took Hudson about twenty minutes of digging in the soft, sandy earth before he struck something firm. He looked into the three-foot-deep hole and saw a patch of white skin.

"I scraped off some sand," Hudson said, "and there were some skivvies."

Two bodies had been dumped on top of each other in a five-foot grave. They were naked except for the under-shorts. Their faces were so badly disfigured that it was not until the FBI lab had had a chance to run through the fingerprints, four days later, that the men were identified as Anthony Spilotro, forty-eight, and his brother Michael, forty-one.

The two had been reported missing nine days earlier by Michael's wife, Anne, and there was some speculation at the time that the Spilotros, both of whom were facing trials within a matter of weeks, had purposely disappeared. Spilotro had gotten the court's permission to visit the Chicago area for eight days to visit his family and to have his dentist brother do some work on his teeth.

Spilotro was going to be a busy man. He was facing the Stardust skim trial. He was about to be retried in the Hole in the Wall conspiracy case; the first trial had ended in mistrial because of a bribe attempt made to one of the jurors. He was also scheduled to be tried for violating the civil rights of a government witness he was suspected of having murdered.

His brother Michael was awaiting trial in Chicago on an extortion sting investigation that showed organized-crime links to sex clubs and prostitutes in Chicago's western suburbs.

Tony Spilotro's standing with the Chicago mob had fallen considerably in recent years. "Tony had developed a lot of negatives," Frank Cullotta says. And wiretaps of Spilotro rapping some of his associates, particularly Joe Ferriola— which were played in court—hadn't helped. On the night of June 14, when Michael and Tony left Michael's suburban Chicago home, Michael told his wife, Anne, "If we're not back by nine o'clock, we're in big trouble."

The grave was about four miles from a farm owned by Joseph J. Aiuppa, Chicago's ex–mob boss, who was at the time in prison on charges that he had skimmed Las Vegas casinos.

"The bodies were not meant to be found," Edward D. Hegarty, Chicago's FBI agent in charge, said, "but whoever killed them didn't count on the farmer coming to apply herbicide." The brothers died from "blunt force injuries around the neck and head," said Dr. John Pless, director of forensic medicine at Indiana University, who performed the autopsies. They had both been beaten severely, but there were no underlying fractures or broken bones. They appeared to have been beaten a few feet from the grave. Their clothes were found nearby. The hole had been dug deep enough so the bodies would not have been plowed up by farmers during the next spring.

"The killers must have carried a tremendous grudge," Spilotro's old nemesis, ex–FBI agent Bill Roemer, said. "Usually, it's one hole, two holes, three holes point-blank in the back of the head, probably a twenty-two. It's quick and the guy doesn't suffer. These guys were beaten to death. Tortured."

◆ ◆ ◆

Today in Las Vegas, the men in fedoras who built the city are gone. The gamblers with no last names and suitcases filled with cash are reluctant to show up in the new Las Vegas, for fear of being turned in to the IRS by a twenty-five-year-old hotel school graduate working casino credit on weekends.

Las Vegas has become an adult theme park, a place where parents can take their kids and have a little fun themselves. While the kids play cardboard pirate at the Treasure Island casino, or joust with knights at the Excalibur, Mommy and Daddy can drop the mortgage money and Junior's college tuition on the poker slots.

The intimacy of Bugsy Siegel's 147-room Flamingo Hotel or even Lefty's early 900-room Stardust has been replaced by the 5,008-room MGM Grand or a series of 3,000- to 4,000-room hotels lining the Strip and shaped like pyramids, castles, and spaceships. A volcano erupts every thirty minutes in front of the Mirage. Right next door on the Strip, a pirate boat appears on an artificial lake six times a day and battles the British Navy.

Only twenty years ago, dealers knew your name. What you drank. What you played. How you played. You could walk right in to the tables and be checked in automatically. A bellman you knew took your suitcase upstairs, unpacked your bags, and filled the room with your favorite booze and ice buckets of fresh fruit. Your room would be waiting for you, instead of you waiting for it.

Today, checking into a Las Vegas hotel is more like checking into an airport. Even the high roller hospitality suites can get stacked up while computers check your credit line against your American Express number for verification that you are who you claim to be.

The Teamsters pension fund has been replaced by junk bonds as the primary source of casino funding; but while junk bond interest rates are high, they're not as high as what the outfit charged. Casino executives who borrow the money don't have to meet their stockbrokers in darkened Kansas City hotel rooms at three o'clock in the morning and be told they're going to get their eyes plucked out.

Tony and Geri are dead and Lefty is gone. Lefty now lives in a house on a golf course in a walled community in Boca Raton. He plays a little, watches his investments, and helps his nephew run a nightclub. Sometimes he sits in a small elevated area in the nightclub and aims a penlight at waiters he believes are not clearing tables fast enough. For years Lefty nursed a hope that he would be allowed to return to Las Vegas, but in 1987 he was placed in the Black Book and was forbidden to set foot in a casino ever again; years of fighting the decision amounted to nothing.

"It should have been so sweet," Frank Cullotta said. "Everything was in place. We were given paradise on earth, but we fucked it all up."

It would be the last time street guys were ever given anything that valuable again.

Index